Marxist Local Governments in Western Europe and Japan

Edited by Bogdan Szajkowski

Frances Pinter (Publishers), London
Lynne Rienner Publishers, Inc., Boulder

© Bogdan Szajkowski 1986

First published in Great Britain in 1986 by
Frances Pinter (Publishers) Limited
25 Floral Street, London WC2E 9DS

First published in the United States of America in 1986 by
Lynne Rienner Publications Inc.
948 North Street
Boulder, Colorado 80302

Printed in Great Britain

British Library Cataloguing in Publication Data

Marxist local governments in Western Europe
and Japan.—(Marxist regimes)
1. Communist parties—Europe—History
—20th century
I. Szajkowski, Bogdan   II. Series
324.24 ′075 ′09   JN94.A979
ISBN 0-86187-458-7
ISBN 0-86187-459-5 Pbk

Library of Congress Cataloging in Publication Data

Marxist local governments in Western Europe and Japan.
(Marxist regimes series)
Bibliography: p.
Includes index.
1. Local government—Europe.   2. Local government—
Japan.   3.   Communist parties—Europe.   4. Communist
parties—Japan.   I. Szajkowski, Bogdan.   II. Series.
JS3000.2.M37   1986   352.04   84-62670
ISBN 0-931477-25-5 (Rienner)
ISBN 0-931477-26-3 (Rienner: pbk.)

Typeset by Joshua Associates Limited, Oxford
Printed by SRP Limited, Exeter

Contents

List of Tables

List of Maps

Preface

The fortunes and misfortunes of the Communist Parties in Western liberal democracies have attracted scholarly interest for many years now. Although there are a number of excellent case studies of the Communist Parties in Western Europe (particularly in France and Italy), most of them concentrate on the involvement of the Communists in central government and institutions. Few have been written from a comparative perspective.

Despite the fact that some of the most numerically important and politically experienced non-ruling Communist parties have over the years been able to build a significant power base in the various tiers of local government, little has been written so far about their sub-national activities. This volume aims at filling a major gap in the literature on the Communist Parties in Western Europe and Japan and their role in a very important aspect of their countries' political process.

The nine chapters included in this study analyse the performance, record and policies of eleven Communist parties, primarily but not exclusively in the context of their involvement in local government. They also provide the reader with some comparative data on and assessment of the Communists' activities in the context of national government. In addition, they identify the main factors that have shaped the evolution of the respective parties' interaction with their domestic environment.

Each of the chapters published in this compendium is based on original research commissioned for this study. Since the context of each of the Communist parties discussed in this volume are different, there are variations in the authors' approach, but such variations are an inevitable feature of a wide-ranging study of this sort. Two of the chapters (on Great Britain and Greece) are much shorter than the others included in this volume. The length of these analyses was dictated, in the case of the CPGB, by the essentially historic nature of the subject matter, and, in the case of KKE, by the non-availability of the essential data required.

This book arose not from a common standpoint but from a common research interest. It aspires to throw new light on a very important but neglected aspect of the workings of some of the most important Communist parties operating in liberal democracies. It should be of major interest to students, specialists and general readership interested in the varying disciplines of social and political science in general and Communist studies in particular.

My thanks go, of course, to each contributing scholar for their cooperation and patience. I am grateful to Dr David S. Bell of the Department of Political Science at Leeds University for his work on this volume. In addition, I should like to thank Dr George Th. Mavrogordates of the Department of Political Science at the University of Athens and Professor Hiroshi Kimura of the Slavic Research Centre at Hokaido University in Sapporo for their help and advice. Special thanks go to Peter Moulson, of Frances Pinter (Publishers), for all his hard work and patient advice.

University College   *Bogdan Szajkowski*
Cardiff

Notes on Contributors

José Amodia is Senior Lecturer in Spanish Studies at the University of Bradford. He is the author of *Franco's Political Legacy* (London, Allen Lane, 1977) and of numerous articles on contemporary Spanish politics.

David Arter is Senior Lecturer in European Politics at Leeds Polytechnic. He is co-author (with Neil Elder and Alastair H. Thomas) of *The Consensual Democracies? The Government and Politics of the Scandinavian States* (Oxford, Martin Robertson, 1982) and he has recenly written *The Nordic Parliaments: A Comparative Analysis* (New York, St. Martin's Press, 1984). At present he is writing on the Finnish governmental system.

David S. Bell is a Lecturer in the Department of Politics at Leeds University. He is the author of *Eurocommunism and the Spanish Communist Party* (University of Sussex European Research Centre, 1979) and numerous articles on Western European communism published in professional journals in the United Kingdom and abroad.

Richard Boyd has worked on Japanese politics since 1976, initially on a Japan Foundation Fellowship held in the School of Oriental and African Studies, University of London, subsequently as Visiting Scholar at Tokyo University (1978–9) and Hiroshima University (1983–4), and is currently Lecturer in Far Eastern Politics at the School of Oriental and African Studies. He is preparing a book on the de-radicalization of the Japanese Communist Party and another more general one with the provisional title of *The Domestication of Liberal Democracy: The Case of Japan*.

John Callaghan is a Senior Lecturer in Politics at Wolverhampton Polytechnic. His main research interests are socialist theory, left-wing movements in Britain, and the history of the Comintern. His publications include *British Trotskyism: Theory and Practice* (Oxford, Blackwell, 1984), which is a critique of the ideology of the far left. He has published articles in *Marxism Today, New Statesman* and other journals, and he is currently working on the ideas of Cole, Laski and Tawney in relation to the state and democracy.

Tom Gallagher lectures in the School of Peace Studies at the University of Bradford. He is the author of *Portugal: A Twentieth Century Interpretation* (Manchester, Manchester University Press, 1983). He has also written widely on the dictatorial era in Portugal and on the transition to democracy via the 1974–5 revolution. Among the journals that have published his work are *Political Quarterly, West European Politics, European Studies Review, The World Today, Iberian Studies*, and *Parliamentary Affairs*.

Stephen Gundle is a Research Fellow of Churchill College, Cambridge. His recently completed Ph.D. dissertation is entitled *Communism and Cultural Change in Post-War Italy*.

Andrew Knapp read History at Peterhouse, Cambridge, before studying at Lincoln College, Oxford, where he wrote a doctoral thesis on the municipality of Le Havre, 1965–80. He has taught at Paris University and at the École Supérieure de Commerce, Le Havre, and is currently a Research Fellow at Nuffield College, Oxford.

D. G. Kousoulas, a Professor at Howard University, Washington, DC, is the author of *Revolution and Defeat: The Story of the Greek Communist Party* (Oxford, Oxford University Press, 1965), *On Government and Politics* (Monterey, Calif., Brooks-Cole, 1968, now in its fifth edition), *Modern Greece: Profile of a Nation* (New York, Scribners, 1974), and many others.

Bogdan Szajkowski, the General Editor of the *Marxist Regimes Series*, is at present a Lecturer in Comparative Social Institutions at University College, Cardiff. His writing on contemporary Communist affairs has appeared in professional journals in Britain and abroad. In addition to contributing to symposia, he is also the editor of a three-volume work, *Marxist Governments: A World Survey* (London, Macmillan, and New York, St, Martin's Press, 1981) and a series of volumes under the title *Documents in Communist Affairs*, which were published annually between 1977 and 1981 and re-established in 1985 (London, Wheatsheaf Books, and New York, St. Martin's Press). He was the founder and editor-in-chief of the quarterly journal *Communist Affairs: Documents and Analysis* published by Butterworth between 1981 and 1985. He is the author of *The Establishment of Marxist Regimes* (London and Boston, Butterworth, 1982) and *Next to God ... Poland: Politics and Religion in Contemporary Poland* (London, Frances Pinter, and New York, St. Martin's Press, 1983). A member of the European Consortium for Political Research, he is also a Consultant to a number of organizations and institutions.

Abbreviations

AD	Alianca Democratica (Democratic Alliance)
ANECR	Association Nationale des Élus Communistes et Républicains (National Association of Communist and Republican Mayors and Councillors)
AP	Alianza Popular (Popular Alliance)
APU	Alianca Popular Unida (United People's Alliance)
ARCI-UISP	Associazone Ricreativo Culturale Italiana–Unione Italiana Sport Populare (Italian Culturo-Recreational Association–Italian Union for Popular Sport)
CCP	Communist Party of China
CFDT	Confédération Française Démocratique du Travail (Democratic Confederation of French Trade Unions)
CGIL	Confederazione Generale Italiana del Lavoro (General Confederation of Italian Workers)
CGTP	Conferacão General de Trabalhadores Portuguéses (General Confederation of Portuguese Workers)
CGT	Confédération Générale du Travail (General Confederation of Labour)
CiU	Convergéncia i Unió (Convergence and Unity)
CP	Communist Party
CPGB	Communist Party of Great Britain
CPSU	Communist Party of the Soviet Union
DC	Democrazia Cristiana (Christian Democratic Party)
DDE	Direction Départementale d'Équipement (Field Service of the Ministère d'Équipement)
DKP	Danmarks Kommunistiske Parti (Danish Communist Party)
DSP	Danmarks Socialistiske Parti (Danish Socialist Party)
DSP	Democratic Socialist Party
EC	European Communities
EDA	United Democratic Left
FUP	Frente Unido Popular (United Popular Front)
GDUP	Grupo Dinamizado de Unidade Popular (Dynamizing Group of Popular Unity)
GLC	Greater London Council
HLM	Habitation à Loyer Modéré (publicly financed, low-cost housing)

JCP	Japanese Communist Party
JICHIRO	All-Japan Prefectural and Municipal Worker's Union
JSP	Japan Socialist Party
KKE	Kommunistikon Komma Ellados (Communist Party of Greece) (Exterior)
LDP	Liberal Democratic Party
MARN	Movimento de Agriculturas e Rendeiros do Norte (Movement of Northern Tenants and Farmers)
MDP	Movimento Democratica Popular (Popular Democratic Movement)
MFA	Movimento das Forcas Armadas (Armed Forces Movement)
NATO	North Atlantic Treaty Organization
ND	New Democracy
NIKKYŌSŌ	Japanese Teachers' Union
NKP	Norges Kommunistiske Parti (Communist Party of Norway)
PASOK	Panhellenic Socialist Movement
PCE	Partido Comunista de España (Spanish Communist Party)
PCE/PEK	Partido Comunista de Euskadi (Basque Communist Party)
PCF	Parti Communiste Français (French Communist Party)
PCI	Partito Communista Italiano (Italian Communist Party)
PCP	Partido Comunista Portugués (Communist Party of Portugal)
PIDE	Portuguese Secret Police
PNV	Partido Nacionalista Vasco (Basque Nationalist Party)
PRD	Partido Democratica Renovador (Democratic Renewal Party)
PS	Partido Socialista (Socialist Party)
PS	Parti Socialiste (Socialist Party)
PSA	Partido Socialista Andaluz (Andalusian Socialist Party)
PSD	Partido Social Democratica (Social Democratic Party)
PSI	Partito Socialista Italiano (Italian Socialist Party)
PSOE	Partido Socialista Obrero-Espanõl (Spanish Socialist Party)
PSU	Parti Socialiste Unifię (Party of Socialist Unity)
SDP	Suomen Sosialidemokraattinen Puolue (Finnish Socialist Democratic Party)
SKDL	Suomen Kansan Demokraattinen Litto (Finnish People's Democratic League)
SKP	Suomen Kommunistinen Puolue (Finnish Communist Party)

UCD	Union de Centro Democrático (Union of Democratic Centre)
USSR	Union of Soviet Socialist Republics
Vpk	Vansterpartiet Kommunisterna (Party of the Left—the Communists).

Communist parties: comparative data

Country	Claimed membership	Election (legislative)			Parliamentary seats		Main publication	Claimed circulation	Union federation	Party leader
		Year	Vote	%	Communist	Total				
Denmark (DKP)	10,000	1984	22,880	0.7	none		Land-og Folke (daily)	6,000	–	Poul Emanuel
Finland (SKP)	50,000	1983	416,000	13.2	27	200	Kansan Uutiset (daily)	45,000	–	Arvo Aalto
France (PCF)	608,543	1981	3,239,201	16.2	44	491	l'Humanité (daily)	100,000	CGT	Georges Marchais
Great Britain (CPGB)	16,000	1983	11,606	0.03	none		Morning Star (daily)	30,000	–	Gordon McLennan
Greece (KKE-Exterior)	73,000	1981	–	10.9	13	300	Rizopastis (daily)		–	Kharilos Florakis
Greece (KKE-Interior)	12,000	1983	–	2.7	none		Avgi (daily)		–	Yiannis Banias
Italy (PCI)	1,670,000	1983	9,579,964	29.9	198	630	L'Unità (daily)	350,000	CGIL	Alessandro Natta
Norway (AKP)	1,000	1981		0.7	none		Klassekampen (daily)	4,500	–	Paul Steigen
Norway (NKP)	500	1985		0.3	none		Friheten (semi-weekly)	100,000	–	Hans I. Kleven
Portugal	187,000	1985	893,180	15.55	39	250	O Diario (daily—semiofficial) / Avante (weekly)		–	Alvaro Cunhal
Spain (PCE)	50,000	1982	824,978	3.8	4	350	Mundo Obrero (weekly)	68,733	(Workers' Commissions) CC.OO	Gerardo Iglesias
Sweden (Vpk)	17,500	1985	–	5.4	20	349	Ny Dag (semi-weekly)	3,000	–	Lars Werner
Japan (JCP)	450,000	1983	5,302,485	9.3	26	511	Akahata (daily)	3,100,000	–	Tetsuzo Fuwa

Note: There are rival Communist parties in several of the countries:

Finland: in April 1986 the Election Organization of the Finnish Communists emerged as a separate party from the SPK. Led by Youko Kajanoja, the Organization claims approximate membership of 5,000. Its daily organ is *Tiedonantaja* (circulation 25,000).

Spain: the Spanish People's Communist Party (PC) was founded in January 1984 by pro-Soviet, anti-Eurocommunist dissidents from PCE. The PC, led by Pere Ardiaca, claims a membership of 25,000.

Sweden: the pro-Soviet Communist Workers' Party (APK) was founded in 1977. It claims a membership of 5,000. The APK leader is Rolf Hagel. The pro-Chinese Swedish Communist Party has been in existence since 1967. Its leader is Roland Petterson. The Marxist-Leninist Communist Party Revolutionary was founded in 1970. It is a pro-Albanian party. It is led by Frank Baude and publishes a weekly *Proletaren*.

1 Communism in Local Government in Western Europe and Japan

David S. Bell and Bogdan Szajkowski

Despite the fact that since the Second World War Communists have held posts in national governments in several of the liberal democracies including Finland, France, Portugal and Italy, the principal area in which they have been able to build up a substantial and consistent administrative record is in local government. The purpose of this introductory chapter is to provide the reader with the necessary background to the discussion of other contributors to this volume.

The Communist Parties of Denmark (DKP), Finland (SKP), France (PCF), Great Britain (CPGB), Greece (KKE), Italy (PCI), Japan (JCP), Norway (NKP), Portugal (PCP), Spain (PCE) and Sweden (VpK) were created at the height of the revolutionary ferment between 1917 and 1923, when for many the seizure of power by the Bolsheviks in Russia was merely the first step towards a world-wide revolution.[1] This period in the history of the Communist movement was dominated by the activities of the Communist International (Comintern, 2 March 1919–23 May 1943), which was founded as an instrument of world revolution. Indeed, to a large extent the parties created at that time were both the product and the victim of Comintern policies and directives. These included the destruction of parliamentary democracy as one of the fundamental conditions for the victorious proletarian revolution all over the world.

The aims and principles of the Comintern, explained in the thesis on *Bourgeois Democracy and Proletarian Dictatorship* written by Lenin and accepted without discussion by its First Congress in 1919, stipulated the immediate and universal establishment of the dictatorship of the proletariat throughout the world. This, among other measures, presupposed the conquest of state power, the destruction of the bourgeois state machine and the replacement of parliamentary democracy by 'self-rule by the masses' (Braunthal, 1967, p. 165). The Communists thus opted for anti-parliamentarianism and revolutionary tactics to reach power. This option not only dictated non-involvement in central but also in local government. Instead, following Lenin's prescription elaborated in his book *Left-Wing Communism: an Infantile Disorder*, the parties invested their energies in working among trade unions. At that stage of the development of the Communist movement the capture of the trade unions became the most urgent task of the party members and their sympathizers.

The International's high expectations for the immediate overthrow of the bourgeois system in Europe were short lived. Although in the aftermath of the foundation of the Comintern a tide of revolutionary ferment swept across the continent, within a year reaction not only regained that ground but also consolidated its position. Consequently the policies of the International in respect of representative institutions began to adjust. At the Third Congress in 1921, its earlier revolutionary tactics were modified by those of the so-called United Front which presupposed the establishment of contacts and cooperation with non-Communist workers' organizations.

In theory, it was a tactic of united action with other parties of the socialist left, in place of attempts at any immediate seizure of power by the Communists alone. In practice, the new policy brought about considerable confusion and had disastrous effects on the Communist parties (Braunthal, 1967, pp. 247–8; Middlemas, 1980, pp. 30–43). There was initially an ambiguity as to whether this meant some kind of open cooperation between Communist and non-Communist leaders (United Front from above), or merely a search for common action with rank-and-file non-Communist workers (United Front from below) (Linderman, p. 268). At the same time, this tactical realignment in essence did not change Communist belief that bourgeois democracy cannot be saved nor indeed that it is worth saving.

Further confusion was added in 1928 when the Comintern turned against the United Front at precisely the moment when unity with socialist parties was most needed to combat the rising power of Nazism and Fascism throughout Europe (Middlemas, 1980, p. 36). The directives of what is known as class against class policy, issued to the Communist parties, required them to reject all alliances with other parties and retain the United Front only from below. In the contorted logic of this sectarian policy, fascism was seen as an inherently unstable phenomenon whose imminent collapse would hasten the advance of communism. Therefore anything that obstructed it, such as the existence of Socialist parties (denigrated as 'Social Fascist') was to be combatted (Middlemas, 1980, p. 37).

A new line—that of the Popular Front—was enforced at the Seventh Congress of the Comintern in 1935. Reflecting Soviet awareness of hostile regimes on all Russian borders, the Communist parties in the West were instructed to rally in the defence of bourgeois institutions and to form a broad coalition of political parties or groups opposed to the foreign policies of the European Fascist states and Japan. Thus instead of class struggle there was now to be cooperation with the bourgeoisie; instead of the Soviet system, eulogy of democracy; instead of internationalism, nationalism (Borkenau, 1953, p. 387).

Comintern's confusing and unrealistic directives for its member parties required fundamental and dramatic changes in their national strategies. These changes more often than not resulted in disastrous consequences on their performance and loss of mass membership. Such a state of affairs has been hardly conducive to the development of appropriate policies that could be applied on a sub-national level. It is worth remembering that for most of the Communist parties local government was only a by-product of the main struggle conducted on a national level and among the trade unions. Involvement in local politics would only divert attention and limited resources from the priority areas.

Thus in the inter-war period the Communist parties operating in the liberal democracies had not developed a consistent local strategy. However, where the Communists were, albeit in a somewhat haphazard manner, involved in local government, they used the institutions they controlled to support their activities elsewhere.

Only after the Second World War did the Communist parties begin to be involved in sub-national politics in a direct and more determined way. A new interest in the representative democratic institutions was facilitated by the dissolution of the Comintern in May 1943 and the consequent absence of central direction of the Communist movement. This, coupled with a general post-war optimism, meant that revolution was off the agenda in Western Europe and Japan. The conquest of the 'bourgeois' institutions by electoral means appeared now a possible strategy for the Communist parties in the liberal democracies and they began to search actively for local responsibility. Thus, except for the period of the Cold War (1947–52), local government provided the Communists with opportunities to display their administrative abilities and capacity to work within the bourgeois system. On the whole, however, sub-national politics did not offer dramatic new openings. On the contrary, the tasks of readjusting a party's priorities and policies, of building alliances with other left-wing forces, of creating a new image and a suitable local environment for the initiation and projection of Communist policies, all this required complex approaches that proved to be long delayed in bringing the desired results. For example, the Communist Parties of Japan, France and Italy found that these changes began to pay off electorally only in the late 1960s and 1970s. By the mid-1980s, the liberal democracies had seen the arrival of the long march through local government institutions by Western Communists. However, evidence compiled by the authors of the monographs included in this volume suggest that Communist advances in local government have already reached a peak and that their electoral appeal is on the decline.

Communist strategy in local government is still on the whole a function of national policies and priorities. Given that all Communist parties operate through *democratic centralism*, which in practice means strict discipline and adherence to directives from central leadership, there remains the possibility of turning away from involvement in local government if so demanded by national strategy. This observation brings about a major reservation as far as Communist involvement in sub-national politics is concerned.

Studies of Communist parties' involvement in local government give no direct indication as to the respective parties' performance in other areas of politics. It does not follow that because a particular party has adopted liberal or conservative approaches on a sub-national level these would be followed in national government. In other words, local approaches should not be seen as the determinant of national strategy. Communists have built up strong positions in local government in many countries and this must now weigh heavily in the calculations of the leadership of the respective parties. However, it should be remembered that in most countries this is not the only consideration nor even a very important one. Local government is still by and large used by the Communists for the purpose of mobilizing for national and international policies as determined by the national leadership of a particular party. It should be borne in mind that local politics is only a part of a Communist party's national strategy. It is with these remarks and reservations in mind that the contribution of local government studies to the understanding of communism and vice versa should be assessed.

This first introductory chapter deals with the general background, strategy and position of the Communist parties under discussion in this volume. It is necessary to review the more general features of these parties before looking at the details of their local government activity. In the remainder of this chapter the national position and national strategy of the parties will be set against the background of their local government record.

In Chapter 2 José Amodia discusses the emergence of Spanish communism after the death of Franco and notes that local government has not been one of the PCE's traditional interests. Communism in Spain has had some minor successes but even at local level it has had very little room for manœuvre, something which led to meagre results in the 1979 and 1983 local elections. The proscribed Spanish Communist Party emerged from the long Francoist era with a reformist strategy; local politics was therefore one arena open to it where it could display its efficiency and responsibility. However, communism was isolated and at the national level the Socialists (PSOE) were able to play *pot de fer-pot de terre*, to refuse any alliance with the Communists and to attain power on their own. Socialist intransigence deprived the Communists of all but a fingertip hold on local affairs.

Spanish Communists have never overcome their political isolation and they have been hampered by internal struggles (Mujal-León, 1983). The PCE emerged from clandestinity with around 200,000 members and the support of diverse groups: Santiago Carrillo, the leader at the time, more or less appropriated the term 'Eurocommunism', openly criticized Russia, and the Spanish Communist Party seemed to be leading the opening-up of old-fashioned Marxism (Carrillo, 1977). But the Communists found themselves competing with a large Socialist Party and at the first election (June 1977) the PCE polled a mere 9.2 per cent of the vote. Carrillo then began the long internal struggle to discipline the Party but found a war on two fronts (internal as well as against the Socialists) debilitating.

Spanish Communists polled slightly better in 1979 when their vote went up to 10.2 per cent, but the 1982 elections, when they sank to 3.7 per cent, were a massive disavowal of the PCE, even in its strongholds such as Catalonia. Moreover, Carrillo's attempts to impose the authority of the leadership had continued through splits and purges and the number of activists fell to about 50,000. Carrillo then resigned as leader and nominated a successor. Gerardo Iglesias had conducted his entire career in Carrillo's shadow but he soon revealed an independent streak and, backed by a union leader, Nicolás Sartorius, was soon engaged in a battle with Carrillo for control of the Party. However, it was not just Carrillo who was dissatisfied; there were pro-Russian groups that felt that the remnants of the 'liberalizers' had excessive influence. The 'Afghans', the Catalonian group that approved the invasion of Afghanistan, were the most important and they left to found the Party of Catalan Communists. Later, in January 1984, the old guard around Ignacio Gallego also quit the Party to establish a new CP—apparently with Moscow's blessing. These groups were followed a bit later by Jaime Ballesteros, formerly number two in the Party, five Central Committee members and an indefinite number of activists; hence the leadership was very much on the defensive in 1985 when a segment of the Andalucian unions was itself on the point of joining Gallego's ultra-orthodox Party. Carrillo claimed that Iglesias had 'liquidated' the Party and, with Julían Ariza of the unions, kept up pressure on the new leadership by threatening to break away. In October 1985 Carrillo abandoned the struggle and left the PCE to found yet another new party.

As José Amodia points out, Spanish Communists do best in industrial areas and the poor rural areas of Andalucia but very badly in Galicia, Navarre, Old

Castile and the Basque Country. In that sense the PCE is not a national party. In the 'Red belts' around Barcelona and Madrid it is well represented in local government, but the Communists have overall control in very few councils, and party squabbles have also had local consequences (policy disagreements, personnel conflicts, explusions, etc.).

Yet even the PCE's 1983 local campaign was run on national issues (primarily against NATO and the record of the central government) and Amodia shows that the Party has not been consistent in its support for local council efforts. It has not provided the necessary help for inexperienced councillors nor given them sufficient attention. This failure is another aspect of the Party's inability to retain intellectuals and professional people and the general run-down of activism. José Amodia notes that the Communists have tried to improve the image of local government (in contradistinction to Franco's local bosses) and to use local councils to promote issues (invariably national), but they have also tried to some extent to use cultural facilities to increase local participation.

Spain and Portugal are often bracketed together but the contrasts on many levels are stark: communism in the two countries is quite different. The Communist Party of Portugal is led by the 71-year-old Álvaro Cunhal who has a heroic image with a long career of opposition to Salazar. Cunhal spent eleven years in a prison at Peniche before escaping to the Soviet Union where he remained until the fall of the dictatorship in April 1974, when he returned to lead the small but disciplined PCP (which may have numbered only 3,000). In the April 1983 legislative elections the PCP managed to poll 18.2 per cent of the vote, which gave it thirty-eight deputies and made it the third party in in the Portuguese parliament, but in 1985 it fell to fourth place with 15.44 per cent of the vote. Moreover, unlike the Italians or Spanish, the Portuguese Communists have not pursued a reformist strategy; they are a closed, secretive party and they have never flirted with the once-fashionable 'Eurocommunism'.

The PCP claimed 200,000 members in 1985, but it is still solidly under the control of the Resistance generation ('700 years in prison', according to the Party's slogan). Iron discipline assures party coherence and, unlike Spain, there have been no purges, expulsions or resignations; it is a party that presents a monolithic front and it has had to sustain few public attacks from ex-Communists (on party function see Middlemas, 1980). Cunhal runs a tight ship: there are no evident splits and there is no 'dauphin' to the venerable but ageing leader.

The Portuguese Communists, as befits a movement moulded by Stalin, are close to the Soviet Union: they never condemned the invasion of

Czechoslovakia; Cunhal declared party support for the 'alliance of people and armed forces' in Poland; and they also supported the Soviet invasion of Afghanistan. The PCP had a ministerial portfolio in General Vasco Gonçalves' provisional (and left-wing) government of March 1975, but in the summer of that year the Party was involved in the closing-down of the journal *Republica* and of the church radio station *Renascenca*. At this time in the mid-1970s the Portuguese Communists tried to exploit a potential *coup d'état* (something which makes it unique amongst modern Western Communist parties), and its unions have frequently carried out harrassing strikes in the industrial belt around Lisbon (Mortimer *et al*., 1979). The Party is deeply entrenched in trade unions (through CGTP Social movements): such tentacular control by the Communists was denounced by Otello Carvalho of the radical Armed Forces Movement.

Notwithstanding the prestige of the party amongst Portuguese intellectuals (a prestige deriving partly from the anti-colonial movement whose leaders were often educated by the PCP), Communists have not quite come to terms with the new situation of Portuguese democracy. Cunhal, whilst a romantic figure, is an austere reminder of the past and the Party has tried to soften its image. Cunhal, in February 1985, took some steps in this direction when he praised the Catholic hierarchy for the 'active and conscientious role which it takes on social questions' and praised President Eanes' 'fundamentally patriotic role'. However, Cunhal has tried to abrade the Socialist Party's left wing (without success) and praise of the President could be seen as part of this tactic (Eanes' party could eat further into the Socialist vote). Cunhal's attempt to gain votes from the extreme left was also unsuccessful and for electoral purposes Communists have fallen back on a conservative defence of the gains made in the Revolution (agricultural reform, union freedom, nationalization, and women's rights).

Another contrast with Spain is that Communists in Portugal have put down particularly tough local roots. Apart from the industrial belt around Lisbon, the Party is strongest in the agricultural plain of the Alentejo where it has nearly an absolute majority of supporters. Alentejo is the region investigated by Tom Gallagher in Chapter 3. In the first local elections in December 1976, the Communist United Popular Front emerged as the largest party in Alentejo (with 40–50 per cent of the vote), despite the PCP's lower national showing of 18 per cent. In Alentejo there is a rural proletariat which developed a strong tradition of solidarity during the years of hardship under the dictatorship. The popular upheavals of 1975 virtually abolished the *latifundia*, which once characterized the region and in their place collective farms were set up. In the mid-1980s the Communists started to make some slight progress in the Catholic, conservative north, where its party head-quarters were attacked during the 1975 coup.

Local government in Portugal is highly centralized so that the Party's local government activity is under Lisbon's surveillance. Although the Party controls some thirty county councils outright and controls about 250 parish councils, and although it has probably concentrated local support, as Tom Gallagher points out, to a greater extent than other Western parties, the Party has not opposed the restrictive local government structure. It has campaigned for more money but, there is no evidence of budgetary discrimination against Communist-controlled areas. The Portuguese Communists engaged in local government work are under tight control from their Lisbon office. Despite the evidence, contained in the chapter on the PCP, that vigorous local government work can achieve results, the Communists have been trying to develop a clientele rather than to build for the future. However, there seems to have been little sign of local discontent over the Party's authoritarian behaviour and it has maintained tight control over the great majority of collective farms in the Alentejo. But there are blockages that arise from the PCP's authoritarian and highly centralized organizational and operational principles, which Tom Gallagher concludes, means that the Party's local strength cannot easily be translated into national advantages.

To move from Portugal in Chapter 3 to Italy in Chapter 4 is to move from the most rigid and disciplined of Western Communist parties to the most open and flexible. It is ironic that the PCP and PCI, the two parties that have best ridden out the storm of the recession, are at opposite ends of the spectrum. In the June 1984 European elections, albeit in special circum-stances, the Italian Communist Party became the biggest party in Italy, ahead even of the Christian Democrats, and confirmed its position as by far the biggest in any of the liberal democracies. However, although Enrico Berlinguer, who died on the eve of the European elections, bequeathed a party of some one and a half million members, his successor Alessandro Natta has inherited a frustrating tactical stalemate and, despite the search for agree-ment with the Christian Democrats that would allow them into government (known as the 'historic compromise'), there has been no movement on that front.

Neither Berlinguer nor any other Communist could find a solution to the Party's difficulties in the 1980s that were compounded by the Socialist-led government of Bettino Craxi which imposed a wages freeze despite Com-munist opposition (both in Parliament and outside) and the small Republican and Social Democratic Parties have had more national impact than the Communists. In this impasse the Party is torn between Giorgio Napolitano who, with the Secretary General of the Confederation of Italian Workers Luciano Lama, appears to want a further 'decommunization', and the powerful but unsure leadership. One of the party leaders, Achile Ochetto, called the rejection of the 'historic compromise' a 'Copernican revolution', but the economic crisis and intellectual heterodoxy have necessitated a deep questioning of Marxist taboos that has only just begun.

Over the years the PCI has built up a diverse network of organizations: cooperatives, trade unions, farmers' associations and, of course, local governments. One of the distinguishing features of Italian communism is the range and depth of its local interests: of the ninety-five prinicpal cities of the Italian provinces, the PCI administers five on its own and twenty-nine in alliance with the Socialists. Italian Communists have been involved in local politics since the Liberation but, as Stephen Gundle points out in Chapter 4, the strategy changed in the 1950s from one of using local party organizations to carry out national policies to one of giving local politics an opportunity to contribute to the shaping of national policy. The increasing local influence is attributed to the loosening of democratic centralism and to the political setback for the Party in the 1980s.

Local government dovetails into the PCI's strategy of reformist politics and the Party has had some success in making a show of its abilities. At the same time it should be remembered that the PCI has not always had such a large local-government interest. The PCI's local base expanded in the 1960s and in particular it developed the 'Emelian consensus model' (from the PCI stronghold of Emilia–Romagna) with intensity. Rapid industrialization and the rise of new industries in the 1960s posed challenges to which the Party did respond nationally, if slowly. It was the June 1975 local elections that marked a distinct shift in Italian politics: those elections, in which the PCI won 32.4 per cent, changed the map of local politics. The PCI improved its vote in places where it was not traditionally strong and it came to power in some of Italy's largest cities (Rome, Turin and Naples).

In the new local governments PCI administrators had a high degree of freedom (there were even complaints about lack of coordination), but they had to face urban decay, the absence of any identification with the cities, and in some places social life on the point of collapse. The PCI's national strategy of a search for alliance with the Christian Democrats ('historic compromise') that would allow them into national government impeded much-needed local reforms (which could be blocked by entrenched groups).

The national leadership of the PCI also finds itself up against a decentralized and restive constellation of quasi-party institutions. In local government the Socialist–Communist polemic has caused the CGIL unions and the

Cooperative League to hesitate, to try and preserve united-left organizations rather than fling themselves into the fray in defence of the PCI. The 150,000 (or so) PCI local officials showed irritation at the inability of the leadership to deal with the worsening national situation. Local Communism has a reformist perspective and it has acquired considerable expertise in dealing with European Community institutions and in developing the regions under its control. The force of PCI local communism stems from the way it has been able to understand and express local needs, and many regional PCI organizations have developed a strong administrative structure that is distinct from the centre. Italian communism has developed an extensive local influence which is where the Party demonstrates its capacity to govern well and in some regions (Emilia–Romagna, for example) it has been in power for many years. 'Red Bologna' is a well-known Communist-governed city but Stephen Gundle shows that the success of the model was somewhat qualified after 1977, when the PCI failed to take the measure of new social demands and power became concentrated in very few hands. But Gundle also points out that the Communists had to find new answers to the pressing local questions of the late 1980s and that they did so despite the resistance of the more traditional sectors of the Party. It should be remembered, however, that Italian communism has, at a local level, been capable of some innovation and flexibility (Blackmer & Tarrow, 1975).

Chapter 5 deals with the communism in the Nordic region where the Communist Party of Finland has had a share of governmental power but where the parties of Sweden, Denmark and Norway have been markedly unsuccessful. The most significant party outside Finland is the Swedish Left-Communist Party (Vpk) which in 1982 polled 5.6 per cent of the vote, which has twenty deputies and which claims a membership of 17,500. Swedish communism has gained a degree of power through the use of its small parliamentary group when the Social Democrats have needed further support, but such power has been very limited. Like other parties, the Swedish Communists have suffered from schisms and from splinter-group competition, but it has established a degree of independence (Albright, 1979, Ch. 6).

The tiny Norwegian Communist Party has a membership of some 500. Since 1945, when most Communist parties profited from their association with the deeds of the victorious Red Army, the Norwegian Communists have been an insignificant force. In Denmark the loyal pro-Moscow Communist Party has an estimated membership of some 10,000 but in 1983 it only managed to poll 1.1 per cent of the vote. At one time in the 1970s the Danish Communist Party polled 4 per cent and in 1957 it managed some 3.1 per cent, but these mark unusual peaks of influence for what is a marginal party.

It does, however, manage to publish a Party daily, *Land-og Folk*, with a circulation of 6,000. In Sweden the Party has made the running on the radical left and as a result has had an impact. But Communists in Northern Europe are, in local elections, usually competing with many radical groups based on 'post-industrial' issues such as peace, feminism, ecology, etc.

However, the largest and most extensively researched Communist party in the region is the Finnish Communist Party which operates the Finnish People's Democratic League (SKDL), a group that has peformed well in elections and that has weighed heavily in politics in post-war Finland. In 1945 the League polled 23.5 per cent of the vote and in 1958 it again almost reached that level with 23.2 per cent, but since then it has been slowly declining even though in the mid-1970s the decline was stemmed for a while. The Finnish People's Democratic League was a regular participant in government during the 1960s and 1970s, but the declining vote and the revival of the Social Democratic Party put strains on the Party, whose splits came into the open in the 1980s (Childs, 1980).

The elections of March 1983 were a severe setback for the League: its vote fell to 13.4 per cent of the votes cast and it held only twenty-six seats in the Eduskunta, the Finnish parliament. In May 1983 the Social Democrat Kalevi Sorsa formed the first government for seventeen years without Communist ministers and the immediate effect of the election losses was to envenom the continuing factional struggle in the Party—the Sinisalo hardliners and the 'participationists' set about each other with renewed energy at the Party's 20th Congress in May 1984. The majority tried to expel the hardliner Esko—Juhani Tennila who had been elected in Kemi on a high personal vote, and further splits have since appeared within the leadership which have neither helped to evolve a way of dealing with the decline nor produced a stable balance between factions. Arvo Aalto, the replacement for Jouko Kajanoja in the party Chair has been criticized by Moscow and several party officials have been dismissed.

David Arter argues that Scandinavian communism has been very much a movement of the geographical periphery and of the isolated, marginal social groups: communism has been relatively weak in the industrial areas although the traditional working class has voted Communist. In Finland the structure of local government has made it difficult for the Communists to have the same impact as the big 'Latin' parties although they polled well locally.

Local issues, as Arter points out, have been important to the Finnish Communist Party which has laid stress on local politics and has tried to develop local welfare and to equalize housing standards. Finnish communism has had influence in local government through informal channels, through the appeal of well-known local Communist personalities and by mobilizing people along the usual Communist lines—through petitions, demonstrations, etc. Arter notes that communism appears to be on the retreat locally but that it may have touched the bedrock of its support in the mid-1980s. As in the rest of Scandinavia, the Communists will have to respond to the new social and economic challenges and put forward a programme acknowledging the demands of modernization and the need to protect human rights. Arter concludes with the view that local government may be the best place to experiment with new models of worker self-government.

As with the Italian and Finnish Communist parties, the French Communist Party has participated in government briefly: from 1944 to 1947 and then, with four ministers, from 1981 to 1984. At the time of the Liberation the Party polled over 26 per cent of the vote (5 million). During the Fourth Republic the Party was a large, seemingly immovable force and in the 1956 elections it polled 25.7 per cent (5,600,000 votes). But the first elections of the Fifth Republic saw the Party reduced to 19 per cent, and in subsequent elections it fluctuated between 20 and 22 per cent, touching 22.5 per cent in 1967 and 20 per cent in 1978. The Party's candidate, Secretary General Georges Marchais, polled only 15.3 per cent in the 1981 presidential elections and in the legislative election which followed the PCF polled only 16.1 per cent. Although the PCF has declined, it is still one of the principal Communist Parties in a liberal democracy; moreover, it is tightly organized around a rigid form of democratic centralism and runs a relatively large union federation (CGT). However, the Party's decline has been visible in its falling membership (which could be as low as 200,000) and the unions in the CGT have also suffered from falling membership (Tokés, 1978; McInnes, 1978).

Under the Fifth Republic the Party looked to an alliance with the Socialists as a way of reviving its fortunes and giving it a place in government. Locally unity of the left benefited the Communist Party which gained from the Socialist abandonment, in the mid-1970s, of the alliance system between centre parties against the Communists. At the same time the PCF were able to come out of isolation and gain control of a large number of cities; it could be said that this was the most tangible pay-off for the Party from the national strategy of left unity it so assiduously pursued. However, the French Communist Party has abandoned the attempt it made in the 1970s to cultivate a more liberal image and since 1984 it has turned its back on a governmental role (though not on its local role). Although the French Communist Party in the early 1980s began to criticize some of the human rights violations in the Soviet Union and Eastern Europe, these criticisms were never as public as those of the PCE nor as steady as those of the PCI. French Communists fell in behind Moscow's view of the world in 1979 when the PCF gave its view that the balance sheet of the Eastern bloc was 'globally positive'; later, the Party refused to condemn the Polish *coup d'état* and supported the Russian invasion of Afghanistan.

French Communist attacks on the Socialist Party became extremely bitter and personal in the mid-1970s and although they quietened for a year or so after Mitterrand's 1981 presidential victory, they began to reappear with the imposition of the Socialist government's austerity policy in April 1983. The alignment with the Soviet Union on foreign policy issues and the attacks on the Socialist government probably contributed to the PCF's inability to stem their steady decline in the polls.

In Chapter 6 Andrew Knapp deals with the long and, except for the war, continuous involvement of the French Communist Party in local politics. He makes the point that, although the Party made great advances in local government under the Fifth Republic, municipal communism is not a fringe phenomenon in France. He shows that in France the Communist-run municipalities do have distinctive policies despite their restricted powers of French local government: Communists appear to prefer business taxes to domestic rates and to rely less on direct payments for services than other comparable cities. Likewise the Communists prefer to give priority to social and educational programmes rather than to 'economic' services, like roads, car-parks, etc., and they support provincial cultural centres in many of their cities. Redistributive policies have also been undertaken to an extent by Communist cities although they have not been profligate spenders. As Chapter 6 shows, the Communist-run cities are not the most indebted in France and Communists have not attempted to provoke head-on clashes with the government on budgetary matters. Social service provision by Communist municipalities is good but the principal difficulty these cities now face is the decline in post-war public housing: the legacy of barren suburbs left by the building of high-rise accommodation and the settlement of large numbers of immigrants in working-class quarters.

Knapp suggests that the French Communist local and national decline are related: the PCF has not answered the basic questions about its identity and commitment to democratic values. However, the local and national situations do not develop in strict parallel and this has enabled the Party to survive several difficulties. But it is not certain that the PCF can continue to stave off local decline whilst the Party's national audience dwindles.

Unlike most Communist parties the Communist Party of Great Britain (CPGB) has had an unbroken history of legality within a liberal democratic system but it has had only limited success at parliamentary and local level during its sixty-five-year existence (Pelling, 1975). British communism has had influence in the trade unions and is the most important of the far left '*groupuscules*' in British politics but it is marginal, especially when compared to the giant parties of the continent. Communism in Britain reached its high point after the Second World War (when it had about 215 councillors), but since then it has steadily declined and in the 1980s was torn apart by factional rivalries. Factional struggles in the CPGB echoed those in other parts of Europe but focused on the control of the Party's major resources, the *Morning Star* daily. CPGB internal struggles also involved the journal *Marxism Today*, the Party's intellectual organ, which espoused 'protest' issues as the way for the Party to regain influence. *Marxism Today* and the leadership were opposed by a coalition of 'tankies' (who supported the Russian invasion of Czechoslovakia) and unionists who emphasized the Party's more traditional constituency in the trade unions.

In Chapter 7 John Callaghan reviews the CPGB's poor local showing and notes that its well-known 'Little Moscows' of the inter-war period came about despite the Party's concentration of effort elsewhere. Up until 1927, when the class-against-class tactics intervened, the Party had had some local success in association with Labour but the record was better immediately after the Second World War. Callaghan notes that the Party did not run an overall version of 'community politics and its literature was an unimaginative assertion of national demands. Full employment, the Cold War and industrial diversification were factors in the disappearance of the "Little Moscows"', but the CPGB was still polling well in some strongholds as late as 1956. The lack of interest in local affairs and the unimaginative nature of the CPGB have meant that the revival of 'municipal socialism' in Britain has come from elsewhere.

The Greek Communist Party (KKE) was responsible for the 1946–9 guerrilla movement and was declared illegal in 1947; it was also, of course, illegal during the dictatorship so that its period of legal history is relatively short—since 1974, (Albright, 1979). However, the Greek Communist movement emerged with two competing parties, the 'Interior' and 'Exterior': the 'Exterior' is the official pro-Soviet party and is the major Communist force in Greek politics, but both parties are a national presence. However, the Interior Party counts for only about 2 per cent of the vote: at the 1985 elections the Exterior Party polled 629,518 votes (9.89 per cent) and the Interior 117,050 (1.84 per cent). In contemporary Greece the Exterior Party is marginal but could have a pivotal position—if the Socialist support slipped any more—but it is chiefly remarkable for having held its share of the vote since 1977 (480, 188 or 9.36 per cent).

In Chapter 8 D. G. Kousoulas discusses the sub-national performance of the two Communists Parties in Greece and their allies, stressing that their successes are partly due to the electoral system which favours the election of Communist candidates, particularly during the second round. Reviewing the structure of Greek local government, the author points out the importance of political patronage in the system which allows the Communist mayors to extend their influence and perpetuate the orientation of the voters.

The Japanese Communist Party (JCP) has since 1950 followed a path familiar to observers of the West European Communist movement. The Party moved out of its 'ghetto' by rejecting the inflexible and hardline policies (in keeping with CPSU imperatives) that verged on 'Maoism' at one time in the 1950s. The JCP was riven with internal conflict and during its period of isolation polled very badly: 2.6 per cent (1952), 1.2 per cent (1953), 2.0 per cent (1955) and 2.6 per cent (1958). What Richard Boyd in Chapter 9 calls a policy of 'deradicalization' was initiated in the early 1960s and the new line became associated with Miyamoto, who rose at that time from the internal squabbles as undisputed leader. The new line of the JCP was based on a programme of reforms and on the parliamentary road to socialism: Japanese communism set out on a route that became increasingly 'reformist', increasingly distant from the old dogmas, and more inclined to criticize the Soviet Union. This strategy brought success of a sort, in that the Party began to rise in the polls as the concept of a 'national, democratic, united front' became increasingly familiar. Coalition policies were proposed by the Party and went hand in hand with an increasing flexibility of the leadership, but the wooing of the Japanese Socialist Party (JSP) has not yet paid big dividends (the JSP must remain the Party's best hope as a partner although mutual suspicion is intense). Nevertheless, despite its distance from power, the JCP increased its vote from 4.6 per cent in 1967 (five seats), to 6.8 per cent in 1969 (fourteen seats), to 10.5 per cent in 1972 (thirty-eight seats), and it reached 10.4 per cent in 1976 (but only seventeen seats). But the JCP vote may have reached a plateau in the mid-1970s because it has not polled well subsequently. Moreover, the Communist Party has suffered a decline both in membership and support in the 1980s. The Party had an estimated membership of 450,000 in 1984 but they polled only 9.4 per cent of the vote in the same year and held only twenty-six of the 511 seats in the Diet. This erosion of support has occurred despite an active policy of contacts with overseas parties and a distinctive line obliquely criticized by V. Zagladin in *Pravda* (23 July 1982).

The JCP has an active press, it publishes periodicals and a daily paper, 'Red Flag' (*Akahata*), which has a circulation of over three million. This paper and the Party's other publications, and its general strategy of alliances, have given the JCP an audience which goes beyond the traditional limits of the Party—in keeping with this it has developed numerous 'front' associations to extend influence into other social groups. The ideological innovations and apparently open nature of Japanese Communism have much to do with its success (as has the 'un-Communist' readability of its papers), but for the same reason there have been clashes with the Communist Party of the Soviet Union (Kaplan, 1978).

In addition to increasing its general influence, the JCP has increased its presence in local affairs (from which it had been almost completely absent in the 1950s). Over the 1970s it became widely represented in local assemblies: as Richard Boyd points out, the 'parliamentary road to socialism' to which the JCP became committed after the hardline attitude was an essential precondition for involvement in local politics. Japanese communism responded to the domination of local politics by independent conservative notables and the 'apolitical' rhetoric of local politics by searching for wider coalitions with what they termed 'democratic forces' and by building up a parallel organization that incorporated the socially and economically marginal. Boyd also considers the extent to which this resulted in distinctive administrative styles and programmes and he examines Kyoto (which could be called the JCP's Bologna) as a show-case of Communist local government. Future prospects for Japanese communism have some features in common with the European position: coalitions have come under strain and the Party has looked to the peace movement as a means of increasing its influence in Japanese politics and its present flexibility allows such issues to be used in the system.

The various chapters that make up this book are an overview of communism in local government in Western Europe and Japan. The Conclusion draws together some of the threads from the separate chapters but there are cross-references made and parallels drawn throughout the book. Local government does not offer much in the way of revolutionary opportunities and the Communist parties involved in local politics to a large extent are usually parties that have sought to exploit the reformist potential of the liberal democratic systems within which they operate. There are some exceptions to this, notably Portugal, but local government activity for the most part ill-befits the heroic vision that inspired the early Bolsheviks. Increased Communist activity in local government in the 1960s and 1970s does not provide irrefutable evidence that the parties have become reformist. They could, like the parties of the 1930s, have decided to occupy such positions as they arose (there to wait for better days), but there is the persistent problem of electoralism and of being drawn into the bourgeois system to the detriment of revolutionary purity. However, the collapse of the party machine is not something that can happen overnight and, as the following chapters show, the forces moving parties in that direction vary from country to country.

Note

1. The *Communist Party of Denmark* (Danmarks Kommunistiske Parti–DKP) was organized on 9 November 1919 in the turbulent aftermath of the First World War and except for the period of the German occupation during the Second World War it has always been a legal party. The oldest of the Scandinavian parties, the *Communist Party of Finland* (Suomen Kommunistinen Puolue–SKP), was founded by 'red' dissident Social Democrats on 29 August 1918 in Moscow. Until 1930 the Party operated through a variety of front organizations before it was forced underground. It became legal in 1944 under an agreement stipulated by the Finnish-Soviet armistice that year. The *French Communist Party* (Parti Communiste Français–PCF) was formed as a French Section of the Communist International during the Congress of the Socialist Party held in Tours on 25–30 December 1920. Except for a short period of illegality (1939–40) following its support of the Soviet-Nazi pact and the clandestine period between 1941–4 of the Resistance, the PCF has operated publicly and legally. Another section of the Comintern was the *Communist Party of Great Britain* (CPGB), founded after a fusion of several organizations and prolonged negotiations during its 1st Congress in London in July–August 1920. The *Communist Party of Greece* (Kommounistikon Komma Ellados–KKE) evolved from the Socialist Workers' Party of Greece which was formed during the 18–22 November 1918 Congress in Piraeus. The Party remained a marginal force in Greek politics for several years, undergoing repeated splits till 1931 when the Comintern installed a Stalin-supported leadership. Its membership and influence grew steadily during the years of depression until 1936 when the KKE was banned. The *Italian Communist Party* (Partito Comunista Italiano–PCI) was founded on 21 January 1921 as a section of the Comintern. Declared illegal in November 1926, the Party conducted its activities underground until April 1944 when it participated in the first post-war royal Italian government. Subsequently it also took part in other governmental coalitions until 1947 when it was excluded from office. For a brief period, between summer 1976 and January 1979, it again became part of a governmental coalition but without holding cabinet posts. The *Japanese Communist Party* (Nihonkyōsantō–JCP) was founded on 15 July 1922 and until 4 October 1945 remained an illegal organization. Between the wars its membership never exceeded about 1,000. However, after its legalization during the American occupation of Japan, the Party's membership and influence, especially among trade unions, grew until 1950 when after expressing an open support for North Korea it was partially suppressed. Some of its leaders went underground and

engaged in extreme activities including acts of terrorism. The Party suffered badly during the 1952 general elections and saw a substantial decline in membership. The party fortunes revived in 1961 when it began to advocate the 'parliamentary road' to power, a platform that became even more pronounced after 1964 when the JCP broke with Moscow over the issue of the test-ban treaty. The JCP Eurocommunist line has remained basically unchanged since then. The *Norwegian Communist Party* (Norges Kommunistiske Parti–NKP) was organized on 4 November 1923 by a few radical politician and trade-unionist members of the Labour Party who decided to remain affiliated to the Comintern. The Party remained weak throughout its existence and, with the exception of parliamentary elections in October 1945 when it received 11.9 per cent of the votes, its electoral support and membership has been on the decline. The *Communist Party of Portugal* (Partido Comunista Portugués–PCP) was founded in February 1921 as a splinter group of the Portuguese Socialist Party. The Party was declared illegal in 1926 and worked underground until the April 1974 revolution which restored democracy and the legal functioning of all political parties in the country. The Party emerged from thirty-eight years of clandestinity as the largest, best organized and most powerful in Portugal and during the following two years it further strengthened its position and control over key areas of national life, in particular, trade unions, the armed forces and the mass media. It openly rejected democratic policies in favour of collaboration with a left-wing dictatorship of the Armed Forces Movement which attempted a coup in 1976. Subsequently its influence has however, been eroded in several sections of the population with the exception of some trade unions and the farm workers of the Alentejo area. The *Communist Party of Spain* (Partido Comunista de España–PCE) was founded on 7 November 1921 and immediately joined the Comintern. It was banned in 1924. During the years of Franco's dictatorship it was the best-organized party and emerged in 1977 as a powerful political force with its membership increasing rapidly from 15,000 in 1974 to 200,000 in 1977. Even before its legalization the PCE adopted the Eurocommunist platform and has continued to be its main exponent ever since, despite several internal divisions and outside pressures particularly from the Soviet and Eastern European Communist parties. The *Party of the Left–Communists* (Vansterpartiet Kommunisterna–Vpk) was originally formed in May 1917 as the Social Democratic left of Sweden. It joined the Comintern in July 1919 and was represented at its founding congress. In 1921 it accepted the Comintern's Twenty-One Conditions and changed its name to the Communist Party of Sweden and became a section of the Comintern. The Party has a long history of factionalism and splits that have dominated its policies and performance throughout its existence. Its widest popular support came at the end of the Second World War during the 1946 elections. In 1967 its name was changed to the present one in order to reflect a political line more independent from Moscow. The Vpk has on a number of occasions played an important parliamentary role despite its small size, since the ruling Social Democrats have had to rely on its support in order to remain in power.

Bibliography

Alba, V., 1979. *El partido comunista en España*. Barcelona, Planeta.

Albright, D. E. (ed.), 1979. *Communism and Political Systems in Western Europe*. Colorado, Westview.

Amyot, G., 1981. *The Italian Communist Party*. London, Croom Helm.

Blackmer, D. L. M. and Tarrow, S. (eds), 1975. *Communism in Italy and France*. Princeton, Princeton University Press.

Borkenau, F., 1953. *European Communism*, London, Faber.

Braunthal, J., 1967. *History of the International: 1914-1943*. London, Nelson.

Carrillo, S., 1977. *'Eurocommunism' and the State*. London, Lawrence & Wishart.

Childs, D. (ed.), 1980. *The Changing Face of Western Communism*. London, Croom Helm.

Darke, B., 1952. *The Communist Technique in Britain*. London, Penguin.

Ellison, H. J., 1985. 'United Front Strategy and Soviet Foreign Policy', *Problems of Communism*, vol. XXXIV, no. 5. Sept–Oct., pp. 45–64.

Gyford, J., 1985. *The Politics of Local Socialism*. London, George Allen & Unwin.

Kaplan, M. A. (ed.), 1978. *The Many Faces of Communism*. Glencoe, Free Press.

Lange, P. and Vanicelli, M. (eds), 1981. *The Communist Parties of Italy, France and Spain*. London, Unwin.

Lindermann, A. S., 1983. *A History of European Socialism*. New Haven, Yale University Press.

Machin, A. (ed.), 1984. *National Communism in Western Europe*. London, Hutchinson.

McInnes, N., 1975. *The Communist Parties of Western Europe*. Oxford, R.I.I.A.

Middlemas, K., 1980. *Power and the Party: Changing Faces of Communism in Western Europe*. London, André Deutsch.

Mortimer, E., 1984. *The Rise of the French Communist Party 1920-1947*. London, Faber.

Mortimer, E. *et al.* (eds), 1979. *Eurocommunism: Myth or Reality?* Harmondsworth, Penguin.

Mujal-León, E., 1983. *Communism and Political Change in Spain*. Bloomington, Indiana University Press.

Pelling, H., 1975. *The British Communist Party: A Historical Profile*. London, A. & C. Black.

Sasson, D., 1981. *The Strategy of the Italian Communist Party*. New York, St. Martin's Press.

Staar, R. F. (ed.), 1977. *Yearbook on International Communist Affairs: 1977*. Stanford, Hoover Institution Press.

Sunday Times, Insight Team, 1975. *Insight on Portugal*. London, André Deutsch.

Tannahill, N., 1978. *The Communist Parties of Western Europe*. London, Greenwood Press.

Tokes, R. L., 1978. *Eurocommunism and Détente*. New York, New York University Press.

Tunon de Lara, M., 1966. *La España del siglo XX*. Paris, Librería Española.

Upton, A. F. (ed.), 1973. *The Communist Parties of Scandinavia and Finland*. London, Weidenfeld.

2 The Spanish Communist Party and Local Government: An Overall Assessment

José Amodia*

Some Introductory Thoughts

When one examines the role played by the PCE in the area of Spanish local government since the death of Franco, two features become immediately apparent. First, the Party's global achievements, despite the success of some individual Communist figures and some Communist-controlled councils, have been rather modest and largely dependent on alliances with the Socialists. And secondly, local government affairs have been low in the PCE's order of priorities. Democracy in Spain was established from above and did not descend to local level till the spring of 1979, some three and a half years after Franco's demise. The PCE involved itself fully in that process of democratization, accepting and following the direction set by those who controlled it. The Party's interest centred excessively, if not exclusively, on major institutional and constitutional matters to the detriment of political problems at lower levels.

The PCE was propelled into prominence by the events of the Spanish Civil War and during the long dictatorship that followed it became a major force in the opposition to Franco. But the Party's clandestine activities never entered the area of local government. In the early years the Communists were involved in guerrilla warfare; later on they organized demonstrations and strikes, tried repeatedly and unsuccessfully to create some kind of united front with the other anti-Franco forces, and became involved in the various protest movements that developed in the universities, in the regions and among the working classes. The PCE even infiltrated the state-controlled Syndical Organization, particularly during the 1960s when it succeeded in having many of its activists elected as shop stewards (Mujal-Léon, 1983,

* José Amodia would like to record his gratitude to Carlos Alonso Zaldívar, PCE's Secretary for Municipal Affairs between 1979 and 1981, and to the successor and present incumbent of that post, Juan Francisco Pla. The long conversations in Madrid were most helpful and illuminating. Thanks must be extended, too, to all the Communist councillors and mayors who offered information and opinions both orally and in writing. Needless to say, their cooperation does not in any way make them responsible for the views expressed in this chapter; that responsibility is entirely that of the author.

p. 58). What the Communists never did, nor even tried to do, was to tamper with or undermine local government structures or processes. As far as it is known in this area there was no attempt at infiltration.

When democracy returned to the country, allowing the Communists to regain legal status, the PCE's attention was diverted away from local government. Factors external to the Party combined with internal tensions and problems to bring about such a state of affairs. The exceptional nature of the process of democratization concentrated the efforts of all political parties on what might be termed matters of state. Certainly, the left-wing parties—the PCE amongst them—had little room for manœuvre in this respect. Parliamentary elections, the consolidation of the monarchy, the new constitution, the legalization of parties, the question of regional autonomy, etc., absorbed all the political energy available during the first few years. In the newly-born democracy, local government matters were left aside as non-urgent. Municipal and provincial councils had to wait until the new *Cortes Generales* and the regional assemblies were established.

Apart from the external factors mentioned above, which generated similar tendencies towards local government in all parties, in the case of the PCE a number of internal crises reinforced such tendencies. It will suffice to enumerate here some of the reasons that motivated those crises: the return to Spain of the historical leaders of the Party—Santiago Carrillo, La Pasionaria, etc.—after many years of exile and the difficulties encountered by these figures to adjust to a new country and to new generations of Communists; the parallel adjustments required to turn an organization developed in clandestinity into a party for open political contest; the more or less profound changes in strategy which the now rather *passé* label of Eurocommunism promised at one time; the apparent renunciation of some long-standing ideological dogmas such as 'Leninism' or the 'dictatorship of the proletariat'; the demands from certain sectors of the membership for internal democratization, that is to say, doing away with 'democratic centralism' and recognizing the existence of currents of opinion or tendencies in the Party; the hope for more decentralization, even a federal structure, that would give the regional branches greater autonomy *vis-à-vis* the central party apparatus.

The combination of all these exogenous and endogenous elements accounts for the low priority that municipal questions have had in the life of the PCE over the last decade. They have always been subordinated to the higher interests of the Party. Very often Communist municipal policies are little more than an echo of what is happening to the Party or what the Party is doing in other areas. Consequently, the study of the role of the PCE in local government requires a wider context to allow cross-references to be made.

Within that broader framework four main questions will be considered: the performance of the PCE in municipal elections; the geographical distribution of Communist support in the country; the relationship between the Party and its local councillors; and finally the local government policies and achievements of the PCE as well as its municipal agreements with the PSOE (Spanish Socialist Party).

It should not be assumed that the subsidiary position of local government in the overall strategy of the PCE devalues the study of such matters. On the contrary, it provides a view of the subject often neglected in the studies of Spanish communism. It also serves to highlight one of the most serious errors committed by the PCE since it returned to Spain and regained legal status: the neglect of grassroots politics. Paradoxically enough, one of the most neglected areas has yielded some of the Party's best results. This may very well be taken in advance as the main conclusion of this study.

The PCE in Local Elections

The change from dictatorship to democracy was slow, gradual and legalistic and, to a large extent, was controlled by those who had their hands on the levers of power at the time of Franco's death. It was to the advantage of these groups to delay the holding of local elections for as long as possible. It was widely assumed that once elections were held they would lose much of the institutional infrastructure provided by Francoist councillors and mayors, which allowed them to extend their control over the transition to the provincial and local levels. In spite of the occasional voice raised on the left demanding the democratization of municipal councils, the first local elections did not take place until the spring of 1979. By then two general elections had been held, a new constitution had been approved, and the status of the PCE as a minor political force had already been established.

Any assessment of local elections in Spain must include some consideration of the multiplicity and diversity of municipalities. The proliferation does not reach French levels—there are over 36,000 'communes' in France—but a figure of some 8,000 is still too high for a country whose population does not exceed 38 million. The very unequal distribution of that population, exacerbated by the large migratory movements during the period 1955–75, adds another dimension to the problem. As a result in 1975 some three-quarters of Spanish boroughs had 2,000 inhabitants or less, with an average of 550 per borough; in contrast, 70 per cent of the population was concentrated in 523 boroughs with more than 10,000 residents each (Díaz-López & F. Morata,

1984, p. 81). When local government reform takes place—and after several aborted attempts it is likely to happen in the near future—new boundaries will be drawn up and the number of councils considerably reduced. But in the meantime the relevance of these inequalities in any electoral study is patently obvious.

Another preliminary comment appears necessary. At this early stage in the development of Spanish democracy municipal elections should not be considered in isolation from other types of elections, both national and regional. This is particularly relevant in this case because over the last few years Spaniards have lived in a kind of electoral fever. From December 1976, when the referendum that set them on the road to democracy was held, to the most recent local elections in May 1983 they were called to the polls no fewer than thirty-one times: seven referendums—two national and five regional ones— three general elections, two municipal elections, and nineteen separate regional ballots to elect the autonomous assemblies, and all this within the span of six and a half years. Hence one can appreciate the need to set municipal voting within this broader and tightly packed electoral context.

When the PCE was confronted with the first local elections, the Communists had already experienced the disappointment of two general elections which had placed them in a subsidiary position to the Socialist Party. In 1977, out of a total of 350 seats in Congress, the PCE had only gained twenty. Even the slight improvement of 1979, when they raised their number of deputies to twenty-three, only served to confirm the ascendancy of the Socialists on the left of the political spectrum—the PSOE obtained 118 seats in 1977 and 121 in 1979. By the spring of 1983, when new local councils were elected, the PCE had already experienced a kind of electoral nadir. The previous autumn its parliamentary representation had been reduced to a mere four deputies. The Communist share of the vote (in percentage terms) in both general and local elections between 1977 and 1983 was as follows:

Type of Election	National	National	Municipal	National	Municipal
Year	1977	1979	1979	1982	1983
Communist vote (%)	9.4	10.81	13.1	4.14	8.18

(Source: El País, Ya and Cambio 16)

As can be seen, the Communist share of the vote in Spain is consistently low, lower than in other countries of Southern Europe with the exception perhaps of Greece. The picture would be even worse if regional elections were included in the figures. The PCE has no deputies in nine of the seventeen autonomous assemblies and only a very small representation in the other eight. Yet the PCE's performance in municipal elections represents, both in 1979 and 1983, an upturn in the fortunes of the Party. This might be explained, partially at least, by the fact that in general the pattern of electoral behaviour differs when the voter moves from the national or regional to the local level, with the left very often doing better at the latter. The reasons are, of course, more complex, resulting from the confused tangle of multiple polls held over a short period of time. The municipal elections of 1979 took place one month only after a general election. A single campaign encompassed both electoral contests. All the parties had to do in the intervening weeks was to adjust their strategy from the national to the local level taking into account the results of the first election. In 1983 the picture is even more involved. Local councils were elected the same day as thirteen regional assemblies. In those thirteen regions the campaigns, the voting and even the results overlapped to a large extent.

So far the PCE's approach to municipal elections seems to have been motivated by two main factors. In the first place they tried to use the local councils as a platform from which to reverse the misfortunes of the Party after the electoral disappointments of 1977 and 1979 and the débâcle of 1982. The Party, having seen its presence in parliament reduced and almost obliterated, started searching for political influence and space in other spheres, for example, the municipal councils and the trade unions.

In the second place, Communist leaders soon realized that even at the municipal level the PCE was not a front runner. The chances of the PCE gaining control of many councils were rather remote. The PSOE was dominant on the left and even though there appeared to be a considerable ideological overlap between both parties, as the opinion polls showed repeatedly there was little likelihood of many voters shifting their support in favour of the Communists. Consequently, the PCE ran its electoral campaigns with an open offer for a municipal pact with the PSOE, or any other progressive party for that matter.

As indicated above, there was a considerable ideological overlap between the electoral offer of the two main left-wing parties. That certainly was the case in 1979. Behind a façade of mutual acerbic attacks at the hustings, there was a fundamental agreement in matters of principle. The electoral campaign of both parties conveyed the same double message to the electorate: first and foremost, the democratization of municipal councils, bringing to an end the corruption, inefficiency and patronage that were endemic in Spanish local government; and, secondly, the promise of a number of improvements in schooling, health care, recreation, housing, etc. The PCE was not presenting the electorate with an image sufficiently different from that of the Socialists. Left-wing voters who a month earlier in the general election had offered their support to the PSOE could see no real reason now to change their allegiance to the PCE. Furthermore, the Socialists, already established as the main opposition party and with more means at their disposal, were able to run a much more sophisticated and intensive campaign.

Nevertheless, the PCE's efforts to gain some ground on the municipal front were not altogether unsuccessful. Impelled by the then newly created Secretariat for Municipal Affairs, the Communists made some noticeable progress in the local elections of April 1979. Their share of the vote—the best in any election to this day—gave them more than 3,700 councillors over all Spain (out of a total of 69,568), putting them in third position on the party table, far behind the Socialists and the centre-right UCD, but ahead of the right-wing Popular Alliance. Even more important was the fact that the combined votes of the PSOE and the PCE gave the left a predominant position in most of the major cities. In many of these cities the Socialist councillors were in a majority, but they still needed the support of the Communists to occupy the *alcaldía* (office of mayor) and control the council. By means of an agreement with the PSOE the Communists were able to take a share in the running of some of the most important local councils over the next four years.

The 1983 municipal elections differed in several ways from that of 1979. The contest could no longer be centred on who should replace Francoist mayors and councillors. There had already been four years of left-wing management in many local councils. At the same time the political scenario had altered considerably. The party system had been shaken by the disappearance of the UCD—the ruling party from 1977 to 1982—and this disappearance had placed a question mark on the ballot papers of several million voters. The general election in the autumn of 1982 had given the PSOE a landslide victory and had transformed the right-wing AP into the second parliamentary force. As for the Communists, the internal crises in the Party, the deep cleavages and splits in their ranks in Catalonia and the Basque Country, the loss of more than one million votes at the general election, and the subsequent resignation and replacement of the Party's General Secretary, had left the PCE in a sorrowful state. The local elections took on dramatic overtones for them. For all these reasons caution should be exercised when comparing the results of 1983 with those of 1979, and the conclusions should not be taken as a safe platform to forecast future development.

In contrast to what had happened in 1979, the electoral campaigns of the Socialists and Communists differed considerably in 1983. Four years of partnership in local government had not reduced electoral antagonism between the two parties. On the contrary, mutual recriminations and acrimonious attacks were the order of the day on both sides. And their electoral images were now looking in opposite directions. The Socialists had an overall majority in parliament and they were still riding on the crest of a wave, with public opinion polls showing a sustained level of popular support. From that lofty position they could afford to look down on their municipal allies. Their campaign was directed very much towards local issues. Even their best-known figures remained mostly in the background. The PSOE tried to avoid the local election becoming a test of the government's record. Five months was too short a time to be able to claim any major achievements.

On the other hand, the PCE decided to run its electoral campaign as a frontal attack on the programme and policies of the recently established Socialist government. Local issues were largely pushed aside and the main thrust of the campaign concentrated on the government's handling of the economy—unemployment and industrial restructuring primarily—and on its ambiguous stance in foreign policy—membership of NATO or the backing for American missiles in Europe (Gerardo Iglesias, *El País*, 27 April 1983). Table 2.1 shows the electoral support and the number of councillors gained

Table 2.1 Results of municipal elections, 8 May 1983

Party	Vote (%)	Councillors		Mayors	
		Number	%	Number	%
PSOE [1]	43.01	23,729	35.05	2,640	33.09
AP/PDP/UL [2]	26.43	21,076	31.13	2,471	30.97
PCE [3]	8.18	2,495	3.68	172	2.16
Independ. [4]	5.75	8,650	12.78	1,184	14.84
CiU [5]	4.17	3,279	4.84	432	5.41
PNV [6]	2.23	1,322	1.95	173	2.17
CDS [7]	1.82	658	0.97	172	2.16

[1] Socialist Party
[2] Conservative coalition centred around the Popular Alliance
[3] Communist Party
[4] Independent Candidates
[5] Catalan Conservative Party
[6] Basque Nationalist Party
[7] Democratic Social Centre

Source: *Anuario El País 1984*, p. 53.

by all the main parties in 1983. On the left of the political spectrum the Socialists obtained two million votes fewer than in the previous general election, but in comparison with the 1979 local election they managed to strengthen their position in the municipal sphere. From now on they would be able to control many important *ayuntamientos* (local councils) without Communist support.

For the PCE the results had exactly the opposite effect. The Communists recovered some of the ground lost at the previous general election. Having sunk to a mere 4.14 per cent share of the vote in October 1982, they almost managed to double it now, recovering in the process the support of some 600,000 voters. The figures, however, look less encouraging when a straightforward comparison is made between these results and those of 1979. The 8.12 per cent share of the vote is well below the 13.1 per cent of four years earlier. The PCE has lost a third of its councillors and almost the same amount of mayors. What is even more important is that in many of the larger cities the PCE is no longer a *partido bisagra*, that is to say, a party on which the control of the local council hinges. In cities such as Madrid, Valencia or Seville, whose councils between 1979 and 1983 had been governed jointly by Socialists and Communists, the PSOE had now an overall majority guaranteeing a Socialist mayor and sole control of the council (a mayor in Spain has wide powers).

The global assessment of the results, then, is not favourable to the Communists. Between 1979 and 1983, the left-wing vote has increased considerably, but the PCE's share of it has gone down. There are, however, some positive aspects. In certain areas the PCE maintained, and even increased, its electoral support. This tended to happen in towns which already had a Communist-controlled council. The voters were thus expressing their satisfaction with the way the Communist councillors had been running their municipal affairs, a fact which the PCE leadership was quick to point out in its own assessment of the elections.

The PCE considers the result of the recent municipal elections as a ratification of the profound democratic process started in 1979 by the councils under Socialist-Communist control, and is pleased to see as an important part of that ratification the support given to the work done by Communist mayors. [*Materiales II* (4/5), January-June 1983, p. 3.]

Where are those PCE mayors to be found? Which are the Communist-controlled councils? Is there a Communist Spain?

Geographical Distribution of the PCE's Vote

Communist support is very unevenly spread over the country. The three general elections held to date show this quite clearly (see Table 2.2). Regional elections produce a very similar pattern. The Communist vote is unevenly distributed and its strong and weak areas are the same ones as in the general elections. Most of the Communist votes come from five regions: Catalonia, Valencia, Andalusia, Madrid and Asturias. Communist support in the rest of Spain tends to fall below the national average for the Party, with Galicia, Old Castile, the Basque Country and Navarre appearing consistently at the bottom of any table. Other national parties are affected by such regional variations but not to the same extent as the PCE. The PSOE is not only stronger but its support is much more evenly distributed, whereas the Communist vote drops to negligible levels in wide areas of the country.

Table 2.2 Variations in PCE Support, 1977–82*

Year	Highest (%)	Lowest (%)
1977	Barcelona 20, Cordoba 16.4	Lugo 1.7, Orense 1.6
1979	Barcelona 19.12, Cordoba 19.11	Lugo 1.5, Navarre 2.23
1982	Oviedo 10.5, Cordoba 9.8	Navarre 0.7, Orense 0.8

* Percentages refer to provincial constituencies.

In the municipal elections of May 1983 the PCE's share of the vote, which averaged 8.18 per cent nationally, did not place the Party ahead in any of the fifty provinces into which the country is divided. Only in twelve did the PCE surpass its national average. All twelve provinces are situated in the regions mentioned earlier as inclined towards the left. Seven are to be found in the south in Andalusia, with one outstanding example: the province of Cordoba where the PCE with 32 per cent of the vote finished a close second to the Socialists. Badajoz, the southern province of Extremadura, which shares many of the socio-economic features of Andalusia, is another one. And, finally, there are the four provinces with big urban centres and a high level of industrialization: Madrid, Barcelona, Valencia and Asturias. At the other end of the scale, the Communist vote was extremely low in Galicia—particularly in the rural and underdeveloped provinces of Lugo and Orense—in the whole of Old Castile, in Catalonia outside the populous area of Barcelona, in Navarre and in the Basque Country.

Table 2.3 Communist support in municipalities with over 200,000 inhabitants

Municipal council	PCE position	Votes		Communist councillors/total in council
		Number	%	
Madrid	3	112,040	6.84	4/57
Barcelona	4	62,421	6.95	3/43
Valencia	3	28,887	7.61	2/33
Sevilla	3	24,099	8.89	2/31
Zaragoza	4	14,150	5.41	1/31
Málaga	3	13,554	7.18	2/31
Bilbao	5	2.764	1.62	0/29
Murcia	3	9,216	7.07	2/29
Las Palmas	4	8,193	6.33	2/29
Valladolid	3	8,315	5.47	1/29
Palma de Mallorca	5	3,905	3.17	0/27
Hospitalet	2	16,835	12.69	3/27
Córdoba	1	79,683	57.97	17/27
Gijón	3	12,664	10.22	3/27
Vigo	4	6,053	5.68	1/27
Alicante	3	5,650	4.95	0/27
Granada	3	5,114	4.40	0/27
La Coruña	4	2,609	2.61	0/27
Badalona	2	35,926	36.30	11/27

The Basque Country is a special case requiring some comment. It is a highly industrialized and developed region with a considerable amount of immigrant labour—at first sight a suitable environment for Communism, but no so in practice. Historically the Basque electorate has shown a proclivity towards the ideological mixture of traditional Catholic values and moderate nationalism represented by the PNV (Basque Nationalist Party). The appearance of some left-wing nationalist parties—*Herri Batasuna, Euskadiko Eskerra* — for example, offers the native workers the possibility of giving their vote to an organization that represents and defends both their class interests and their Basque identity. As for the immigrant workers settled in the industrial hinterland of Bilbao—Santurce, Basauri, Baracaldo, etc.—their preference is for the PSOE rather than the PCE. This Communist weakness in Euskadi has been further compounded by the crisis in the EPK (Basque Communist Party) during the course of 1981, which led to the expulsion of its General

Secretary, Roberto Lertxundi, and the division of the Party into two irreconcilable organizations (Vega & Erroteta, 1982, pp. 232–52).

Let us now move from the provincial to the municipal level. There are in Spain 156 municipal boroughs with an electoral register of more than 20,000 voters each (*Anuario El País 1984*, pp. 61–6). They encompass, of course, all the large population centres of the country. In 1983 the PCE surpassed its national average of 8.18 per cent of the vote in fifty of these municipalities. The towns where the Communists achieved their best results—those in which they were the leading party or gained at least 20 per cent of the vote (see Table 2.4)—all have a high proportion of working-class voters. As was to be expected, the PCE is a working-class party, although not the party of the working class, an honour which up to now had been held to a large extent by the PSOE (Linz *et al*., pp. 388 ff). These muncipalities with broad Communist support are to be found in the 'Red belt' of immigrant settlements surrounding Barcelona and Madrid, in the mining region of Asturias, and in the *latifundium* areas of Andalusia. In only seven of them did the PCE obtain overall control of the council. These were Sabadell, Santa Coloma, San Feliú de Llobregat and Rubí—all four industrial towns situated in the metropolitan area of Barcelona; Coslada, also an industrial town to the east of Madrid; Puerto de Santa María, a municipal area in the province of Cadiz, famous for its sherries and wines; and the city of Cordoba, the only provincial capital in which the PCE gained an absolute majority.

Cordoba and Its Communist Mayor

Cordoba has become the municipal showpiece of the Communist Party. Even though the PCE lost a lot of its councillors and mayors in 1983, it was able to defend and strengthen its position in some key councils, like those mentioned above, or others with similar characteristics such as Arganda and Pinto in the province of Madrid, or San Fernando and Sanlúcar de Barrameda in the deep south. Cordoba was one such council, but with the added glamour of being a provincial capital.

In many ways the city of Cordoba is not a typical Communist municipality. Santa Coloma de Gramanet (Barcelona) or Coslada (Madrid), whose accelerated growth was the result of successive waves of immigrant labour, fill the bill much better. Cordoba is the capital city of one of the eight provinces of Andalusia, a region where the Communists enjoy above-average support. It is a city of some 280,000 inhabitants and in its economically active population, its socio-economic structure, income per head, amenities, etc., it does not differ noticeably from other Andalusian cities. And yet in the municipal

Table 2.4 Municipalities with a population exceeding 20,000 in which the Communists took more than 20 per cent of the vote

Municipality	Province	Communist vote (%)
Rubí (1)	Barcelona	63.81
San Feliú	Barcelona	62.72
S. Martín del Rey Aurelio (3)	Asturias	60.31
Cordoba (4)	Cordoba	57.97
Sanlúcar de Barrameda (5)	Cádiz	53.84
Coslada (6)	Madrid	53.30
Sabadell (7)	Barcelona	51.47
Prat de Llobregat (8)	Barcelona	47.13
Santa Coloma (9)	Barcelona	45.91
Cornellá (10)	Barcelona	39.50
Badalona (11)	Barcelona	36.30
Puerto de Sta. María (12)	Cádiz	33.25
Dos Hermanas (13)	Sevilla	30.27
Algeciras (14)	Cádiz	27.41
Mollet del Vallés (15)	Barcelona	24.61
Mieres (16)	Asturias	22.82
Langreo (17)	Asturias	22.04

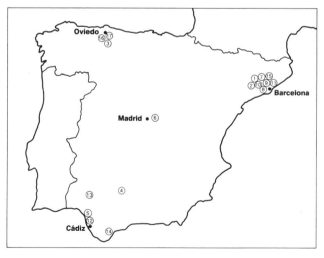

Map 2.1 Communist vote in large municipalities

elections of 1979, and even more so in 1983, the Communist vote in Cordoba was far higher than in Seville, Granada or Málaga. Part of the explanation is to be found in the stronger infrastructure and better organization of the PCE in the whole of the province of Cordoba. In all the elections, both general and regional, Cordoba has been the Andalusian province where the Communists have done consistently better, with the 19.1 per cent in the general election of 1979 being their highest figure to date. But Communist performance in the municipal elections in Cordoba far outstrips that kind of figure. In 1983 they gained 57.97 per cent of the vote. Seventeen of the twenty-seven members in the local council are Communists. The PCE had come out on top in 1979, too, though on that occasion without an overall majority. Between 1979 and 1983 the Communists ran the Cordoban council with the support of the Socialists.

The most convincing reason adduced to explain the growing Communist success in the city of Cordoba is the *fenómeno Anguita* (the Anguita factor). Julio Anguita is the Communist mayor of Cordoba. His personal qualities seem to have played a major role in the victory of the PCE. He could also be taken as the prototype of the new generation of Communist militants whose presence in the Party during the last few years has been so prevalent and controversial. Julio Anguita is a 42-year-old Andalusian with his roots in the lower-middle classes. He trained and worked as a teacher for a number of years; later he took a university degree in Contemporary History. He joined the PCE in 1972. He belongs to a generation of well-educated Spaniards who, feeling imprisoned by the narrow-mindedness of Franco's political system, saw in the PCE a vehicle to bring democracy to Spanish society. Once inside the Party, they fought outwardly to gain democracy for Spain and inwardly to renovate and democratize the Party organization; hence the label '*renovadores*' (renovators) that is often applied to them.

In the first democratic elections in 1977 Anguita stood as a Communist candidate in Cordoba, but did not get a seat. Two years later he headed the PCE list in the municipal election and led the Party to victory. He was elected mayor of Cordoba and from that moment on his political career soared. A certain personal magnetism, a handsome presence, and his public-speaking qualities gained him rapid popularity and the colourful title of 'Red Caliph of Cordoba'. His ascending influence rests, however, upon a more solid base. His love of teaching is reflected in his political work. He is what might be termed a didactic politican (an opinion echoed by a number of Communists interviewed by the author). In his own words, it is necessary to awaken doubts in people's minds, so that they do not applaud but go away thinking (*El País*, Suplemento dominical, 7 August 1983, p. 12). In his running of the council he has been receptive to pressures and suggestions from below. In so far as it is possible he tries to maintain a constant dialogue with the voters of Cordoba by means of edicts and open letters published in the local press and written in a colloquial, populist style (Anguita, *passim*).

In relation to the other parties represented in the Cordoban council, Julio Anguita has usually adopted an open attitude. His proposals, his policies, his leadership are obviously inspired by the party he represents, but the council has normally been run upon the basis of consensus politics (Anguita interview in *Materiales II* (4/5) January–June 1983, p. 10). During his first four years as mayor he was sustained in office by an agreement with the Socialists. However, the coalition was abruptly terminated when the mayor, carried away perhaps by his own success, took one or two important decisions without prior consultation with his Socialist allies.

Another important ingredient of Julio Anguita's popularity has been his willingness to confront the challenge of conservative attitudes and traditional institutions surviving from the previous period. Famous in this respect was his public polemic, conducted through the pages of the local newspaper, with the Bishop of Cordoba over the council's decision to return to the Muslims a Catholic temple which had previously been a mosque (Anguita, pp. 58–62).

The PCE has scored its finest victory in the sphere of local government in the way explained above. It cannot be attributed to the mayor exclusively, but it is highly unlikely that without him the Communists would have been so successful in Cordoba. Julio Anguita has now become an important figure in the Party's hierarchy. He presided over the PCE's 11th Congress held in Madrid in December 1983 and he was at that time elected a member of the Party's Central Committee. It is safe to assume that his political career will take him to higher things within the Party. His imprint will still be there when he moves on, but his departure may very well explode the Communist myth of Cordoba.

The Relationship between the PCE and Its Local Councillors

The relationship between a party and its councillors flows along two parallel channels. Through one, the party offers technical and material help in order to increase the efficiency of its representatives in local government. Through the other, the party provides ideological guidance and secures the implementation of its municipal policies by its own councillors. Put in a more controversial way, it can be said that in this dual relationship the balance tilts sometimes in favour of a managerial or administrative view of the councillor's role and at other times it takes on a more political dimension. In the first case the councillor will limit himself to running the affairs of the people he represents as if he were the manager of a commercial enterprise; in the second, the councillor becomes a kind of conveyor belt bringing to the local council the policies and decisions of his party's hierarchy. The taxonomy is too simplistic as the two established categories overlap and cannot be mutually exclusive. But the correlation between the two does throw light on the party–councillor relationship.

The Spanish electoral system adds complexity to the problem. It is usually assumed that in local elections the voter is swayed more often by the personal qualities of a candidate than by the ideology of the party he represents. However, the system of closed lists used in Spain forces the elector to choose between parties and not between candidates, so that it can be argued that the party stands between the voter and the local councillor who, in his turn, owes allegiance to the party first and only through the party to the electorate. This subject has exercised the attention of all parties in Spain and it has given rise to bitter disagreement, disciplinary measures and even expulsions.

The PCE's attitude is that the councillors elected on the Party's ticket or list have the obligation of implementing, as far as it is possible, its municipal policies. The Party, through its provincial committees, controls the names of candidates and the order in which they will appear on the electoral list. In the case of Madrid such control falls to the Central Committee (in December 1983 the 11th Congress altered the statutes; in future the Committee only has to be consulted). Once elected and in office, 'the councillors must be simple instruments of the party's committee', according to the view of the previous General Secretary, Santiago Carrillo (*Mundo Obrero*, 4–11 December 1981). This point of view can also be found—though with a much greater degree of flexibility—in the Political Report submitted by the Central Committee to the Party's 11th Congress:

It must be stated quite clearly that the general lines of our work in local government have to be drawn up by the party's municipal leadership, but granting councillors broad autonomy in their application. [The full text was published in an undated special issue of *Mundo Obrero* a few weeks before the 11th PCE Congress.]

This combination of centralized policy-making with some degree of independence for the councillors encapsulates the opinion prevalent in the Party at the present time. It is certainly the one favoured by Juan Francisco Pla, head of the PCE's Secretariat for Municipal Affairs (as stated in an interview in April 1984), and acceptable to all the Communist mayors and councillors consulted. The following quote can be taken as indicative of the latter groups point of view:

> The members of the Town Council enjoy total autonomy in the running of local government, subject to the condition that they apply the programme and general guidelines approved by the party. The party does not interfere with the decision-making process. [L. Hernández i Alcácer, Communist mayor of Sta. Coloma de Gramanet, Barcelona, in letter addressed to the author.]

There is no reason to question the coincidental views of Communist leaders and practitioners in the field of local government. Broadly speaking, they both express a considerable degree of agreement, and even satisfaction, with the system as it stands. But a more detached observer can easily detect the following flaws:

(a) that within the party structure the department in charge of municipal affairs has had, from the moment it was set up in the not very distant past, a rather slow and uneven development, and that as a result of this, the amount of material help and technical advice provided to Communist councillors has been lacking in many respects;

(b) that in those occasions when the party apparatus felt ignored or threatened by an independent or dissenting attitude on the part of its councillors, the leadership did not hesitate to apply disciplinary measures, including expulsion from the Party.

The PCE decided to create a department to take charge of its municipal affairs on the eve of the first local elections in the spring of 1979. The task was entrusted to Carlos Alonso Zaldívar, one of the leading 'renovators' in the Party. He studied the way in which the PCF and the PCI organize such matters, and leaning more towards the Italian model he set up a Secretariat for Local Affairs whose aims were: firstly, to establish channels that would allow information and communication to flow between the Party and its local government representatives; secondly, to offer these representatives technical help and advice in those areas that required specialized knowledge; and, thirdly, to awaken in the Party an awareness of the meaning and importance of municipal affairs (a summary of Alonso Zaldívar's views as expressed in an interview in April 1984).

The lack of political experience amongst the new Communist councillors was patently obvious. Most of them had not held public office before. In many cases, particularly away from the big cities, the councillors also lacked the necessary knowledge and expertise to deal with legal, financial or urban problems on a large scale. The newly established department aimed to make up for such deficiencies and to provide some measure of ideological co-ordination in the application of the PCE's municipal policies. With such aims in mind a new publication was founded, *Materiales* (full title, *Materiales de Política Municipal y Movimiento Ciudadano*), a magazine for internal circulation dealing with the latest issues in the sphere of local government and conveying the official views of the Party about them. At the same time, the Secretariat headed by Alonso Zaldívar, tried to gather a team of experts to whom the 3,700 Communist councillors could turn for help and guidance.

Such at least was the theory. Reality fell far short of those goals. For a number of reasons the Secretariat for Local and Regional Government Affairs was unable to discharge its duties satisfactorily. Lack of material means was one of its main handicaps. Even the publication of *Materiales* has been rather erratic. The internal crises in the PCE brought to a sudden halt the work initiated by Alonso Zaldívar. In 1981, after the stormy confrontation in the PCE's 10th Congress, he was excluded from the Executive Committee and lost his post as Secretary for Local Government Affairs. His dismissal was followed by the resignation, as a sign of solidarity, of all the members of his departmental team (Vega & Erroteta, pp. 228–31).This undid much of the work that had been started, leaving the Party's mayors and councillors out in the cold. Some of those consulted expressed such views and complained of having to rely almost exclusively on their own initiative and resources.

The other side of the coin might be the apparent absence of political control exercised by the PCE over its local councillors. Whether this was the result of a real democratic spirit or just motivated by a certain indifference on the part of the PCE's leadership towards municipal matters is not easy to say. There are some indications of the latter. In November 1980, Santiago Carrillo, as General Secretary, submitted to the Central Committee a political report in preparation for the forthcoming party Congress. Several Central Committee members—the 'renovators' who were demanding an overhaul of party structure—adopted an openly critical attitude towards the General Secretary's report. Their attack included the denunciation of the absence in it of any analysis of or reference to municipal issues (Claudín, 1983, p. 326). And this was happening at a time when the real political strength of the Party was to be found in the area of local government.

Whatever its motivation, its uppermost limit was clear. Communist councillors could enjoy their independence as long as the party apparatus did not see any danger in it. Any sign of threat brought about pressure and disci-plinary measures from the leadership. In the 1979 municipal election, the PCE won nine of the fifty-seven seats in Madrid's local council. Out of those nine Communist councillors only one served his four-year term, the others fell along the way. Disillusion led some to resign, the rest were expelled from the Party, thus losing their right to remain as councillors. (In 1983, the Constitutional Council declared that the dismissal of councillors who had been deprived of party membership was unconstitutional).

The story of these and other subsequent expulsions is rather involved, too long and complex to be even summarized here (contrasting accounts in Azcárate, 1982, pp. 241–88 and Carrillo, 1983, pp. 105–12). It is one of the least edifying events in the Party's recent history, and one that the Party has come to regret. It stemmed from two main factors: the unwillingness of the PCE's central organs to listen to and satisfy the demands for decentralization originating from some regional sections of the party; and the inability of that same leadership to accommodate the many intellectuals, professionals and artists who had joined the Party during the years of Franco's rule. This latter subject merits some attention here.

The image the PCE enjoyed for many years as the symbol of the anti-Franco struggle attracted to its side the support of dozens of intellectuals, artists and members of the liberal professions. During the dictatorial period they shared their Communist ideals and democratic aspirations with little or no interference from the leaders of the PCE who were at that time in exile. Their return to Spain and the legalization of the Party altered that peaceful equilibrium. The adoption by the Party of a territorially-based structure destroyed the homogeneous groups or cells that had protected such intellectuals from the hurly-burly of party politics and had allowed them to live their political experiences in common with like-minded people. At the same time the old-guard Communists brought back from exile a hierarchical view of party authority against which the demands and expectations of these intellectuals would soon collide. In January 1981 a group of disgruntled Communist intellectuals gathered in Madrid to give expression to their grievances (Vega & Erroteta, 1982, pp. 306–4). Santiago Carrillo addressed the meeting and, though renowned for his avoidance of self-criticism, he had to admit to his audience that the leadership was partly to blame for the uneasy relationship between the Party and what he called 'the forces of culture'. The leadership had not encouraged the independence of such forces, neither had they consulted them nor collaborated with them (full text in Carrillo, 1983, pp. 203–12).

Yet the PCE did try to put to some use the wealth of talent offered by the new generations of Communists. It was a way, too, of neutralizing some of their criticism by means of incorporating them into the work of the Party. Some stood as parliamentary candidates for the PCE. Many had the opportunity of becoming local councillors. In the municipal elections the

Communist lists included a large number of intellectuals, artists, doctors, lawyers, etc., particularly in the big cities. Amongst the Communist councillors in Madrid there were an architect, an economist, a university professor, two laywers, a political scientist and a surgeon. The ploy, however, did not diminish the unrest and criticism. Even as representatives of the PCE in public posts, many continued to demand a profound renovation of the Party's organization. As time went on frustration turned to disillusionment and finally to resignation from the Party. The departure of Ramón Tamames, well-known economist and deputy mayor of Madrid, in May 1981, became a *cause célèbre*, but it was by no means the only significant loss to shake up the PCE at the time.

Others remained in the Party in the hope of achieving some renovation from inside but had little success, and their mounting efforts would soon encounter the intransigence of the leadership. Amongst them were five local councillors from Madrid who in November 1981 were forced to give up their party membership because they had publicly supported a meeting at which one of the speakers was a Basque Communist already expelled from the PCE. The political repercussions of such a measure were extremely serious—other expulsions and forced resignations followed right up to Central Committee level—and a great deal of damage was done to the reputation of the Communists (as recognized by Juan F. Pla in an interview). Relations between Party and councillors were soured, many valuable members were lost, and the electoral image of the PCE was badly dinted. Since the Party's 11th Congress in Madrid in December 1983, the new leader, Gerardo Iglesias, has been trying to rebuild some bridges to make it possible for some of those who left to return.

The PCE's Municipal Policies and the Pacts with the PSOE

At the end of the Spanish Civil War the PCE found itself in total isolation, rebuffed by all the other political groups that had been forced into exile after Franco's victory. The situation remained like that for many years, with the Party experiencing what has been aptly described by I. Fernández de Castro as *exilio en el exilio* —exile in exile (Mujal-León, 1983, p. 12). On the face of such obstinate rejection the Communists searched in vain for willing partners. In the words of Santiago Carrillo, 'pacts, agreements and alliances have been the aplha and the omega of our Party's struggle throughout its history' (Carrillo, 1983, p. 212). This strategy, aimed at establishing contacts and cooperation with other progressive forces, did not yield any fruit till the mid-1970s. Once the transition to democracy gained momentum after Franco's demise, the PCE found itself playing an important role in the consensus politics that resulted in a new constitution. But the most tangible success of the PCE in its pursuit of alliances was the signing of a municipal pact with the Socialists after the 1979 local election.

The 1979 electoral results were the decisive factor in the signing of the agreement. During the preceding campaign the two parties held opposing views with regard to any possible alliance. The Socialists, well established as the major left-wing force in the country, could afford to disregard the overtures from the Communist camp; whereas the PCE's awareness of its own electoral weakness reinforced the Party's proclivities towards compromise and agreement. The results of the election placed the PSOE well ahead of its left-wing opponents, but the PCE had gained enough votes to oblige the Socialists to accept some kind of pact. In most of the major cities the Socialists would only be able to control the council with the help of the Communists. In a few councils the situation was the same but in reverse, with the Communists requiring Socialist support. There were some town councils, too, particularly in Catalonia and Andalusia, where the pact had to be broadened to include other parties such as the PSA (Partido Socialista de Andalucía) and CiU (Convergència i Unió).

The municipal pact signed by the PCE and the PSOE on 18 April 1979 had more symbolic value than real substance. For the first time since the end of the Civil War the left was going to wield some effective power in Spain, even though only at local level. This was enough to alarm some of the more conservative politicians such as former Franco minister L. López Rodó into denouncing the pact as 'a new version of the Popular Front' (*La Vanguardia*, 18 April 1979). But as a result of the PSOE's reluctance to full commitment in any alliance with the PCE, the document signed was very modest in scope (*Materiales*, spring 1979). The pact was little more than a device to allocate municipal posts between the two parties in accordance with the number of councillors each one had. No common programme was agreed. A few and very generic references were included about the need to democratize town councils, to improve local finances, to increase popular interest and participation in local government affairs, and to push for greater decentralization. The clauses in the agreement dealing with the distribution of power were adhered to in nearly all the councils where the Socialist and Communist councillors together formed a majority. The net yield in terms of policy was much smaller and resulted, rather than from the pact itself, from the capacity of certain individuals and local committees to compromise and to find common goals.

The existence of the pact renders difficult the task of isolating the main features of Communist municipal policy. But even without it, in 1979 the local government objectives of most left-wing parties could not have differed greatly. It was, in the broadest sense, a question of bringing democracy to local government. The obstacles Socialists and Communists had to surmount were also the same, requiring specific solutions regardless of party ideology. Municipal legislation was totally unsuitable for the new Spain. Even today, in the mid-1980s, the 1955 Local Government Law has only been partially abrogated. The financial state of many muncipalities verged on bankruptcy. Scant help from central government funds, confused accounting and increasing debts, incurred particularly during the years of political transition, were compounded by high expectations on the part of citizens, who assumed that the new councils would provide more and better services (Díaz-López & Morata, 1984, pp. 90-8). Corrupt practices and inefficiency were deeply rooted in the running of municipal councils. Civil servants at local government level, either for ideological reasons or more often as a result of mere professional inertia, were not always inclined to cooperate with the new left-wing councillors. In short, the legacy of forty years of dictatorship had to be shaken off before any serious consideration could be given to more party-orientated measures.

Consequently, much of the work carried out by Communist and Socialist councils can be gathered under the heading of *política necesaria* (necessary policies). The decisions taken and the policies carried out were determined by need rather than ideology. Julio Anguita, Communist mayor of Cordoba, went as far as admitting that 90 per cent of what the Communists had achieved could equally have been done by a moderate right-wing council (*Materiales II* (4/5), January-June 1983, p. 10). This is not to say that the predominance of Socialist and Communist councillors in the main areas of the country was devoid of political significance. On the contrary, it accelerated and gave credibility to the process of democratization. It awoke in many Spaniards the hope of real change in their cities—a feeling poetically expressed by Tierno Galván, mayor of Madrid, when he announced in the spring of 1979 that 'the sparrows would soon be returning to Madrid'.

It is in this evasive area of feelings, attitudes and aspirations that one has to look for the distinguishing features of the work done by Communist councils. When asked to establish the differences between the PCE and the PSOE, after four years of joint experience in local government, Julio Anguita can only do so in a negative way by denouncing the absence of a Utopian outlook in the Socialist ranks (*Materiales*, ibid.). The enumeration of the party's strengths in local government coming from similar sources is not much more precise. The Communist mayor of Grado, a small town in the northern province of Asturias, sees as characteristics of his party's local government policies the following:

(a) the capacity to offer popular solutions, based on the interests of the rural and the urban working classes;
(b) the exemplary behaviour of Communist councillors as shown by their integrity in financial matters and by their total dedication to work;
(c) an open political attitude, close to the people and far removed from the despotism displayed by other parties;
(d) the search for alliances with other political forces in order to produce and guarantee lasting results. [J. Sierra Fernández, PCE mayor of Grado in Asturias, letter dated 25 May 1984.]

The list is vague in the extreme. Indeed, any Socialist would see it as applicable to his own party. But it does provide some idea of what the PCE has been trying to achieve in the sphere of local government.

The Party's programmes, documents and publications, the public pronouncements of some of its leaders, the activities of Communist councils, all point in the direction suggested above. An analysis of them discloses the reiteration of certain traits which can be taken as characteristic of the Party. Amongst them three stand out. The most obvious one is the emphasis placed on popular participation. Communist councils have encouraged it to the maximum through the provision of cultural facilities, the revival of popular *fiestas*, the mobilization of citizens, or the support given to neighbourhood associations. In short, the Party has been trying to shift the centre of gravity of local democracy from representation to participation. Secondly, the PCE, together with the Socialists, has also been trying to improve the image of local government in the public eye. Open-door government and greater public accountability have been some of the tools used by Communist mayors and councillors to regain people's interest after so many years of corruption, *caciquismo* (power of local bosses), and inefficiency in local councils. Thirdly, Communist councils have often been used by the leadership as carriers of the PCE's banners on issues of a national rather than a municipal nature, such as opposition to nuclear arms, the legalization of abortion, unemployment, or Spain's membership of NATO.

The 1979 municipal pact between Socialists and Communists gave some 70 per cent of the Spanish population a taste of life under a left-wing council. On balance the pact yielded positive results for all concerned. The democratization of Spain was undoubtedly strengthened by the pact. The voters showed their satisfaction with it when in the 1983 election they again lent their support to left-wing councils. As for the two parties concerned, their assessment was on the whole favourable—nevertheless, the municipal pact was one of the most controversial issues at the 11th PCE Congress. Of course, the benefits accrued by each party were in proportion to the number of councillors they had. The PSOE profited much more because it had many more mayors and controlled many more councils. At a much lower level the PCE did equally well.

However, by 1983 the circumstances that had led to the signing of the pact four years earlier had altered considerably. The PSOE's meteoric ascent and the collapse of the PCE removed the need for agreement in most of the councils where that agreement had been necessary to guarantee left-wing control in 1979. The PCE still campaigned with the hope of renewing the alliance, whereas the Socialists remained aloof and unwilling. The results gave the Socialists an overall majority in many of the most important towns and cities. Any new pact between Communists and Socialists was bound to be circumscribed within a very narrow area. Felipe González, General Secretary of the PSOE, in a letter addressed to his Communist counterpart, would only offer the PCE the partial collaboration of his party because, in his own words, 'the small number of municipalities where mutual support is required to elect the mayor obviates the need for a national agreement, which, in any case, would always be more complex and difficult to achieve' (*El País*, 18 May 1984). This is exactly what happened. The left-wing municipal pact was renewed only on a local basis and in a small number of towns situated for the most part in the southern part of the country. Where the renewal occurred it did not extend beyond the 1979 limits. The pact was signed in each specific case just for the purpose of securing control of the council, but without any agreement on policies. A good example is provided by Oviedo, the provincial capital of the mining area of Asturias. The PSOE and the conservative AP gained the same number of seats in the council, thus leaving the only Communist representatives with the deciding vote. It was enough to guarantee the election of a PSOE mayor, but since then the relations between the Socialist group and the Communist councillor have been far from friendly or cooperative.

There is little doubt that the outcome of the 1983 municipal elections has had the effect of altering and complicating the balance of power in local government, and not only as a result of the breakup of the national agreement between Socialists and Communists. Alliances have become more diversified than they were in 1979. In Madrid the Socialists, with overall control of the council, have given the PCE councillors a share in government, whereas in

Barcelona, with a similar distribution of seats, the Communists find themselves in opposition. In a number of towns both Socialists and Communists, unable to agree among themselves, have supported, or have been supported by, conservative councillors. The picture is made more complex by the Socialist control of the Cortes and most of the regional assemblies. The 1979 municipal pact had created, at local government level, a left-wing front which, although not very solid, was clearly in opposition to the centre–right national government of UCD. During the last three years the Communists have found themselves in the paradoxical situation of frequently having to denounce the PSOE government whilst at the same time seeking closer ties with the Socialists at municipal level.

All these changes have weakened the PCE's position in local government. Undaunted by them, the leadership continues to adhere to the hope of turning the local councils into 'fully democratic institutions open to popular participation', as a recent resolution of the Party's Executive Committee put it (*Mundo Obrero*, 13–19 April 1984). As things stand at the moment, they seem to lack the strength, both internally and externally, to transform such high hopes into reality.

Bibliography

This work relies primarily on interviews and correspondence with members of the PCE, party publications and information gathered from the Spanish press. The following lists includes other books and articles consulted.

Alba, V., 1979. *El partido comunista en España*. Barcelona, Planeta.

Anguita, J., 1983. *Textos y discursos (1979-1982)*. Cordoba, n/p.

Azcarate, M., 1982. *Crisis del eurocomunismo*. Barcelona, Argos–Vergara.

Bell, D. (ed.), 1983. *Democratic Politics in Spain*. London, Frances Pinter.

Borja, J., 1977. *¿Qué son las asociaciones de vecinos?* Barcelona, La Gaya Ciencia.

Campos Vidal, M., 1981. *El PSUC y el eurocomunismo*. Barcelona, Grijalbo.

Carmona Guillén J. A., 1979. *Estructura electoral local de España*. Madrid, Centro de Investigaciones Sociológicas.

Carrillo, S., 1983. *Memoria de la transición*. Barcelona, Grijalbo.

Claudín, F., 1983. *Santiago Carrillo. Crónica de un Secretario General*. Barcelona, Planeta.

Díaz-López, C. and Morata, F., 1984. 'L'Espagne', in Y. Mény, *La réforme des collectivités locales en Europe*. Notes et Études Documentaires No. 4755, pp. 73–100.

Esteban, J. and López Guerra, L., 1982. *Los partidos políticos en la España actual*. Barcelona, Planeta.

Hermet, G., 1971. *Les Communistes en Espagne*. Paris, A. Colin.

Linz, J. J. *et al*., 1981. *Informe sociológico sobre el cambio político en España: 1975–1981*. Madrid, Editorial Euramericana.

Maravall, J. M., 1984. *La política de la transición*. Madrid, Taurus.

Mujal-León, E., 1981. 'Cataluña, Carrillo and Eurocommunism', *Problems of Communism*, March–April, pp. 25–47.

—, 1983. *Communism and Political Change in Spain*. Indiana University Press.

Preston, P., 1980. 'The PCE in the Struggle for Democracy in Spain: A Eurocommunist Gamble', *Proceedings of the Third Conference of Hispanists in Polytechnics and Other Colleges*, Bristol, pp. 205–32.

Subiranchs Martínez, A., 1979. *Las elecciones municipales*. Barcelona, Plaza y Janés.

Vega, P. and Erroteta, P., 1982. *Los herejes del PCE*. Barcelona, Planeta.

3 The Portuguese Communist Party

Tom Gallagher

The Portuguese Communist Party (PCP) has yielded up few secrets since it was founded in 1921. Although it is the country's oldest political party and the only one operating today that dates back to Portugal's first experiment with liberal democracy, the parliamentary republic of 1910–26, far more is known about its non-Communist rivals even though they are hardly more than a decade old.

The PCP's underground role during the long, right-wing dictatorship, which stretched from the mid-1920s to the mid-1970s, meant that its affairs had to be cloaked in secrecy—otherwise its very survival was at stake. Unfortunately for this and other studies of the Party, the embargo about revealing party information has not been subsequently lifted and there is far less hard knowledge available about the PCP than any other West European Communist Party. Dr Álvaro Cunhal, its veteran General Secretary, remains deeply hostile to revealing its past history even in the comparatively relaxed conditions of Portugal's ten-year-old democracy. Despite interesting testimonies by ex-members (Ventura, 1984; Silva Marques, 1976), much of the Party's past and present history remains a blur. One commentator was even driven to conclude that only two types of people know about the PCP's history—its leadership and the now defunct secret police known as the PIDE (Pacheco Pereira, 1982, p. 269).

Withholding information about events past and present is an integral element of Portugal's political culture in which civic consciousness and the public's 'right to know' are feeble concepts that command little respect from the practitioners of politics and government functionaries (Gallagher, 1984, p. 480). For a long time Cunhal refused to confirm that he was married and had a family. This austere and dogmatic Communist chieftain has ruled his party in much the same way one assumes he would have established control over Portugal if the turbulent revolution which in 1974–5 accompanied the transition from dictatorship to democracy had succeeded in transferring power to what then, as now, is the largest and best-organized party in the country. The spectre of a Communist Portugal was described in terms of a Cuba on Europe's doorstep by nervous commentators back in the 1970s. But Álvaro Cunhal resembles the flamboyant Fidel Castro far less than he does the ruthless and introspective Enver Hoxha of Albania. Portugal's geographical and political isolation from the rest of Europe makes possible a tentative comparison between her Communist Party and the unrepentently Stalinist one-party state of Albania, due allowance being made for the different historical experience of each one.

But leaving aside the vagaries of local political culture and Portugal's marginal location in Europe, the long night of persecution by and resistance to the dictatorship of Dr Oliveira Salazar was undoubtedly the formative influence alongside which its present behaviour at local and national level must be viewed. The chief hallmarks of the PCP identified by commentators during and after the revolution—suspicion, determination, orthodoxy, ruthlessness, tactical skill—became key elements of its corporate personality during the stiff ordeal it faced for almost forty-eight years, approximately two-thirds of its entire existence. Perhaps if Salazar had sought to wipe out physically the PCP membership in the way that his Iberian confederate General Franco strove to do in the 1940s (instead of merely imprisoning its leaders for years on end), a more flexible party might have emerged in the absence of the Stalinist old guard who had come to the fore in the 1930s. But despite the omniscience of the secret police, the PCP managed to avoid a complete rupture in its activities and the early cadres were able to mould and indoctrinate successive waves of activists in their own implacable image.

Today the PCP is the most important political legacy bequeathed to Portugal by Salazar and his *Estado Novo* (New State) political system. Of his own political system practically nothing remains and the non-Communist parties all emerged in or around the revolutionary period. This is not to suggest that there is a direct affinity between the two, other than the fact that they are the chief authoritarian political movements of twentieth-century Portugal and hence comparisons are unavoidable. Like the *Estado Novo* in its heyday, we only usually learn what the PCP sees fit to divulge, or what can be divulged from election results at national or local level or strikes and trade-union elections.

Experience has shown that in other West European countries with numerically strong Communist parties much can be learnt about their essential character by the way they function at local level. They often tend to be more flexible and outgoing in municipal politics because here their activists are interacting outside strict party confines, sometimes with citizens and politicians from other parties and they may be prepared to negotiate, compete or compromise in order to boost the Party's standing in the local community.

In Portugal, local politics have still not proved to be a means whereby the PCP can be observed at close quarters and information about the determinants governing its behaviour pieced together. Theoretically since 1976,

Portugal has had a system of local government that gives directly elected councils some fiscal autonomy and control over a wide range of services and resources. In theory, county and parish councils can impose a number of taxes, expropriate some land, grant commercial licences and set the number and salaries of municipal employees (Opello, 1981, p. 274). In practice, local government officials are the agents of national government. The policy-making process remains highly centralized, communications flowing from the top down, and local initiative being pre-empted by a flow of directives and administrative decrees which the county and parish councils are obliged to enforce (Opello, 1981, p. 273).

Provisions in the 1976 constitution, allowing for the creation of a regional tier of government with directly elected regional assemblies, have been shelved on the mainland and only implemented in the Azores and Madeira in 1978 in the face of separatist unrest (Gallagher, 1979 (1), pp. 353-9). Public figures such as President Eanes and the respected politician, António Barreto, have decried the absence of strong local government which they see as con-tributing to the national malaise into which the country plunged so quickly after the restoration of democracy. But there has been no serious backlash in the country against the failure to devolve political power to the different regions and to encourage involvement with democratic institutions at the grassroots of society, even though discontent with the highly centralized nature of rule from Lisbon has always been manifest, no matter what political system has prevailed. The assertion by politicians and commentators in 1974–5 that democracy could only acquire strong roots if the people were involved in the direct management of their own affairs at local level was soon forgotten and gave way to the prevailing fatalism about the weakness of small communities in the face of the Lisbon-run bureaucracy.

Ever willing to castigate the non-Communist parties for betraying this or that gain of the revolution in the period since 1976 when they have ruled in alternating coalitions, the PCP by contrast has been relatively silent about the weak structure of local government. Instead it has campaigned for more money to be allocated to local councils even though there is no evidence that its southern strongholds have been receiving less than other parts of the country. Central government makes available funds on the basis of a district's needs, not according to the amount it pays to the central exchequer in taxes—a system that probably benefits the poorer areas in the south where the PCP is strong. So far the PCP has not sought confrontation with central government in those areas where it commands sweeping local majorities: the Party has always distrusted forms of popular mobilization that may slip from its grasp, and in the twilight of post-revolutionary Portugal morale among its supporters may simply not be strong enough for a local challenge against central government to be successfully promoted.

Being more centralized than any other party, perhaps the PCP may not see Portugal's weak system of local government as being particularly anomalous. Centralization has been imposed by the left as well as the right during the periods radical forces have been able to influence the direction of the country. When the *ancien régime* was toppled in the revolution of 1820 by liberals influenced by Jacobin values, they adopted the Napoleonic forms of administration that emerged in the post-1789 centralizing French state, the beginning of a tradition whereby Portugal has borrowed heavily from French government norms. Portugal's long epoch as the nerve-centre of a far-flung maritime empire had already laid the basis for rigid centralism which then reached its zenith in the twentieth century with the imposition of Europe's most durable authoritarian right-wing regime in Lisbon from 1926 onwards. It was characterized by one-man rule, disregard for civil liberties, contempt for political pluralism, and the advance of centralized bodies like the church, the military, and a number of large economic combines (Barreto, 1984, p. 15).

After carrying out an in-depth study of local government in one Portuguese rural county at the end of the 1970s, political scientist Walter Opello was forced to conclude that 'the actual structure and policy formation of local government is little different from that of the previous regime' (Opello, 1981, p. 273). The parish (*freguesia*) is still the primary unit of local government. A number of parishes from a municipality or county (*concelho*) which is governed by a mayor (*presidente de camara*). The counties are combined into eighteen districts on the mainland, each of which is presided over by a civil governor appointed from Lisbon.

The only major change is that elections for the parish and county councils are held every three years on the basis of universal suffrage. Since 1976 local elections have received plenty of media coverage in Portugal but nearly always from the perspective of what the results say about national shifts in party support (Table 3.1); specifically local issues, even if they have relevance over a large area, are usually downplayed or edged out completely by the media and if parties shape their campaign around local issues, it is often in a half-hearted or opportunistic manner.

Though the PCP gives little away about its internal deportment at local level, it is possible to learn about the nature of its electoral support and its relationship with voters by studying its performance in local politics. In 1976 the PCP won outright control of thirty county councils and around 250 parish councils. Since then, it has been the largest party in the industrial zone south of Lisbon located around the district of Setúbal and it also enjoys

Table 3.1 Percentage of the Communist (or APU) vote in Portuguese local and national elections since 1976

	Local election	General election
1976	18.0	14.6
1979	20.5	19.0
1980		16.9
1982	20.7	
1983		18.1
1985	19.4	15.5

predominance in the adjacent districts of Évora and Beja which make up the sprawling agricultural province of the Alentejo (see Map 3.1). Indeed probably more than any other West European Communist Party, its strength is highly localized. In Portugal, where the Communists are strong, they tend to be very strong but in the areas of weakness they are virtually non-existent (Cabral, 1983, p. 196).

Map 3.1 Portugal with the administrative districts of the south indicated

The PCP's local strength is confirmed not so much by its electoral successes but by the semi-autonomous power bases which the Party has built up in the trade-union movement and, more especially, in the hundreds of cooperative farms that were created in the Alentejo out of land seized from *latifundists* (absentee landowners) in the 1974–5 revolution. In the north of Portugal, where the land tenure system is different and Roman Catholicism is a powerful force among the smallholding peasantry, the Party's behaviour locally also had important repercussions since major unrest followed attempts by it to take over local political institutions in the absence of a strong electoral base there.

While an examination of the relations between the central Party and its local adjuncts can only be tentative, given the amount of reliable evidence available, this will be attempted along with a more thorough assessment of the geographical spread of Communist support and the reasons for its continued hegemony in large areas of the country.

To understand PCP behaviour at local level under democratic conditions better, it is necessary to probe slightly deeper into its formative years before 1974. On doing this, it quickly becomes apparent that there is striking continuity in the way it responded to government interference with its activities and laid stress on the maintenance of a highly developed party apparatus under differing hostile circumstances. There was also surprisingly little fluctuation in the nature and location of its support even though it was able to organize throughout Portugal only after 1974.

It was during the 1930s that the Portuguese Communist Party began to evolve from a small sectarian body on the fringe of political life to a party that would strive to achieve hegemony over the Portuguese working class. Its only real competitor on the left were anarcho-syndicalists who had dominated the small but highly conscious working class mainly located in the Lisbon-Setúbal industrial zone, until their labour unions were crushed by the secret police in the 1930s.

By 1945 the Party was establishing a second power base in the Alentejo province which dominates the southern half of the country. The landless rural labourers, who comprised 80 per cent of the Alentejo's population, had been politically disaffected even before the PCP began to organize among them (Cutileiro, 1971, pp. 15–24). Then, as now, they might have had high levels of illiteracy, but they were a tight-knit group living together in towns and large villages and possessing a strong oral political culture. They had shown little respect for the local priest ever since the religious orders had been replaced as the owners of large estates by *nouveaux riches* from Lisbon. This happened in the 1830s and was the crowning economic achievement of

Portugal's liberal revolution initiated in the 1820s, but it deprived the Alentejan labourers of the use of common lands and placed them at the mercy of *latifundists* who fuelled their collective sense of grievance by exploiting them badly. When a republic was declared in 1910, strikes broke out in the region in the following year. The object of the movement was not the distribution or nationalization of land, but better wages and conditions.

The Alentejan peasantry was thus a rural proletariat rather than a class of would-be smallholders. Its class consciousness stemmed from the uniform pattern of life and work which the region's inhabitants mostly shared and from a tradition of solidarity borne out of hard and unremitting deprivation. In the much more densely populated north of Portugal, rural dwellers escaped hardship by emigrating to the Americas; but if the Alentejan peasants moved at all, it was in the direction of the Lisbon–Setúbal industrial zone. The fact that new members of the industrial working class were likely to have some radical traditions of their own and were not merely backward rustics encouraged their politicization and linked city and countryside in southern Portugal, thus enabling the PCP to operate fairly effectively in both environments during the era of Salazar.

Whatever social gains had been made during the parliamentary republic vanished under its authoritarian successor. Probably the *jornaleiro* (day labourer) of the Alentejo suffered more than any other social group at the hands of this dictatorship of the privileged. While the *latifundists* of the Alentejo were possibly its staunchest supporters, grinding poverty and, in some years, outright starvation became the lot of their employees. The farm labourers were regularly employed for only five months of the year and left to fend for themselves as best they could for the other seven. The bitter memories of the hard times before 1974 were worth many votes for the PCP afterwards, thus making it necessary to pause and examine the formative experiences that would later shape the preferences of the electorate in the Alentejo.

Despite the region's traditional militancy, there were relatively few examples of outright confrontation with the repressive agencies of the state during the years of the dictatorship. Ever since 1934, when a virtual uprising in some industrial centres had resulted in the seizure of many activists, the PCP had been wary of pursuing armed resistance or even sanctioning social agitation against a regime whose chief institutional prop was a deadly efficient secret police. The need to preserve the organization of the Party was deemed greater than any short-term political gains that might be made against the *Estado Novo*. This concern with maintaining the party apparatus still greatly influences its behaviour in its regional strongholds in the democratic era.

Despite its implantation within the proletariat, many of the Party's cadres were intellectuals, professional men, or small businessmen from a lower-middle-class background or else were skilled workers. Álvaro Cunhal, the Party's *de facto* leader from 1943 onwards in the years he was not in prison, came from a comfortably-off background (through his mother he is related to Alentejan big landowners). The organization was perpetuated by recruiting and training members, printing and distributing papers, raising finance, etc. Perhaps Cunhal's distrust of '*putschism*' stemmed from an awareness that the dictatorship could collapse suddenly leaving the PCP as the best-organized political party in the resultant power vacuum. The *Estado Novo* was not as internally cohesive as Franco's dictatorship in neighbouring Spain and in 1961 it had almost collapsed due to factional infighting about whether Portugal should fight a guerrilla war in order to keep her colonies in Africa. In 1962 the PCP thus remained aloof from the last military uprising against Salazar before the regime was successfully toppled in 1974—even though it took place in its Alentejan stronghold of Beja.

The PCP played no part in the coup of 25 April 1974 when young officers radicalized by long years of warfare in Africa swept away the old order. Though heterodox in their political opinions, the centurions grouped in the Armed Forces Movement (MFA) soon found that the PCP had its uses in the huge power vacuum that had opened up. Its credibility in the working class and its organizing abilities meant that activists were put in charge of state agencies such as press, radio and television. Within days of it being legalized, party leader Cunhal became the first communist in thirty years to enter the government of a major West European country. In a parallel development which time would show to be possibly even more significant, members of the Popular Democratic Movement (MDP) were placed in charge of local government throughout Portugal. Time gradually revealed the MDP to be not a broad opposition front but a Trojan horse composed of members loyal to the PCP. Local government remained in the hands of this pro-Communist body until 1976 and proved an enormously powerful weapon that enabled the PCP to step up the momentum of the revolution at key moments.

As the young officers' movement shed its moderate elements so as to effect a rapid withdrawal from Africa, relations between the PCP and the MFA blossomed. The danger that local elections would be quickly held, thus revealing the Party's narrow regional base, was averted with the resignation of President Spínola in the autumn of 1974. At the time the PCP was still more concerned with cementing its authority within the working class and the existing social order than in taking advantage of the post-dictatorial chaos to launch a revolutionary grab for power.

The PCP was facing active competition from a variety of Maoist, Trotskyite or non-aligned groups on the far left led by former party members who had long ago rejected its ideological rigidity and tactical caution. To the right, the PCP was confronted with a fast-growing Socialist Party (PS) which demonstrated that its rival did not have a monopoly of working class support by winning the largest percentage of votes in elections for a constituent assembly held on the first anniversary of the 1974 coup. The PS got 39 per cent of the vote, compared with the 16 per cent mustered by the PCP and its front party, the Popular Democratic Movement (MDP), whose alloted role was to draw middle-class and rural votes desirous of change but fearful of the PCP's militant communism. The result showed that the Party was unable to win support outside those parts of the country where it had traditionally been strong.

At its 7th Congress held in Lisbon in the autumn of 1974, the PCP had sought to create a moderate image by repudiating the dictatorship of the proletariat as its ultimate aim and by pledging support for Portugal's membership of NATO, while reaffirming its loyalty to Moscow and having no truck with Eurocommunism. But this difficult balancing act came undone in January 1975 when the PCP sought to sanctify in law the monopoly role the Party already effectively exercised in the trade-union world. Not without difficulty, the PS wrung an assurance from the MFA that the union world would not be allowed to become the preserve of one party. The revolution then entered its most tumultuous phase in March 1975 when a foiled coup by moderate officers triggered off wholesale seizures of capital, property and land throughout the country. PCP activists and ordinary members were in the forefront of the wave of expropriations that were ratified within days by the military-led government when it announced the nationalization of the domestic banks, insurance companies, and most of Portugal's top firms. Without the Party's effective control of the infra-structure of local government (through the MDP), it is doubtful if this assault on economic power could have been carried through so quickly and with such apparent ease. The events of March 1975 signalled the end of the PCP's moderate phase in the revolution. The Party's own polling samples had shown that studied moderation was not going to bring it an electoral windfall and so, with the MFA beginning to lose control of events, the Party revised its strategy, placed far less reliance on seeking power by constitutional means, and began to think in terms of a bolder assault on power using classical Leninist percepts.

The Alentejo witnessed some of the greatest popular upheavals in 1975. Within a few months the *latifundia* which characterized the region were virtually abolished and the power structure of the rolling wheatlands of southern Portugal completely altered. By the end of 1975, 480 estates comprising 2.5 million acres (one-fifth of Portugal's farmland) had been occupied and transformed into cooperative farms, a change ratified by law in July 1975 (*World Bank*, 1978, p. 13). Meanwhile within the working-class, approximately two and a half million strong, two million workers had been enrolled into the Communist-controlled *Union Intersindical* and the Party was seeking new ways to expand its influence in the army and government.

But its drive for power came to a shuddering halt in the summer of 1975, when serious anti-Communist violence broke out throughout Northern and central Portugal. By the autumn over 200 party offices had been burnt out or damaged in a *Jacquerie* that swung the revolution back into the hands of more moderate officers (Gallagher, 1979 (2), pp. 212–13). Lacking a strong presence in the north, the PCP/MDP had behaved clumsily by installing party loyalists in all the state bodies that operated at local level. Non-elected MDP mayors were accused of directing municipal work and other favours to comrades; farmers complained that agricultural credit was granted according to party colours; while much heat was generated about the hold that local Communist lawyers had gained over licensing and civil litigation (*Sunday Times* Insight Team, 1975, p. 258).

Having failed to establish a strong foothold in the northern half of the country during its years of clandestinity, the PCP had been prone to dismiss the inhabitants of Portugal's most populous region as docile folk who had no minds of their own and were too easily manipulated by reactionary priests and local bigwigs. Although reactionary elements were implicated in the anti-Communist violence, much of its was spontaneous and occurred when wholesale land seizures began to spread into central Portugal. With the MFA in increasing disarray, the non-Communist parties began to demand a rapid transition to democracy and revolutionary fervour was confined to the PCP's urban and rural strongholds of southern Portugal. Rather than provoke civil war by coercing the majority of Portugal's 8.5 million people into a Marxist state, the Party vacated the revolutionary high ground for ultra-leftists and was on the sidelines when the revolution finally spluttered out in November 1975.

While the victorious military pragmatists and the non-Communist parties spent the first half of 1976 putting the finishing touches to a liberal-democratic system that would be functioning by the year's close, the PCP concentrated on establishing its hegemony over the radical left and on consolidating its position in those urban and rural areas where it already had a commanding local presence.

In the general election for a new parliament held in April 1976, the Party held its ground in these areas, winning over 41 per cent of the vote (but only 14.4 per cent nationally) in conjunction with the pliant MDP. But in the elections held two months later to elect a head of state who would wield much power in Portugal's semi-presidential political system, the PCP suffered a devastating reverse in every one of its local strongholds. Major Otelo Saraiva de Carvalho, an ultra-left hero of the 1974 revolution, halved the Communist vote in Évora, Beja, and Setúbal and emerged as the clear victor in the south, although winning only 16 per cent of the vote nationally. Overall, the PCP candidate got only 7 per cent of the vote and the result was especially dispiriting in urban and manufacturing areas. Here a minority of politically-aware workers, alienated by the regimentation that so often characterized the PCP at local as well as national level, pledged their support to a variety of far-left parties. Self-managing neighbourhood groups called Dynamizing Groups of Popular Unity (GDUPs), which had emerged in working-class zones during the most radical phase of the revolution, provided the embryo of a far-left political alternative to the PCP. Often more egalitarian and internally democratic than the Communist Party, the GDUPs lacked its cohesion and efficiency and were too dependent on the fleeting electoral popularity of their champion, the mercurial Major Otelo.

When local elections were held for the first time under universal suffrage in December 1976, the far-left challenge melted away. Aware of how much of a negative symbol the word 'communism' had become in Portugal, the Party proclaimed itself the United Popular Front (FUP) and, standing in conjunction with the MDP, recouped its earlier losses. In the Alentejo and Setúbal, it emerged as the largest party with between 40 and 50 per cent of the vote. Nationally the PCP got 18 per cent on a low turn-out of 65 per cent (over 90 per cent had voted in April 1975 for the first free elections in half a century). This was the third set of elections fought in just over eighteen months, this time for local councils that most people knew had few powers—hence the disappointing turn-out. With the most efficient party organization, the PCP was the only Party to improve on its general-election turn-out. It would do likewise in the 1979 and 1982 local elections, its more politicized supporters being more prepared to vote than those of any other party.

The PCP won control of 250 municipal assemblies, mainly in the south, but it also got improved results in a few isolated areas of the north where the composition of the labour market bore a resemblance to that in the Alentejo. The party-sponsored Movement of Northern Tenants and Farmers (MARN) has enjoyed some success in organizing wage labourers in the wine-growing country of the Douro and Dão valleys, but the corresponding electoral benefits were generally slight. The political breakthrough which the PCP experienced in the county of Sobral de Monte Agraço, inhabited by a mixed population of small farmers, labourers and industrial workers, was a relatively isolated event. In a county adjacent to more conservative voting districts, the Party emerged with an outright majority in 1982 thanks to its councillors winning a reputation for efficiency and hard work at the service of their constituents. This breakthrough demonstrated that opportunities existed for parties to make a local reputation by their performance in government, even though the tight constraints on the powers of local councillors meant that much of their time was taken up with administering relatively unimportant local matters.

The weakness of local government attests to the dead hand of centralizing tendencies in the Portuguese state even in the new democracy. Indeed, the structural changes Portuguese society witnessed in 1974–5, were more significant for further advancement of state power than for their socialist content. Some democrats were openly stating after the 1974 coup that if local government was granted to the rural masses, 'the grey-suited notables' of the Salazar era would simply re-emerge from the shadows to manipulate gullible rural folk (Saraiva, 1980, p. 80). This view prevailed even though it was the PCP with its regional power blocs in southern Portugal that soon looked like the chief excuse for not devolving major executive responsibilities on to local and proposed regional tiers of government.

Much more would be known about the Party and its inner workings if it were running important tiers of local government rather than merely staffing parish–pump assemblies. Most weekly council meetings are open to the public but usually there is little local interest in them. If locally elected members had found themselves with important executive responsibilities, they would be under closer scrutiny from the media and local voters, and the chances are that central headquarters would find it less easy to exercise the rigorous control that has been accepted usually without question ever since the underground era. Different tendencies could at last become visible. The Party might conceivably be forced to grant more autonomy to activists whose formative experience is no longer dodging secret policemen. The greater opportunity to exercise local responsibility—the corollary of a strong system of local government—would over time probably give rise to a more pragmatic and less introspective party. As it is, the number of functionaries employed by central government has risen much quicker than the number employed by local government since 1976. In fact, there has been a relative decline in the numbers employed by local government from 21 per cent of the total in 1968 to 16 per cent in 1983, while the percentage of employees in central government has gone up from 79 to 84 per cent in the same period (Barreto, 1984, p. 32).

So far, the PCP has not complained very loudly about the centralizing features of government and administration inherited from the authoritarian era and to which a democratic gloss has been added. The absence of powerful local assemblies where party activists might have gained too much independence has undoubtedly enhanced the tight-knit and monolithic character of the Party. Power does not reside with the forty-plus elected deputies to the national parliament or with its hundreds of councillors, but with full-time officials located in the Secretariat and the Political Committee of the PCP. These bodies are elected by the Central Committee but it is in fact the smaller Political Committee that puts together the single list on which internal elections are fought and decided (Kohler, 1982, p. 215). Further down the hierarchy, the Party is organized in such a way that rank-and-file members have no means of interfering with the essential decision-making process (Cabral, 1983, p. 187; Kohler, 1982, p. 216).

So far, there is no hard evidence that the leadership around the veteran Cunhal, whose 70th birthday nearly coincided with the 10th Party Congress in 1983, is finding it difficult to maintain its grip over such a large apparatus. The Party Congress is invariably a smooth and well-orchestrated affair with none of the open-power struggles which, for instance, accompanied the replacement of Santiago Carrillo at the 1982 gathering of the Spanish Communist Party. Defections of Central Committee members or parliamentary deputies are infrequent but two prominent defections ought to be noted: Candida Ventura, the first woman on the Central Committee, and Álvaro Veiga de Oliveira, Minister of Public Works in 1975 and ex-leader of the PCP parliamentary group.

At local government level, enterprising figures have been brought to heel if their policies run counter to those of Lisbon headquarters. The best-known example occurred during the early 1980s in the district of Setúbal where the president of Palmela county council had earned a reputation as an efficient administrator. He electrified 85 per cent of the county and pressed ahead with improving drainage and roads. But instead of being congratulated by the party bosses in Lisbon, he was pilloried. By demonstrating that even with the small amounts of money at his disposal it was possible to achieve a lot with efficient management, he contradicted the argument of the Party that its locally elected officials had not enough money to do things. This hapless official also showed up the shortcomings of his colleagues in other municipalities. Many have preferred to channel local finance into prestige projects like crèches, pre-school educational facilities, and cultural events. Such policies have the advantage of giving employment to social workers, teachers, or intellectuals with party cards, while the poor state of roads or the water supply can always be blamed on the parsimony of central government.

PCP councils have also expanded their local bureaucracies by taking on non-members who they hope will back the Party at the polls out of gratitude. But this form of clientelism rests on rocky foundations since, during 1984, many of these surplus bureaucrats had to be dismissed because no more money was available to pay their salaries and it now seems quite likely that many will prove fair-weather friends for the party.

The electoral system in Portugal plays an important role in enabling PCP headquarters to exercise control over local parties. In local as in national politics, elections are fought under proportional representation, constituencies are vast, and each party presents a slate of candidates that is usually drawn up in Lisbon. The great size of constituencies makes it difficult for local parties to agree on a single list and enables Lisbon headquarters even to place candidates in order of preference for local activists to campaign around. The 1974 electoral law encouraged such centralization in order to deter the appearance of local political bosses or *caçiques* and to give some ballast to political parties which in Portugal have been prone to fragment. But the end result has been to destroy the vitality of local politics and leave disproportionate power in the hands of national *caçiques* or party bosses located in the capital. Thus the centralized nature of the electoral system fits in with the authoritarian style and proclivities of the PCP. With no tradition of local democracy to inspire them, the membership of each of the parties usually complies with the decisions handed down from Lisbon. The individual placed at the top of the victorious electoral slate usually becomes mayor or president of the council (*camara*). If he gets into difficulties, like the mayor of Palmela, he is replaced by the next person on the slate. In the cities of Setúbal, Évora and Beja, the key PCP provincial centres, the president of the local council has usually tended to be a member of the PCP's Central Committee which only serves to tighten Lisbon's grip on the Party's provincial strongholds.

At local level, there has been little sign of outward discontent over the lack of flexibility or internal democracy. The tradition of secrecy and silence inherited from the authoritarian era still serves the party well in the less paranoid atmosphere of the democratic Third Republic. Many party members, especially in its rural strongholds where the illiteracy rate was still over 30 per cent in 1984, are poorly educated or illiterate and they defer naturally to the professional organizers who are often from an industrial or lower-middle-class background. Often local mayors are outsiders drafted in by the central party because of the absence of local talent or for some other reason which Lisbon thinks important. In 1984 the president of Setúbal council was from Lisbon, Beja's was a Goan originally from the Indian sub-continent, and Odemira's was from Madeira. These outside cadres are likely to have greater loyalty to the party machine than to their adopted locality.

In one prosperous Alentejan town known to the writer, a doctor originally from Mozambique was thought to be a more suitable choice for mayor than the incumbent who had not got further than technical school and was from a more humble background. He was duly replaced in a bid to attract the support of radical professional people who were reluctant to vote for somebody lacking a degree. Access to higher education is the principal path to social mobility in Portugal. A university degree counts for more there than in any other West European country. So in its own behaviour the Party still reflects the elitism that continues to be rampant in Portuguese society. And in terms of its leadership, it is far from being the most proletarian in Western Europe, a claim that was made during and after the revolution.

With regard to PCP membership, card-carrying members are predominantly male (83 per cent), as indeed are PCP voters. But the Party has greater rural support than any other West European Communist party, with the exception perhaps of the Italian PCI, and an examination of its voting figures since 1975 suggests that its regional support in the southern countryside is possibly the most loyal of that enjoyed by any Portuguese political party. The isolation of the Alentejo's few, large populated centres and the persistence of illiteracy affecting upwards of 30 per cent of the adult population may explain why the region has so far remained impervious to cultural influences that might weaken the PCP's hold.

The PCP's strong if highly localized rural profile has also much to do with the fact that the takeover of the *latifundia* brought improved living standards and greater job security for the farm labourers who made up three-quarters of the population. Conditions had already started improving for the *jornaleiros* in the 1960s when a sharp increase in emigration resulted in a labour shortage and higher wages. But the 1975 upheavals brought two fundamental economic benefits that have cemented the loyalty of 150,000 rural dwellers to the Party. Tens of thousands of new jobs were created when land previously allowed to remain fallow or else used for hunting was brought into cultivation. The increase in production now guaranteed work all the year round for the members of the cooperative farms (Smith, 1979, p. 194) and the collective also provided a guaranteed minimum wage, low by international standards but an improvement on what had gone before.

The PCP exercised tight control over the functioning of a great majority of the cooperative farms in the Alentejo, dubbed by hostile commentators as the scene of the first experiment in Soviet-style communism outside the Eastern bloc. Local government had minimal influence over these activities. In Lisbon, the Ministry of Agriculture played a more crucial role. It supplied the cooperative farms with financial credits which became crucial for the survival of an increasing number during the late 1970s as they were bedevilled by poor harvests and, in a lot of cases, poor management. The PCP, true to its aim of winning power by infiltrating government departments rather than by popular mobilization, had placed supporters in the Ministry of Agriculture during the revolution but its influence here was curtailed after the Socialist Party formed Portugal's first freely-elected government in July 1976. Soon collectives were getting into trouble for taking their orders too blatantly from the Party rather than the Ministry which had statutory control over them. Some had their credits reduced for flouting the orders of the Ministry. Money was stopped altogether to others when satisfactory accounts could not be produced or where it was suspected to be going into the coffers of the PCP (McLoughlin, 1979).

A far more serious threat to the unique experiment in the Alentejo was posed by government attempts to reduce the size of the cooperative farms. In July 1977 the Socialist government passed a law under which the previous owners of land were given back some of their property. Steps had already been taken to hand back the land of small and medium-sized farmers which had been seized in the maelstrom of 1975. Ultimately the government hoped to return 1.5 million of the (slightly more than) 3.5 million acres expropriated in 1975 (*Economist*, 14 June 1980). Since the *reservas* being restored to the former latifundists often constituted the best land on the collective farms, the PCP cried foul and characterized this measure as a deliberate attempt to undo the changes carried out in 1975.

Throughout southern Portugal, PCP-controlled councils came to the fore in organizing protest meetings or passing council motions deploring state measures against the collective farms. But the Party acted to much greater effect in Lisbon by threatening to oust the minority Socialist government if it put the 1977 Barreto law (named after the minister responsible) into effect. In retrospect, the attempt to undermine the PCP's agricultural power base did far more damage to its instigators than to the Communists. By 1980 less than half the land earmarked for removal from the collective system had been taken, but at the start of the year a right-wing coalition government known as the Democratic Alliance (AD) was elected. The collective farms lost substantial amounts of land in that year and the work-force, having declined from 72,000 in 1975–6 to fewer than 60,000 in 1978–9, suffered a further big drop in 1980-1 (*Economist*, 14 June 1980). Under the centre-right Sá Carneiro government, the first to be elected with an overall majority, the collective farms seemed a distinct anomaly. In a land which imported half of its food and three-quarters of its grain, the AD placed its faith in private farming along intensive lines. During the era of collective agriculture, grain yields had remained between one-third and one-quarter of those elsewhere in Europe in what is supposed to be Portugal's grain basket.

At the 1979 local elections, the parties making up the right-wing AD were not damaged by their controversial plans for the Alentejo which were partly carried out over the next two years. They made gains among former tenant farmers but at the expense of the PS not the PCP. While the Socialists were pushed out of second place in many parts of the south, the PCP tightened its hold on the three large districts of Setúbal, Évora and Beja. Standing as the United Popular Alliance (APU), the Party increased its vote nationally from 18 per cent in 1976 to 20.5 per cent in 1979, and to a further 20.7 per cent in 1982. Undoubtedly the PCP benefited from receiving protest votes that would normally have gone to the other parties, especially the Socialists. Since 1976 it had been in opposition at a time when the other parties, constituting short-lived coalition governments, had been coping badly with mounting economic problems and pressing austerity measures on the public.

In 1982, APU had won control of all twenty-eight county councils in the two districts of Beja and Évora that comprise the Alentejo. In no other mainland region of Portugal has any one party ever enjoyed such absolute sway at the municipal level. Bearing in mind the degree to which the PCP's chief agricultural show-case was under steep pressure as a result of internal shortcomings and governmental hostility, this was an impressive demonstration of the depth of support for it in the Alentejo.

Electorally, APU did well in its remaining power base in the industrial zone south of Lisbon where a hostile government had also sought to check its power. Given the weakness of local government, the Party's control of the trade-union movement was a much greater source of authority among workers concentrated in the iron and steel, shipbuilding, metal manufacturing, paper and chemical industries to be found in Portugal's 'red belt'. In 1977 a Socialist attempt to create the '*Carta Aberta*', a rival trade-union confederation to the CGTP—Intersindical (General Confederation of Workers-Intersindical—its new title since that year), flopped badly. In April 1979, the Party finally succeeded in floating a successor, the UGT, but it hardly dented the size of the CGTP—Intersindical which was more badly affected by the recession, with membership down to one-third of the total labour force by

1980 (Middlemas, 1980, pp. 202–3, 208). A majority of CGTP–Intersindical members are probably non-Communist voters, most of these being in the north and centre of the country, but by its continued hegemony in the trade-union world the PCP has made itself and the labour movement coterminous. The Party's sway in the industrial proletariat is one of the reasons why multinational companies are reluctant to invest in the petro-chemical complex and deep-sea harbour which the state has built at enormous cost at Sines in southern Portugal. But in the working-class heartland of Setúbal, APU expanded in each of the local elections fought between 1976 and 1982 despite grim economic times. By 1982, it was gaining over 53 per cent of the vote there and similar pluralities in Évora and Beja.

The well-defined vote of the PCP shows no sign of collapsing in the way that the electoral strength of the Spanish PCE and French PCF did in the early 1980s. The Party has benefited from the fact that working–class values and behaviour have not greatly altered since 1974. Living standards remain low and there has been no dramatic rise in expectations that might have opened up a credibility gap between upwardly mobile workers and the PCP. The bourgeois parties (including the PS) remain an object of suspicion to many workers in the south who are mindful of the way they have governed the country since 1976. Of all the parties, the PCP is most closely associated in the popular mind with the revolution that brought changes such as a strong labour law and initially steep wage rises for workers.

The very narrow regional and social composition of PCP support has enhanced stability and discouraged change within the Party. If its national constituency had been more disparate, a more ideologically bland party would probably have been the result. The PCP is an anti-system party and still possesses many of the hallmarks of a closed society even though it is now a mass organization. It is the only party not to have participated in government since 1976 and at local level it enters no coalition with any other party to its right.

But the PCP has paid a high price for its ideological purity. It shows every sign of having exhausted its membership potential among industrial workers and peasant labourers (Kohler, 1982, p. 215), while at the same time being unable to achieve a breakthrough among any other social groups. Latterly, wages have risen much faster outside the collectives whose lustre has diminished. In order to boost its vote in the south, there is evidence that the PCP has been drafting in militants from other parts of Portugal who register as voters and stay in their adopted localities until election time. Such ploys may become increasingly necessary owing to the fact that the Party lacks credibility among the young, even in the most Communist-orientated parts of the country. Evidence for this claim is provided by the results of elections for school assemblies in 'Red' towns like Barreiro and Almada, where for year after year the Communist ticket has been repudiated. If the children of Communist parents continue to reject the PCP at the national ballot box, it will spell trouble for the Party. But with no tradition of participatory democracy behind them, older voters, industrial workers and farm labourers are less repelled by the authoritarian temper and Soviet sympathies of the PCP than are the young or the Party's shrinking middle-class and intellectual constituencies.

In 1985 the PCP suffered a big electoral reverse mainly as a result of the emergence of the populist, left-leaning Democratic Renewal Party (PRD), newly created by the supporters of Eanes, the retiring head of state. It traded on widespread disillusionment with the record and image of the existing parties to get 18.5 per cent of the vote on its first outing. Even though out of government for a decade, the PCP was not immune from the backlash and its vote in the October general election fell to 15.5 per cent.

In local elections in December 1985 the PRD did further damage to the PCP. Its intervention in the city of Setúbal pushed APU (the Communist electoral front) down to 39 per cent so that it lost power to a centre-right coalition. The number of local councils it controlled fell from fifty-five to forty-six but the result could have been even worse since, in many areas where APU was in office, the PS and PSD had formed an electoral pact with the express aim of dislodging it from town halls in both the rural and industrial south. Overall, APU's vote (19.4 per cent) was up on its dismal October showing while down on its performance in the previous local elections. The Party took comfort from its ability to stave off the sharp erosion in Communist support witnessed in France and Spain, but the lesson of 1985 is that its electoral base is far less cohesive than the party apparatus itself. There is every sign that the lesson will be confirmed in the presidential election of 1986 where a lively radical candidate lacking the Party's endorsement nevertheless gathered support in Communist strongholds and won the backing of the MDP, the junior partner in the APU coalition.

Prospects of future growth are tied up with the need for a more modern and less sectarian image and with the fate of both the Socialist Party and the PRD. The PS has drifted steadily to the right since 1976 due in part to having been in coalition with centre-right parties. The centre is less well defined than the edges of the political spectrum and if the PS were to enter precipitous decline, the PCP might be a beneficiary. The process of decline has already occurred in the Alentejo and Setúbal where the PS has lost almost 40 per cent of its vote since 1975. But these regions are very distinctive politically and not representative of the rest of the country where the great bulk of the population resides, which is the primary reason why they have proved such fertile ground for the PCP.

The PCP's highly localized presence reveals how the dictatorship and the revolution had a disproportionate impact on the south of the country. But the chronic weakness of local government and its own centralizing tendencies mean that, on present trends the Party is highly unlikely to be able to turn this local strength to its own decided advantage.

Bibliography

Barreto, António, 1984. 'Centralização e Descentralização em Portugal: antecedentes e evolução desde a revolução de 1974', paper for International Conference on Portugal, University of New Hampshire, USA.

Cabral, M. V., 1983. 'The Portuguese Communist Party: the weight of fifty years of history' in H. Machin (ed.), *National Communism in Western Europe: A Third Way for Socialism*. London, Methuen, pp. 180–99.

Cutileiro, José, 1971. *A Portuguese Rural Society*. Oxford, Clarendon Press.

Economist, 14 June 1980. 'Almost there: Portugal, a survey'.

Gallagher, Tom, 1977. 'Peasant Conservatism in an Agrarian Setting: Portugal 1900–75', *Journal of Iberian Studies*, vol. 6, no. 2.

Gallagher, Tom, 1979 (1). 'Portugal's Atlantic Territories: the Separatist Challenge', *World Today*, September, 353–9.

—, 1979 (2). 'The Portuguese Communist Party and Eurocommunism', *Political Quarterly*, vol. 50, no. 2, pp. 205–18.

—, 1984. 'Salazar's Portugal: The "Black Books" on Fascism', *European History Quarterly*, vol. 14, no. 3, pp. 479–87.

Kohler, Beate, 1982. *Political Forces in Spain, Greece, and Portugal*. London, Butterworth.

Lomax, Bill, 1983. 'Ideology and Illusion in the Portuguese Revolution: The Role of the Left' in L. Graham and D. Wheeler (eds), *In Search of Modern Portugal, the Revolution and Its Consequences*. Madison, University of Wisconsin Press.

McLoughlin, Robert, 1979. 'Small Farms in Portugal', *New Statesman*, 29 July.

Middlemas, Keith, 1980. *Power and the Party: Changing Faces of Communism in Western Europe*. London, André Deutsch.

Opello, Walter, 1981. 'Local Government and Political Culture in a Portuguese Rural County', *Comparative Politics*, vol. 13, no. 3, pp. 271–89.

Pacheco Pereira, José, 1982. 'Problemas da História do PCP', in *O Fascismo em Portugal*. Lisbon, A Regra do Jogo.

Saraiva, António José, 1980. *Filhos do Saturno*. Lisbon, Livararia Bertrand.

Silva Marques, José, 1976. *O Partido Visto Do Dentro*. Lisbon, Livros Horizonte.

Smith, Diana, 1978. 'The Alternative: Portuguese Communism' in P. F. della Torre (ed.), *Eurocommunism, Myth or Reality*. London, Pelican.

Sunday Times Insight Team, 1975. *Portugal: The Year of the Captains*. London, André Deutsch.

Ventura, Candida, 1984. *O Socialismo Que Eu Vivi*. Lisbon, O Jornal.

World Bank, 1978. *Portugal, Agricultural Sector Survey*. Washington, DC.

Yearbook of International Communist Affairs, 1978. Stanford, Hoover Institute.

4 Urban Dreams and Metropolitan Nightmares: Models and Crises of Communist Local Government in Italy

Stephen Gundle

More than any of its sister parties in Western Europe, the Italian Communist Party (PCI) can lay claim to be a party of power. Much of its thinking and political culture is geared to the actual or potential exercise of authority as a consequence of the real influence it exerts in various quarters of society. This is in part a result of the size of the Party but it is also linked to the profound realism of its political practice. In his speeches of the 1945–6 period, Togliatti, the party leader up until his death in 1964, constantly underlined the need to intervene in specific conflicts and problems. The Party could not simply say that things would be better under socialism; it had to be able to offer realistic potential solutions both to great national issues and to individual people's concerns. Ever since the expulsion of the Communists from central government in 1947, local government has been the PCI's largest stake in state power and the terrain where the Party's credibility as an alternative administrative force has been most measurable. It has also been the ground where the Party has had the most opportunity to experiment and innovate in public policy and illustrate the sense of its pragmatism.

The PCI's participation in local government may be divided into two broad phases (Table 4.1). Before 1975, Communist government was more or less limited to those areas in the centre of the country, and in Emilia–Romagna in particular, where the Party's strength was most concentrated. Between the 1940s and the early 1970s, therefore, the scale of Communist local government may be said to have reflected the Party's confinement to opposition and lack of institutional legitimation. Following the local elections of 1975, which brought left–wing coalitions to power in most Italian regions and major cities, the Party's position changed radically. Its high level of participation and undisputed leadership role in the key cities of Rome, Naples and Turin, reflected not only diminished isolation, but also a growing legitimation in society and increased credibility as a potential force of government in the national arena. With the defeat of the PCI in the local elections of May 1985, this second phase may be considered closed and a new

Table 4.1 Percentage of votes obtained by the PCI in general elections, 1946–83 (by region)*

Region	1946	1948	1953	1958	1963	1968	1972	1976	1979	1983
Piemonte	20.8	32.0	21.4	19.0	23.2	26.0	26.3	34.1	30.5	30.1
Liguria	28.4	39.1	25.7	24.6	28.4	30.9	31.6	39.1	35.5	35.7
Lombardia	20.1	33.2	17.8	18.7	20.1	22.9	23.8	31.5	28.4	28.0
Trentino A. Adige	8.1	9.5	8.9	5.2	5.8	6.7	7.5	13.2	11.1	11.1
Veneto	13.7	24.0	14.2	13.4	14.8	16.7	17.3	21.4	21.7	20.8
Friuli v. Giulia	13.2	22.3	15.2	16.3	18.3	19.7	20.4	27.8	25.3	24.5
Emilia–Romagna	37.5	51.2	36.7	36.7	40.7	43.4	43.6	48.8	47.4	47.5
Marche	21.8	34.2	23.1	25.7	30.0	32.3	32.8	39.9	38.1	37.7
Toscana	33.6	48.1	35.0	34.4	38.5	41.0	45.3	50.3	45.8	46.5
Umbria	28.0	47.1	28.2	30.8	38.8	41.8	41.7	45.2	45.5	45.1
Lazio	14.1	27.3	23.0	22.8	25.5	27.6	27.1	36.0	30.2	29.5
Campania	7.4	18.8	19.3	21.8	22.3	23.3	22.7	31.8	24.9	24.2
Abruzzi–Molise	10.1	23.5	20.1	20.1	22.7	25.5	25.5	33.4	29.2	27.6
Puglia	14.7	26.6	23.7	24.0	26.2	27.1	25.7	31.6	26.7	25.5
Basilicata	13.0	25.6	25.9	25.9	28.9	26.2	24.9	33.3	28.9	27.9
Calabria	12.2	29.5	20.8	23.0	26.3	24.0	25.9	33.0	26.6	26.2
Sicilia	7.9	20.9	21.8	21.9	23.7	22.5	21.2	27.5	21.1	21.6
Sardegna	12.5	20.3	21.2	19.8	22.5	23.7	25.3	35.6	31.7	28.8
Italy	18.9	31.0	22.6	22.7	25.3	27.0	27.2	34.4	31.5	31.2
Total vote	4.36m.	8.14m.	6.12m.	6.70m.	7.80m.	8.56m.	9.07m.	12.62m.	9.85m.	9.86m.

* The percentages reported for 1948 are those obtained by the Democratic Popular Front, an electoral alliance in which Communists, Socialists and left independents presented a single list of candidates.

phase opened in which the Party faced the risk of a return to its pre-1975 position.

In this chapter an attempt will be made to provide a global overview of Communist local government in Italy since 1945. The experience of administration in Emilia–Romagna and later in the major cities of the north and south will be examined in relation to both structural changes in Italian politics and society and to evolutions in the national strategy of the PCI. It will be suggested that the model of government developed in Bologna, for thirty years the largest city led by the Communists, rested on a compact and stable local society subject to controlled development. The progressive disappearance of such qualities of compactness and stability from Italian cities in the 1970s undermined the 'Emilian model' of local government and created serious problems for the new left-wing administrations elected in 1975. The substantial failure of the PCI to bridge the gap between public institutions and a changing society with effective government and novel forms of participation both compounded the Party's difficulties in presenting itself as a national alternative following the collapse of its proposal for a 'historic compromise' with the ruling Christian Democrats (CD) and led to defeat in 1985.

The first section will deal with the emergence of local government as a central field of political struggle between right and left in Italy, the second with the Emilian model, its significance and principal characteristics. The third section will examine with the rise of the PCI in the 1970s and its accession to power in many of the major regions and cities. Finally, the reasons behind the Party's failure to consolidate its power in local government in the 1980s will be assessed.

Local Power and National Strategy

In this section the nature of the society in which the PCI elaborated its postwar strategy will be outlined. The conditions under which the Party came to view local government as both a key theme and a field in which it could build its claim to legitimacy as a force of democratic government will also be illustrated. First, however, let us sketch the distinctive features of Italian Communist politics.

Although the PCI would remain a Moscow-orientated party up until 1956 and arguably beyond, its political line displayed certain notable elements of originality even in 1944. Returning to Italy in March of that year, Togliatti set out a vision of Communist politics and organization that did not fully correspond to the norms of the Third International. Insurrection was rejected in favour of action inside the political sphere of the state; capitalism and political pluralism were accepted as the necessary bases of reconstruction; the Party dispensed with old models of cadre formation in favour of the recruitment of a mass membership; the formulation of constructive and practicable policies was deemed a priority and wide social and political alliances a practical necessity.

Togliatti's decision to recast the politics of the PCI in the light of specific national conditions, laying the basis for the strategy that would explicitly be termed the 'Italian road to socialism' after 1956, was related to the backward state of a society that for twenty years had sustained a Fascist regime. It was felt that until a process of democratic education and cultural integration had been completed, Communists could not realistically hope to win the support of a majority of the population. In the 1940s Italy was largely a peasant country that lacked a national language and common culture embracing the subordinate classes. In addition, traditional patterns of authority marked social relations in much of the country and the Catholic Church was extremely influential in civil life. But if the PCI did not expect to achieve the conventional goals of a Communist party it none the less expected to remain a force of government. Despite the hostility of the terrain, the experience of the Resistance in the north of the country, a diffuse desire for change, and a common faith in participation and progress facilitated the rapid growth of the Party and its conquest of almost 20 per cent of the vote in the elections to the Constituent Assembly in 1946.

The conduct of Communist leaders in the Assembly's discussions of the new Republican constitution may be interpreted in relation to two goals. First, the PCI worked to preserve the framework of unity between the democratic parties that had characterized the whole process of institutional change following the fall of Fascism. Second, it aimed as far as possible to ensure that the new state took a unitary, centralized form. The first goal reflected a recognition that for the present the left could exert its influence most effectively within the context of a coalition, the second an expectation that in the foreseeable future the left would gain the upper hand and be able to use the state apparatus to carry out major social transformations. It was for these reasons that the PCI voted with the Christian Democrats in favour of the inclusion within the constitution of the Lateran Pact forged by Mussolini between the Italian state and the Church, yet with the Socialists and Liberals against the Christian Democrats to block decentralization of some of the legislative functions of central government to elected bodies in the regions. Greater autonomy for municipal government was seen as desirable, but any

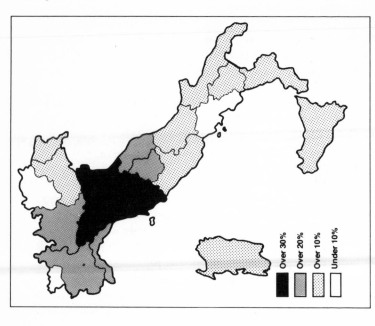

Map 4.2 Electoral strength of the PCI in the general

Over 30%
Over 20%
Over 10%
Under 10%

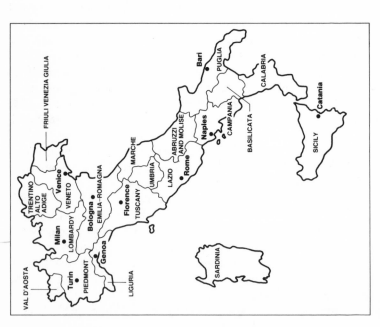

Map 4.1 Italy

VAL D'AOSTA
Turin
PIEDMONT
LIGURIA
Genoa
Milan
LOMBARDY
Bologna
EMILIA–ROMAGNA
TRENTINO ALTO ADIGE
Venice
VENETO
FRIULI VENEZIA GIULIA
Florence
TUSCANY
MARCHE
UMBRIA
LAZIO
ABRUZZI AND MOLISE
Rome
Naples
CAMPANIA
BASILICATA
Bari
PUGLIA
CALABRIA
SICILY
Catania
SARDINIA

form of federalism or devolution might have acted as an impediment to the enactment of a programme of radical reforms.

The final draft of the constitution, and the way it came into effect in 1948, fully reflected the contradictory aspirations of different political forces. Despite the fact that the Fifth Article established the principle that elected assemblies should be set up in regions, provinces and communes to conduct the business of local government, a range of interests combined to ensure that in reality the state remained highly centralized. Democratic municipal governments had been set up immediately following the Liberation but, with the exception of areas of the country marked by particular ethnic, cultural, or linguistic features, no regional assembly would actually be established for over twenty years.

At no time in the period between 1944 and early 1947 did Communist leaders imagine that the PCI would suffer a serious political setback. Indeed, continuity in the framework of national unity was one of the key assumptions of Togliatti's political strategy. Thus the sequence of events that took place in 1947-8, which saw the expulsion of both Socialists and Communists from government, the defeat of the left in the bitterly ideological election of April 1948, and the successive consolidation of Christian-Democratic power over the state, represented a very major blow. The Party that had devoted its efforts to the conquest of a legitimate role in society and the state suddenly found both its influence and legitimacy as a component of national life sharply questioned. Although Togliatti did not revise Communist political strategy in the new circumstances—the commitment to wide social and political alliances and the construction of a national consensus remained key themes—certain changes of approach were obviously necessary. The position occupied by the PCI after 1948, for example, largely invalidated the motivation behind the commitment to the unitary state that had been adopted in the Constituent Assembly. The centralization of powers no longer represented a political means of facilitating reform, but a threatening instrument for the consolidation of a very different type of social order from that envisaged by the PCI.

Such fears would rapidly be confirmed. At the helm of the state, the Christian Democrats soon forgot the causes of devolution and decentralization that it had championed in 1946. Indeed, the consolidation of its power involved a marked concentration of central authority. On the one hand, this meant the further postponement of the establishment of the regions (since in central Italy this would have implied conceding platforms and resources to the left) and the imposition of rigorous controls on the policies and budgets of town and city councils. On the other, it involved, through the Interior

Ministry, a widespread use of extensive police and prefectorial powers inherited largely intact from Fascism. In those areas where Communist strength was such that the breakup of political unity did not result in its exclusion from local government, central intervention was particularly harsh. Prefects acted to ban demonstrations, forbid the distribution of propaganda material hostile to the government and arrest the leaders of unofficial rallies and protests. On occasions mayors were also dismissed and elected councils judged to have exceeded or abused their authority dissolved (Fried, 1963, pp. 236–9).

Even before the elections of 1948 formally established the subaltern position of the PCI in the political system, however, a significant change in the Communist conception of the role and value of local government took place. The change affected both attitudes towards the structure of the state and perceptions of the function of Communist local government. Let us look first at the PCI's view of the form of the democratic state.

Forced out of power centrally, yet retaining a commitment to the institutional framework it had helped shape, the Party embraced the theme of local autonomy as both a neutral instrument with which to attack the Christian Democratic state and a terrain on which it could give proof of its democratic credentials. The reasoning behind what would come to be a highly significant change of approach was first set out in an article published in the party monthly *Rinascita* in July 1947 (Laconi, 1947, pp. 182–4). At the Constituent Assembly, the article's author explained, the regional autonomism of the Christian Democrats had constituted a 'diversion from the social and economic aspirations of the Italian people' that 'exploited the local spirit and contrasts that still exist between different cities and regions'. The division of the country into eighteen or twenty regions endowed with wide legislative powers, it was argued, would necessarily have fragmented and deflected the 'great unitary struggle of the working masses'. In the new circumstances, the PCI still adhered to the unity of the state, but it also recognized the necessity for decentralization. The campaigns for regional assemblies, greater autonomy for the communes, abolition of the prefects and a curtailment of central police powers were seen as key battles around which the PCI could construct a new political role for itself in relation to public institutions.

In opposition, the PCI also adopted a different view of the role of Communist local government. During the period of the Constituent Assembly, this had been seen as a lever on central government, a sort of formally constituted pressure group within the state that could act as support to the national action of the Party. After 1947 its function was perceived in a

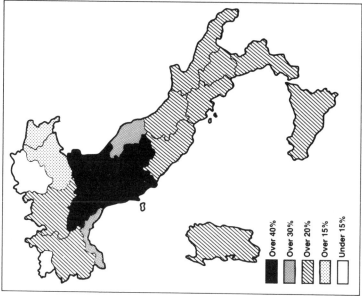

Map 4.4 Electoral strength of the PCI in the general elections of 1968: regional distribution

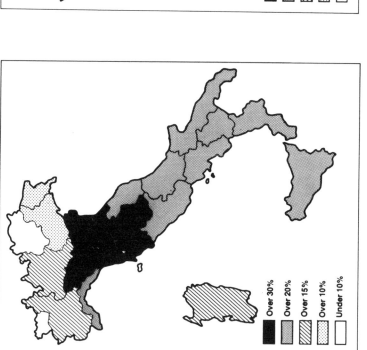

Map 4.3 Electoral strength of the PCI in the general elections of 1958: regional distribution

quite different way. Deprived of any leverage over central government, municipalities where Communists governed in conjunction with their Socialist allies provided the material ground on which the left, within obvious constraints, could best construct a model of government that, in its priorities and expenditure, contrasted with standard models of local administration in the rest of the country.

Communist Local Government in Emilia-Romagna

Although Communist local government was a feature of much of central Italy in the late 1940s, Emilia–Romagna and the regional capital Bologna provided the scene of the most developed experiment in left-wing power in post-war Italy. In this section the principal characteristics of what came to be known as the 'Emilian model' will be investigated, with special attention being paid to the role of the Party and the form and quality of its influence over civil society in Bologna. It will be shown that a unique social alliance between the leading working-class party and the middle classes underpinned left-wing domination of the city and that the preservation, consolidation and institutionalization of this alliance became the guiding theme of Communist action for over forty years. The terms of alliance, however, would change significantly from the mid-1950s with the beginning of a process of industrialization in the region and the resulting alteration in the balance between urban and rural classes. From this time it may be said that the distinctions and interplay between party, institutions and society became less clear and the PCI progressively assumed a role of social integration that would later lead to serious problems in its ability to mediate and represent a broad range of interests.

From the very earliest days of the Liberation, it was clear that Emilia-Romagna was the Italian region where the PCI could count on greatest support. The rapid expansion of membership, organized presence of the working-class movement, high level of electoral support and consequent leadership of local government meant that, within a short space of time, it came to be regarded as Italy's 'red region' *par excellence*. The only large city to have a Communist mayor throughout the 1950s and 1960s, Bologna was for Italian Communists a symbol of immense importance. No figure better symbolized the general battle waged by the Party against the consolidation of the CD regime than Giuseppe Dozza, Bologna's charismatic first citizen for some twenty years who, in the face of mounting checks, controls and interventions, spoke out vigorously in favour of the merits of left-wing local government (Dozza, 1951, p. 7). It was in these years of repeated attempts to undermine and undo the authority of the PCI in its principal strongholds that the legend of left-wing rule in Emilia–Romagna, its honesty, effectiveness and popularity, its contribution to the quality of life and different forms of collective involvement in decision-making, was first born. The legend occupied an important place in Communist mythology but, more significantly, it constituted a tangible source of credibility, a proof of responsibility and expertise to which Communist leaders would often refer in claiming a greater role for the Party in other localities and on the national plane.

In 1946 Togliatti himself sensed that there was 'something new and different' in Emilia (Togliatti, 1974, p. 32). 'Here there is an ardour and intensity of movement', he said, that contrasted sharply with the torpor encountered elsewhere. Even on 'the faces of the men and women who in great numbers cycle along the roads' he detected a particular sense of satisfaction and involvement. 'It seems that the blood circulates more rapidly, that the nation's heart beats more quickly here', he commented. These flattering observations, however, were but the prelude to what, at the very beginning of the Reconstruction, was to be the first authoritative elaboration of a politics of alliance that took the social structure of the region at its point of departure.

In his Reggio Emilia speech, Togliatti proposed the strategic consolidation of the unity of action between working class, agricultural labourers and rural middle class that had been a feature of the region both in pre-Fascist times and in the struggles leading up to the Liberation. The prevalently agricultural character of Emilia, combined with an industrial presence sufficiently developed to sustain a significant working-class movement, constituted the ideal terrain for the realization of the unity between classes that Togliatti had stressed as a necessary objective long before in the lectures on Fascism he had conducted in Moscow in the early 1930s (Togliatti, 1970).

The analysis of the social categories and classes that had coalesced in the past in support of socialism and anti-clericalism and now in support of the PCI was neither ritualistic nor purely formal for Togliatti. Nationally, the social alliance between landed and landless peasants and industrial workers was the essential formula that the party of the working class had to struggle to achieve. In Emilia-Romagna it was the reality that, through its political action, the Party had to turn into progressive public policy (Anderlini, 1978). Togliatti's analysis is of significance here above all because it illustrates the extent to which the PCI's conception of power in the region was sociologically founded (that is, the degree to which the interaction between party and society was seen as determinant upon the relationships between party and institutions and between institutions and society) and also because it shows how far Communist rule was not seen to rest purely on the dominant position of the working-class movement (trade unions, cooperatives, etc.), but on a more heterogeneous social base.

Before discussing the consequences of these conceptions on policy and on the forms of political participation and mobilization adopted, a look at the degree of Communist influence in Emilia–Romagna will serve to illustrate the context of the relationships under examination. What, to put the question plainly, was the extent of Communist dominance of the local political system? First of all, it needs to be said that apart from occasional experiences in single cities where, for one reason or another, Socialists were unwilling to enter into coalition and the PCI was sufficiently strong to govern alone, local government in Emilia–Romagna has been founded on a long-term coalition of Socialists and Communists. This coalition finds expression in local government but is also rooted in the trade-union movement, in the management of industrial and agricultural cooperatives, and in the common organization of an extensive network of labour clubs and recreational circles. But, until the early 1980s at least, the Socialist Party (PSI) was a passive ally confined in virtually all circumstances to a secondary position. At no time, for example, has any non-Communist held the position of mayor in a city where the Party was the major political force. The PCI's dominance was above all a product of the balance of electoral forces, since the post-war vote of the PSI in Bologna, for example, has fluctuated between 8 and 12 per cent, while the PCI can command up to 49 per cent. However, the sheer numbers of Communist membership made it difficult for the Socialists to assert themselves forcefully on any plane. Even in 1946 the PCI could count on a membership of 424,000 in Emilia–Romagna, making the region a party political stronghold probably without equal in the Western World (Ghini, 1982, p. 247). For this reason it is legitimate to talk in terms of a 'centrality' of the Party, not just in the political system but in virtually the whole of civil life. Nowhere was this more evident than in the diffusion of a progressive ideology capable of integrating the principal social groupings in the region under the banner of its central themes. The ideology of the Resistance first, but also the themes of democracy, progress and participation, all were, and to a more limited extent still are, mechanisms of mass politicization and of the perpetuation of Communist centrality.

If the period between 1948 and 1956 may be seen principally as one of consolidation in which the PCI gradually assumed the tasks of mediation between the various interests in the dominant social bloc and of the resolution of a variety of demands in a general programme, the years after 1956 can be seen as a period in which the quality of Communist rule changed considerably and assumed a much closer identification with the actual tools and offices of local administration. This second period is of particular interest here since the PCI had not merely to assume the leadership of a social alliance that to some extent already existed, but to recreate a set of alliances and adequate policies in new conditions. Industrial development and the consequent transformation of significant sectors of the rural population into urbanized working and middle classes created a complex of conditions and problems that placed a great demand on the local authorities. Thus there was also a significant recasting and development both of local government activity and of the mechanisms of legitimation of Communist rule.

Table 4.2 Votes obtained by the PCI in elections to the commune of Bologna, 1946–85

Year	Votes	%
1946	71.369	38.3
1951	93.043	40.3
1956	121.556	45.3
1960	138.090	45.6
1964	149.433	44.8
1970	149.339	42.5
1975	179.622	49.0
1980	158.622	47.7
1985	151.109	44.5

It is often remarked that PCI local government in Emilia is of a 'reformist' type, not simply because of emphasis placed on the alliance with intermediate social strata but because of the decisive influence of the latter on public policy (Serafini, 1974). For, through local government policy, the political formula of the anti-monopoly alliance, under which Communists seek to win small and medium-sized producers to their side in the battle against big capital, became economic reality. From the mid-1950s, industrial development in Emilia–Romagna followed a pattern that made the region unique in so far as the Party was able to condition and negotiate industrialization in such a way as broadly to favour the small industrial and commercial middle class and block the penetration of monopoly capital. Even today the economy of Emilia–Romagna is largely composed of a network of medium, small and very small enterprises: despite the fact that it is the third industrial region of the country, the large industrial concerns typical of Piedmont and Lombardy are practically absent.

If the alliance between working class and rural middle class in the immediate post-war years had been first and foremost an ideological one from which the PCI had benefited politically, the alliance with urban middle classes was constructed in a more active way. Beyond the issue of ideological sympathy, business people, artisans, and commercial and industrial managers identified with the PCI because the Party translated their demands into basic economic policies and promoted and defended their interests. What the Party was able to provide through its control of local government was centralized planning, directed public spending, coordinated urban development and infrastructural provision, capital investment in support of small enterprises, export promotion and the setting of agreed commercial priorities and targets. It was, in short, able to structure and organize economic life in such a way that the fruits of development came to the region without displacing the Party's position of political dominance (cf. PCI, 1959). Indisputably, there were many ambiguities and contradictory elements in the PCI's approach to the intermediate classes but, equally indisputably, the singular role of local government in Emilia produced a model of development that was among the most pacific and successful in Italy.

Nowhere was this more evident than in the striking cultural continuity that marked the process of development. This passage from a peasant culture to an industrial culture in the decade between the mid-1950s and mid-1960s involved a series of breaks in traditional values and cultures. In some of the northern regions of the country and among the rural masses of the south, uprooted from the land and forced to migrate north in search of employment, these breaks were radical and potentially disorientating. In other sectors of society the transformation was negotiated with less dramatic consequences. But only Emilia–Romagna can be said to have undergone a process of industrialization characterized by a large measure of cultural continuity. The model of development based on small and medium-sized production, planned and controlled from above by an institutionally dominant political force, preserved the balance between city and countryside and avoided the fragmentation of established communities, life styles, values and patterns of socialization. A robust and dynamic peasant culture, far from disappearing, constituted a vital matrix, capable of uniting and aggregating wide groups of rural and recently urbanized classes even in the face of the growing challenge of the modern alternatives of television and other mass media. Even in Bologna the basic compactness of society and its mechanisms of integration were scarcely disturbed in the 1960s.

What made the Emilian model unique was not only the unusual inter-action established between a Marxist party and capitalist development, but also the role exercised by the former in pursuing a social policy designed to limit the tensions arising out of the latter. The structure of the Party, with its centralized command and extensive organizational presence in society, permitted a very high level of political intervention in all spheres of social and economic activity. Thus its role was not purely one of reaction, limited to dealing with the consequences of a process taking place outside its control. The PCI both guided development politically and evolved itself as a force of mediation in the context in which development took place. At the national level this dynamic new role occasioned a widespread interest in Emilia-Romagna in the late 1950s. Both the formative alliance with an industrial middle class about to undergo a rapid expansion in the country as a whole and the capacity to provide a model of local government that combined planning, stability, equity and democratic participation made Bologna a precious example which the PCI argued could be of general value.

In the new phase a transformation of the function and the role of the Party took place that effectively shifted the emphasis from activity in society (in economic struggles, the recreational field, social organizations and popular mobilization) to institutional management. In the ideology of the Party and in its conception of politics this redefinition took place slowly and in an incomplete way, but in terms of practical activity the change was more rapid. First, the task of shaping public opinion in a way favourable to left-wing rule passed from the Party to the town hall. Communist organizations still played an important part in winning and maintaining support, of course, but support came to depend more on the enactment of policies that produced tangible results in terms of economic growth and the quality of life. Naturally, relationships inside the Party tended to reflect this qualitatively higher degree of institutional penetration. If the key figure in Communist circles before the late 1950s was invariably the secretary of the local party federation, afterwards it tended to be a core group of elected administrators whose actions were less subject to party control (Frilli, 1949, p. 9). A second aspect of the institutionalization of the PCI may be noted in the novel use of the centralization of decision-making. A cardinal condition of the PCI's ability to act as a central component of economic and social life and to order the latter in accordance with a general design lay in the command structure of its own organization. Through this the Party could simultaneously provide decisive leadership and rapid execution of decisions on the one hand, and widespread acceptance for those decisions on the other. This quality was important in overcoming trade-union opposition to the promotion of the interests of small and medium-sized industry: democratic centralism provided a unique means of squaring the circle of contradictory interests (Sechi, 1980).

To these two features of Communist local government may be added a third: the absorption within the Party itself of the normal interplay between political forces, public institutions and demands thrown up by society. In the conditions created in the late 1950s a trend towards the obfuscation of distinctions between state and society emerged that would reveal dangers and problems of wide significance in the 1970s. During the 1960s, however, the concern that the nature and extent of PCI dominance might distort the regular channels of political representation was of more theoretical than practical interest. Despite a plethora of centrally imposed political and finan-cial controls, Bologna's administration won a reputation for combining efficiency with innovation. By careful planning and experimentation in the application of powers conceded to local government, the commune managed to evolve a model of administration and forward planning that won many admirers. The quality of transport, educational, health and welfare services was often higher than elsewhere. Moreover, a genuine attempt was made, from 1960 onwards, to decentralize government to neighbourhood councils and seek wider participation in public-policy initiatives. Both in the PCI's own propaganda concerning its achievements and in comparison with other cities, Bologna appeared to be an island of urban harmony in a hostile capitalist world, the best possible model for progressive city government.

In 1960 Togliatti once again proposed municipal government in Bologna as a national example. In contrast to other major Italian cities that were, he said, pawns in the hands of great industrialists, victims of poor services and corruption, prey to traffic problems and inadequate administration, Bologna provided a model of intelligent local government sensitive to infrastructural demands raised by industrialization, to the need for new schools, housing and services, and to an improved quality of life (Togliatti, 1974, pp. 537–8). In asserting this, Togliatti was not simply engaging in a self-serving exercise of party pride. His praise of Bologna had a political function in that it was designed to show that the Communists were a valid national force more than capable of developing policies equal to the challenges raised by the economic boom. In 1960 this was particularly necessary since the breakup of the alliance between the PSI and PCI in national politics after 1956 and the former's gradual move towards participation in Christian Democrat-led gov-ernments threatened to leave the Communists isolated in opposition. The centre-left coalition, however, would not prove sufficient to shore up Christian Democratic authority in a rapidly changing society.

Governing the Major Cities

The 1960s were a decade in which the position of the PCI in Italian society began to change radically. While centre–left governments sought to marginalize the Party and reduce its political importance, a range of transformations and conflicts in the social body sharply undermined the hold of the traditional forces of government and opened the way to the great electoral advance of the PCI in the mid-1970s. Despite the Christian Democrats' strategic cooption of the Socialists, the PCI became the almost unwitting vehicle of a widespread demand for reform that followed sharply on the heels of economic growth. In this section the conditions and dimensions of the Communist advance in the local government field will be assessed and the consequences analysed. First let us sketch the backdrop to change in Italy's large cities.

Implicit in the transformations of this period was the decline of a traditional social order, the immediate consequences of which were a blow to the Church's influence, historically stronger amongst the rural population, and a drop in the electoral strength of the Christian Democrats in the larger cities (Compagna, 1959, pp. 35–49). The PCI did not directly benefit from this situation immediately, but the undermining of Catholic dominance in national life both created the conditions for success in the long-term battle for more local and regional autonomy and provoked a political gap that afforded the PCI an unprecedented opportunity to seize the initiative.

For many years Communists had advanced the cause of local government autonomy as both a necessary practical reform and a means of striking at the form the central state apparatus had taken under Christian Democratic rule. Thus when the battle to set up elected regional authorities was finally won in the late 1960s and the new assemblies established in 1970, it was legitimately hailed as a great political victory. Significantly, it was also seen as the basis for a major shift in the balance of power that gave the PCI a real possibility of dismantling one of the main levers of Christian Democrat dominance. The future Communist mayor of Florence, Elio Gabbuggiani, declared in 1968 that 'our task is to ensure that the introduction of this reform has the maximum disrupting effect on both the traditional and more recently added scaffolding of the bureaucratic, centralized state' (Gabbuggiani & Bianchi, 1968, p. 226). In 1972 Enzo Modica, the PCI's local government spokesman, talked of the role of the battle for autonomy in bringing about 'the irreversible breakdown of the centralized and authoritarian mechanism' on which capitalism and reactionary governments had always based their power in Italy. These assertions may have been exaggerated, but in the centre of the country, at least, the new tier of local government did furnish the PCI with a new power base and a direct input into the formulation of state policy for the first time since 1947.

Within the large cities, conditions favoured a new role for the Party in a quite different way. In the wake of the student movement and the great industrial disputes of 1968-9, urban social movements sprang up to protest about conditions in crowded satellite towns, to demand economical housing and to impede the breakup of working-class communities. These movements often took shape in opposition to, as well as outside, the PCI, but where the Party was not in power such politicized protest activities provoked it to take on broad new issues and ultimately benefited it electorally (Seidelman, 1979, pp. 20-2). Changes in organization were effected and a major effort made to develop new policies on urban problems.

Electoral advantages were not slow in coming. Although the strategy of 'historic compromise' between Catholics and Communists, of which the PCI made itself the bearer throughout most of the 1970s, broadly failed to offer an outlet to mounting pressures for reform, the Party none the less found itself to be the chief beneficiary of changing aspirations. In the local government elections of June 1975 the PCI received a striking increase in its share of the vote and achieved a victory that would be repeated and even improved upon in the parliamentary elections of the successive year. The scale of the Communist success in 1975 was such that it was seen in terms of an earthquake by some observers (Ghini, 1976). The Party won 5 per cent more of the vote to take 32.4 per cent and change the map of local government power. In many regions, including Sardinia, Campania, Lazio and Liguria, where the PCI was not traditionally strong, its vote improved by between 6 and 7 per cent to top 30 per cent for the first time.

Together with the Socialists (and on occasion other small parties) the PCI formed left-wing governments in the majority of Italy's cities. In several of the largest, including Rome, Turin and Naples, Communist mayors acted as the symbolic representation of an experiment in left-wing rule that could soon have become a national reality. Let us now look at the nature of this experiment, the context in which it took place, and the mechanisms of its initial success.

In the run-up to the June 1975 elections, there was a clear desire in some quarters of the PCI to present future left administrations as extensions of the Emilian experience. In recommending his city's style of government as a model of general value, Bologna's mayor Renato Zangheri spoke of the 'courage and fantasy' of a potentially exportable 'historic project' (Mussi 1975, pp. 13-16), while Aniello Coppola asserted in *Rinascita* that 'the "good

Table 4.3 Votes obtained by the PCI in elections to regions created in 1970

Region	1970 Votes	%	1975 Votes	%	1980 Votes	%	1985 Votes	%
Piemonte	728.455	25.9	1,032.842	33.9	932.885	31.7	871.364	28.9
Liguria	383.754	31.3	500.483	38.4	445.177	36.1	429.124	34.8
Lombardia	1,208.968	23.1	1,770.540	30.4	1,623.352	28.2	1,633.159	26.7
Veneto	417.291	16.8	636.251	22.8	612.059	21.7	615.051	20.4
Emilia–Romagna	1,149.172	44.0	1,363.594	48.3	1,359.255	48.2	1,383.008	47.8
Marche	275.110	31.8	349.962	36.9	355.444	39.2	355.324	35.7
Toscana	984.227	42.3	1,169.616	46.5	1,159.489	46.5	1,184.167	46.2
Umbria	215.044	41.8	257.881	46.2	253.874	45.2	258.716	44.3
Lazio	708.082	26.5	1,041.693	33.5	959.401	30.7	1,007.327	29.9
Campania	551.800	21.8	788.874	27.1	726.007	24.1	729.968	22.7
Abruzzi	513.813	22.8	230.501	30.3	213.823	27.5	233.446	26.9
Molise	26.710	15.0	35.621	17.9	32.049	15.7	35.093	16.2
Puglia	488.654	26.3	607.175	28.5	540.058	24.6	581.325	24.4
Basilicata	74.675	24.0	93.625	27.1	89.223	24.9	92.563	24.2
Calabria	218.685	23.3	270.477	25.2	263.918	24.1	266.505	24.4

Table 4.4 Percentage of PCI votes in council elections to selected large communes, 1970–85

Commune	1970–1	1975–6	1980–1	1983–5
Milan	22.9	30.4	28.0	24.9
Turin	28.9	37.8	39.9	35.4
Venice	26.6	34.3	33.6	30.5
Genoa	33.5	41.7	39.6	36.5
Florence	35.0	41.5	40.5	39.9
Rome	25.4	35.5	35.9	30.8
Naples	26.0	32.0	31.7	27.0
Bari	20.7	27.9	15.9	15.8
Catania	15.4	18.3	13.2	12.0

government" of the "red" regions' would act as 'a contagious reference point for a much vaster area of administration' (Coppola, 1975, p. 6). Yet many Communists in Italian cities were extremely diffident about even attempting to copy the Bolognese model. In the first place, the economic and social conditions in which they were called to operate were quite different. Furthermore, outside traditional areas of Communist support there was little or no 'red' subculture, party organization was often weak despite a substantial electorate, and there had been no recent experience of government in the local parties. However, these were ot the only grounds for diffidence. In some cases there was an active rejection of Emilian-style communism. Hellman has argued that in Turin, where the PCI won power thanks mainly to its previous record of opposition, there was no desire to copy the Emilian model of social consensus and class alliance (Hellman, 1979, pp. 174–5). In such cases there was a strong commitment to breaking with previous models and evolving a genuinely new style of governing, in which the Party maintained a role distinct from the local institutions and conserved its oppositional orientation.

The will to formulate a novel approach to city government was underscored by a generational dimension to the Communist advance in 1975. Of PCI councillors elected in provincial capitals, no less than 45 per cent were under the age of 30 (Belligni, 1982, p. 505). Hence the Communist administrator in the large city was often very different from the type of figure traditionally associated with left-wing local government. The new generation was not only younger than it predecessors, but also better educated, more in tune with the attitudes and aspirations of non-Communist peer groups and less attached to old policies and approaches.

Inside the Party, newly elected administrators enjoyed a relatively high degree of autonomy that further enhanced the potential for innovation in policy. At local level few formal controls over councillors existed where the PCI had little or no experience of government and the rapid transfer of senior officials from party activity to public office after 1975 made the setting-up of rigorous mechanisms of accountability difficult. At national level, attempts at creating a common set of policy priorities and establishing channels of communication between the party leadership and local administrators went in a broadly informal direction. The 'Local Government and Autonomy' department of the Central Committee was relaunched, a Consultative Assembly set up and new courses introduced in party schools, but there was no imposition of policies or guidelines from above.

Before examining the content of new policies, let us look briefly at the problems facing local government in the mid-1970s. What, in outline, was the situation the left was called to govern? In the first place, it must be said that in the space of fifteen to twenty years a dramatic change had taken place in the urban landscape. Bologna constituted a major exception in apparently having conserved a sense of homogeneity and socio-cultural compactness. Elsewhere, the large Italian city could no longer be seen as an orderly, culturally unified entity, in which the various classes found common ground in a local culture and shared pattern of values. With industrial expansion and massive emigration from the country to the city and from the south to the north of the peninsula, the character of cities such as Milan, Turin and Rome had been completely altered. On the peripheries of these cities massive estates had sprung up whose inhabitants lacked integration into traditional sub-altern cultures or any link with working-class value models based on social solidarity, the dignity of labour and a sense of belonging to the community. The model of ordered coexistence associated with urban life had been over-turned, and replaced by a general disorder and the emergence of once scarcely-known social problems. In this context, the task before the PCI was not so much that of governing the city, even on an extended scale, as of governing the society in its changed cultural form. There could be no question of seeking a semblance of governability in a limited local dimension based on organized, well-represented interest groups and the use of established tools of administration. Administrators had to reach out and find a way of integrating contrasting values and cultures, a vastly more complex set of social strata, and a range of new social claims into a renewed framework of civil life. Beyond conventional patterns of alliance, therefore, there was a need to identify new, perhaps fluctuating, alignments of forces, categories and movements, and win their support for innovative uses of local power (Tronti, 1981, pp. 54–5).

For the PCI the principal task was to take local administration to the people, to involve them in decision-making and invent policies that met popular needs. Fulfilment of such a task involved action on four levels. First, the role of the mayor needed to be redefined and promoted as the symbolic expression of the popular will. A charismatic figurehead could do much to ensure people's sympathy and give a human identity to local administration. Second, a major effort needed to be made to recreate a collective culture of participation in the large cities. Third, through the creation of new democratic forms and specific action on social issues of pressing concern, a new link between fragmented and heterogeneous popular strata and the traditional organizations of the workers' movement needed to be forged. Fourth, a record of efficient administration, responsive to complex demands and free of corruption, was indispensable to the development of a genuinely new style of government.

It may be argued that the left-wing administrations succeeded in meeting the first and second demands, whilst the fourth was achieved completely only in the first five-year period of government. For various reasons the third demand, arguably the most crucial one to the establishment of a stable new electoral base, was scarcely accomplished at all. This balance of success and failure furnishes a key for explaining the short-term triumph of left-wing city governments and their failure to continue to offer a convincing and appealing model in the mid-1980s. In the next section the causes of the electoral defeat of May 1985 will be assessed. Here, the basis of the Communists' early success will be briefly examined.

There can be little doubt that in terms of energy and image the Communist-led governments of Italy's large cities succeeded brilliantly in the second half of the 1970s. At a time when the great hopes for change that had propelled the PCI forward in 1975 and even further forward in 1976 risked disappointment and dissipation in the highly cautious institutional orientation taken by the party leadership in its search for a compromise with the Christian Democrats, Communist city governments provided tangible proof that the party represented a real break with past methods and constituted a genuine alternative to the political forces that had governed Italy for thirty years. Moreover, the initial successes aided the PCI in its claim to be ready for participation in national government.

These successes were due principally to the ability with which Communists proved able to lead the major cities and to a spectacular redefinition

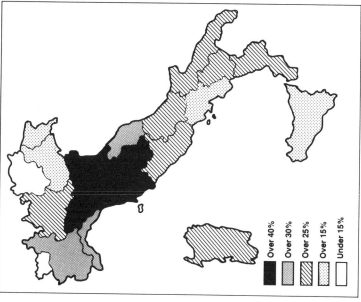

Map 4.6 Electoral strength of the PCI in the general elections of 1983: regional distribution

Over 40%
Over 30%
Over 25%
Over 15%
Under 15%

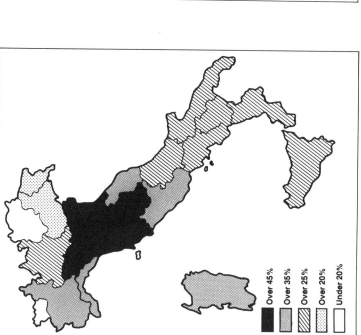

Map 4.5 Electoral strength of the PCI in the general elections of 1976: regional distribution

Over 45%
Over 35%
Over 25%
Over 20%
Under 20%

of cultural policy in a way that captured the public imagination. Diego Novelli in Turin, Maurizio Valenzi in Naples and, after the brief rule of Argan, Luigi Petroselli in Rome, all provided personal examples of integrity and human concern for citizens' problems that contrasted sharply with the often less than proud records of their predecessors. The left aimed, and to varying degrees succeeded, at improving social services and reforming the mechanisms of popular involvement in local government; but it was in a series of cultural initiatives that the new administrations most successfully affronted the task of recreating a collective, participatory framework within the fragmentary texture of metropolitan life.

These initiatives, piloted by Renato Nicolini, culture assessor in Rome, and fruitfully adopted elsewhere, involved the popularization of cultural policy and the use of mass culture in an attempt to move the socio-cultural relations of the city towards greater collective participation. Publicly sponsored theatrical and film festivals, musical events, dances and exhibitions, often held in open squares or the grounds of ancient monuments, brought the PCI in touch with the popular classes, and particularly the younger members, in a quite novel way. In July 1979, for example, some 50,000 people attended a film festival held in Rome's Massenzio Basilica and a programme of over seventy theatrical and musical shows attracted some 210,000 spectators (Petrone, 1979, p. 17). In several cases there was an attempt to decentralize the shows to the popular estates on the edge of the city and involve district representatives in their organization.

The popularity of these events was particularly important at this time since they continued to furnish the PCI with an image of vitality and modernity at the very moment when its national strategy was collapsing. The first six months of 1979 saw the brusque interruption of the Party's collaboration with the Christian Democrats in parliament and a sharp decline of approximately 4 per cent in a new set of national elections. Moreover, its cultural policy helped the Party achieve a form of management of the city that it could not have hoped to achieve by conventional political means. Thanks to Nicolini, a means was found whereby unorganized and un-represented social categories could be integrated into the cultural main-stream of metropolitan life. However, the recourse made to Hollywood blockbusters and rock music did not attract universal approval even within the PCI itself. In addition, the integration achieved left a vast range of social problems and political issues untouched. Whatever the temporary success of enterprising figures like Nicolini, in the long term the Party's ability to provide models of local government equal to the pressures placed on it depended on its capacity to give shape to more permanent bridges between administration and people.

In the next section it will be shown that in the conditions of the early 1980s neither the model of local government formulated within the stable and integrated urban context of Emilia–Romagna in the 1950s, nor the novel administrative resources of the left-wing coalitions in the large cities proved to be politically effective. Although it may be argued that the PCI's return to opposition in virtually all the cities in whose governments it had participated since 1975 was more directly associated with the decision of Socialist and Christian Democratic leaders to seek an extension of their renewed national alliance at local level than to any dramatic popular rejection of the PCI as such, the fact remains that by 1985 neither old nor newer Communist-led local governments any longer constituted positive advertisements capable of winning new electoral support or of sustaining the Communists' demand for a role in national government.

Decline and Fall

The root of the crisis of Communist local government, it can be suggested, lay in the lack of properly political responses to the emergence of a range of social issues consequent upon Italy's rapid urbanization and industrial growth. The collapse of traditional mechanisms of political socialization, the decline of a common patrimony of values and ideals, and the associated disorientation of youth undermined the PCI as much as they did any mass organized force. In Bologna, and the rest of Emilia–Romagna, the most disturbing effects of these transformations had been avoided or contained, with the result that the best-known model of Communist local government rested on a stable pattern of classes, cultures and interests that elsewhere was in decline even in the early 1960s. In the large cities conquered in 1975 an attempt was made to formulate a model of government equal to the challenges raised in a context in transformation but, despite the notable if transitory success in the cultural field, this attempt was broadly a failure in the long run. Despite the lack of an articulated organizational presence or previous administrative experience, the Party's perception of local government in the large cities either presupposed or, more commonly, sought in some way to recreate the organic, compact social model that had characterized Italian cities prior to the economic boom. To put the problem in a nutshell, the Party was politically and culturally ill equipped to deal with the conflicts and disorder that characterized metropolitan life.

Even in Emilia–Romagna these features would manifest themselves in the 1970s. Taking a long view, the beginnings of the crisis in the Emilian model may be dated from the region's first contact with monopoly capital in the mid-1960s and the incorporation of small and medium industrial enterprises into its circuits. The gradual formation of links between the small machine-parts factories of Bologna and Modena and industrial giants such as Fiat undermined the independence of the local economy from negative trends in the national economy and indirectly contributed to the emergence of forms of unofficial and casual labour on the fringes of the traditional working class (Serafini, 1974). With the economic crisis of the mid-1970s, sharp conflicts flared up between organized and unorganized interests which for the first time introduced elements of the disorder of the large city into the con-solidated stability of Bologna's Communist-dominated socio-political sytem. Although the region was able to weather the storm of inflation and stagna-tion in key sectors of northern industry better than elsewhere, the reduction of employment and sharp cuts in central government financing struck at the framework of local planning and impeded the maintenance of a high level of services. If anyone had ever really believed that Emilia could be a happy island in the troubled waters of mainstream Italy, then the grounds for this belief were cruelly dissolved in the second half of the 1970s.

The appearance of a range of 'new subjects' on the fringes of the political system created severe problems for local leaders in Bologna, not so much because a new series of demands were raised that might have been difficult to satisfy as because it demonstrated an unpredictable element of autonomy in the social sphere: a detachment of at least part of society from the local state which, under the dominance of the PCI, had tried to include all interests and categories within a complex institutional system managed by one key force. The impact of modern social problems (Jaggi *et al.*, 1977, pp. 144–5) and the appearance in 1977 of a peculiarly violent student movement hostile above all towards the PCI revealed the extent to which the myth of order and stability had ceased to have any real foundation. Such phenomena, it was suggested, also exposed how the PCI's model of extended government had tended to become an 'organized democracy' that occupied all channels and left no space for voices that did not fit into its scheme (Stame, 1978, p. 53). Under new conditions the 'articulated and complex relationship between the Commune and civil and political society', which the PCI's national local government spokesman had described as a feature of the Party's rule in Bologna, could become not a means of opening up local administration to a wider range of inputs but of ensuring its closure to the unofficial and the unorganized (Modica, 1972, pp. 24–5). Similarly, the 'daily and organized presence of the working masses' in the deliberations of government through 'a network of collaboration, support and also control' circumscribed influence to those actors and interests that were already a part of the network.

In both its early responses to these developments, when the solid and respectable working-class organizations identified with the city government closed ranks against the troublesome new underclass, and in its more considered reactions, which saw the deployment of measures designed to integrate marginalized groups into formally constituted structures on the fringes of the institutional system, the PCI show a lack of comprehension of the necessary distinction between society and the political sphere heralded by the greater complexity and instability of the former. In Bologna after 1977 the adoption of a Nicolini-style cultural policy of open-air film festivals and dances represented not so much a new departure as an attempt to shore up the old with bread and circuses.

The difficulties encountered by the left-wing governments of large cities in the early 1980s cannot be directly compared with those experienced in Bologna due to the diversity of context and the very different organizational and electoral strength of the PCI. Moreover, the two principal causes of the decline in credibility, the failure adequately to renew popular mobilization and participation and the lack of a pristine record of efficiency and honesty, were specific to the administations formed after 1975. Nevertheless, certain general features of Communist practice, reducible to the Party's institutionally-orientated conception of the Gramscian notion of hegemony and its centralized decision-making structure, were present and produced negative effects in both instances. Neither in Emilia–Romagna, nor in cities such as Rome and Naples, did the Party succeed in separating political questions from administrative ones or the party apparatus from the offices of local government. The consequence was the imposition of political decisions in spheres such as the organization of public transport or the conservation of ancient monuments, where professional expertise may have produced more effective and considered solutions. Furthermore, in appointing politically supported candidates to offices within the jurisdiction of the commune, left-wing local governments imitated the very practice (*lottizzazione*) that the PCI had long denounced as an abuse of power when operated by central government.

Certainly these practices contributed to the lack of efficiency in local services which the PCI would find itself accused of in the early 1980s. But a more general problem concerned the failure to maintain popular mobilization, that is, contact with the populace in the resolution of major issues and the formalization of that contact in a network of decentralized administrative units. In part this difficulty was a result of the policy of minimum conflict adopted towards the Christian Democrats during the phase of the historic compromise. Hellman has shown how national priorities at this time all but frustrated local attempts at institutional reform in Turin (Hellman, 1979, p. 176). However, it was also the result of a lack of sensitivity to unchannelled social demands and to the quiet frustration of aspirations raised in 1975. The bold cultural policy initiated in Rome was undoubtedly a valuable experiment, but the vast sums of money involved in sponsoring entertainments could perhaps more usefully have been employed in improving health and welfare facilities. On the key issues of housing, employment, services and general urban conditions, the PCI failed to capture the public imagination or provide radical new policies. Without this the PCI could scarcely have hoped to maintain a high degree of popular mobilization in support of local government. Following electoral defeat, the PCI leader Natta was obliged to admit that, despite the achievements of the left in the big cities, there had been a loss of energy and a failure to grasp the implications of social changes and pressing new demands (Natta, 1985, p. 19).

A further factor in the decline of left-wing local government after ten years in office was undoubtedly the series of corruption scandals that hit left administrations in Turin, Liguria, Naples, and, latterly, Emilia–Romagna. In truth, these scandals directly involved amost exclusively Socialists or local government employees, but it was the PCI, with its oft-repeated claim to be the party with 'clean hands', that suffered the most in terms of public image. The credibility of the Party's boast that it was the only force capable of providing honest administration was severely dented.

The elections of May 1985 confirmed the tendency of decline first shown in the outcome of the extraordinary poll held in Naples in November 1983, following the collapse of administration headed by the Communist Valenzi. In 1985 the PCI lost no more than 1.3 per cent compared to its 1980 position, but the drop was a sharper 4.3 per cent on its results in the European elections of 1984. Moreover, the left was now without a clear majority in Turin, Milan, Bari, Venice and Genoa. In some of the large cities and some Communist strongholds the decline was notably more serious (−3.2 per cent in Bologna, for example). The significant, if not substantial, increase in the votes of both PSI and Christian Democrats rendered possible both the definitive breakup of Socialist–Communist alliances, and the consequent construction of centre–left coalitions in all major Italian cities except Bologna and Florence. If the PCI remained strong electorally (30.2 per cent overall), the collapse of its political alliances nevertheless created a situation in which, in terms of power, the Party risked a return to the post-1948 and pre-1975 position, when it controlled barely one-tenth of Italian cities and none between Rome and Palermo.

Conclusion

In conclusion let us restate the two themes that have dominated the discussion of this chapter. First, it can be said that between the 1940s and the late 1970s the relationship between Communist local government and the national strategy of the Party was radically if gradually changed. If in the late 1940s and 1950s local power was seen as a means of implementing at least some of the preconstituted general goals of the Party and a source of pressure for their advancement in wider areas of local government, by the mid-1970s the extension of Communist influence across much of urban Italy provided powerful support to the Party's claim to be mature for a role in national government. However, the failure of the attempted historic compromise with the Christian Democrats obfuscated the possibility of Communist inclusion in government and heralded the beginning of a new period of political isolation. To compound this position, the failure of left-wing administrations to fulfil popular expectations risked reversing the Party's claim that its example of good government in the communes and the regions was proof of the contribution it could make to the government of the country at large. Failure in one camp augured badly for Communist aspirations in the other.

The second point concerns the more fundamental reasons behind the declining efficacy of Communist models of local government. It may be said that, with the transformation of the city from the late 1950s onwards, the Communists' ability to project a coherent and ostensibly alternative model of government in the local context diminished. The forms of social alliance and institutional management traditionally operated by Communist administrators proved inadequate in dealing with the complex demands and political expressions of a heterogeneous and conflictual society. The Communist model rested on the premise of a relatively high degree of cultural integration and uniformity within the city whereas, in the wake of the great processes of socio-economic change to have taken place in Italy, such conditions could by the 1970s only be found in smaller towns and localities industrialization had passed by. Hence the key challenge facing the PCI in the second half of the 1980s, is to produce an effective, socially-orientated form of local administration that does not seek to include all of society within the state or repress the conflictual interplay of contrasting cultures and interests. The formulation of such a model, however, can only follow from a substantial revision of the Party's traditional conceptions of the proper relationship between a political force and the spheres of society organized under its influence.

Bibliography

Anderlini, F., 1978. 'Società, economia, politica e istituzioni nella esperienza dei comunisti italinai', *La Società*, no. 14–15, pp. 12–24; no. 16, pp. 42–53; no. 17–18, pp. 98–107, Bologna.

Belligni, S., 1981. 'Gli amministratori comunisti: un profilo provvisorio e alcune ipotesi' in M. Ilardi and A. Accornero (eds), *Il Partito comunista italiano: struttura e storia dell'organizzazione 1921/79*. Milan, Feltrinelli, pp. 499–552.

Compagna, F., 1959. *I terroni in città*. Bari, Laterza.

Coppola, A., 1975. 'Ondata di fondo che scuote un regime', *Rinascita*, vol. 32, no. 25, pp. 5–8, Rome.

Fried, R. C., 1963. *The Italian Prefects: A Study in Administrative Politics*. New Haven, Yale University Press.

Frilli, T., 1949. 'I rapporti tra Partito e amministratori comunali a Poggibonsi', *Il Quaderno dell' attivista*, vol. 3, no. 5, p. 9, Rome.

Gabbuggiani, E., and Bianchi, G., 1968. 'Implicazioni politiche e lineamenti organizzativi d'un democratico assetto delle autonomie locali minori' in U. Terracini, *et al.*, *La Riforma dello Stato*. Rome, Editori Riuniti, pp. 225–42.

Ghini, C., 1976. *Il terremoto del 15 giugno*. Milan, Feltrinelli.

——, 1981. 'Gli iscritti al partito e alla FGCI 1943/79', in Ilardi and Accornero, *op. cit.*, pp. 227–92.

Hellman, S., 1979. 'A New Style of Governing: Italian Communism and the Dilemmas of Transition in Turin 1975–1979', *Studies in Political Economy*, vol. 1, no. 2, pp. 159–97, Toronto.

Jaggi, N. *et al*., 1977. *Red Bologna*. London, Writers and Readers' Cooperative.

Laconi, R., 1947. 'La regione nella nuova Costituzione italiana: storia e risultati di un dibattito', *Rinascita*, vol. 5, no. 7, pp. 182–4, Rome.

Modica, E., 1972. *I Comunisti per le autonomie*. Rome, Edizioni della Lega per le autonomie e i poteri locali.

Mussi, F., 1975. 'Intervista con Renato Zangheri, sindaco di Bologna: il coraggio e la fantasia di un progetto storico', *Rinascita*, vol. 32, no. 23, pp. 13–16, Rome.

Natta, A., 1985. 'Natta parla del voto e dopo', *L'Unità*, 19 May, pp. 1 and 19, Rome.

PCI—Emilia-Romagna, 1959. 'Atti della Conferenza regionale del PCI', Bologna.

Petrone, F. M., 1979. 'Tutta la città ne parla', *Rinascita*, vol. 36, no. 27, pp. 16–17, Rome.

Sechi, S., 1978. 'Politica delle alleanze ed egemonia del PCI in Emilia', *Inchiesta*, vol. 8, nos. 35–6, pp. 60–1, Bologna.

Seidelman, R., 1979. 'Neighbourhood Communism in Florence: Goals and Dilemmas of the Italian Road to Socialism', unpublished Ph.D. dissertation, Cornell University.

Serafini, M., 1974. 'Emilia–Romagna: elementi per una riflessione politica' in 'Atti del Congresso nazionale del PDUP', Rome.

Stame, F., 1978. 'Sistema politico e conflitti sociali: la strategia della sinistra', *I Quaderni de La Squilla*, no. 11–12, pp. 53–5, Bologna.

Togliatti, P., 1970. *Lezioni sul fascismo*. Rome, Editori Riuniti.

——, 1974. *Politica nazionale e Emilia rossa*, L. Arbizzani (ed.). Rome, Editori Riuniti.

Tronti, M., 1981. 'La metropoli e i conflitti', *La Società*, no. 45–6, pp. 51–6, Bologna.

5 Communists in Scandinavian Local Government

David Arter

Like it or not, one is bound to look up to Scandinavian communism. The local bastions of the Communist movement in Scandinavia have been in those remote, depopulated and climatically harsh regions in the extreme north of Finland and Sweden that border the Arctic Circle—the lands of Rudolf the Reindeer. This is *par excellence* communism in the geographic and economic periphery, the protest voice of the rural poor, the lumberjacks, smallholders and fishermen, together with the workers in the isolated industrial villages. It has a parallel in the support of the French Communist Party in the foothills of the Massif Central or the Italian Communists in parts of the Mezzogiorno. (In this last-mentioned case, the small depressed town of Montemilone in Basilicata in the deep south of Italy, which recently elected its first Communist mayor, springs to mind.)

In several communes in Finnish Lapland, the Communists polled an absolute majority of the vote in the 1950s and 1960s and, despite something of a slump in the Party's fortunes, it still managed 44.2 per cent in the town of Kemi at the 1980 local elections. In the most northerly Swedish province of Norrbotten, the Communists have consistently managed about one-sixth of the vote in a number of communes and in Pajala it was as much as 19.2 per cent in 1982. Immediately after the Second World War, the Norwegian Communist Party also claimed a significant local government poll—18.8 per cent in 1947—in the Arctic province of Finnmark, a fact denoting not only the relative strength but also the genuinely cross-national character of peripheral communism in Scandinavia.

In contrast, communism has been relatively weaker (as a proportion of the active electorate) in the more developed industrial districts and urban centres in the south, although in a number of traditional working-class wards in the capital cities, Copenhagen, Oslo, Stockholm and Helsinki, the Communists have polled creditably. In the multi-party systems of the Nordic states, the Communists have competed for votes in a crowded market-place: there are, for example, nine parties presently represented in the national assemblies in Denmark and Finland and seven in Norway. The Finnish Communist Party, however, has occupied a distinctive place on the Nordic radical left: it was the largest single party in both national and local elections in 1958 and 1960 respectively; it declined, following a deep split in its ranks, in the 1970s (see Table 5.1); but with 13.2 per cent of the poll at the local elections in October 1984 it remains one of the strongest parties of its kind in Western Europe today.

Table 5.1 Performance of Communist parties at General Elections in the Nordic region, 1945–85

Denmark		Norway		Finland		Sweden	
Year	Vote (%)	Year	Vote (%)	Year	Vote (%)	Year	Vote (%)
1945	12.5	1945	11.9	1945	23.5	1044	10.3
1947	6.8	1949	5.8	1948	20.0	1948	6.3
1950	4.6	1953	5.1	1951	21.6	1952	4.3
1953	4.8	1957	3.4	1954	21.6	1956	5.0
1957	3.1	1961	2.9	1958	23.2	1958	3.4
1960	1.1	1965	1.4	1962	22.0	1960	4.5
1964	1.2	1969	1.0	1966	21.2	1964	5.2
1966	0.8	1973	–	1970	16.6	1968	3.0
1968	1.0	1977	0.4	1972	17.1	1970	4.8
1971	1.4	1981	0.3	1975	18.9	1973	5.3
1973	3.6	1985	0.2	1979	17.9	1976	4.8
1975	4.2			1983	13.4	1979	5.6
1977	3.7					1982	5.6
1979	1.9					1985	5.4
1981	1.1						
1984	0.7						

Two ground rules of the local political process have militated against the Finnish Communists taking control of towns and communes in the manner of their French and Italian counterparts. First, the local political system is not based on the parliamentary principle: all the parties with (a sufficient minimum number of) seats in the plenary council, *valtuusto*, are represented on a proportional basis on the executive committee, *kunnan/kaupungin hallitus*, which in turn is not dependent on the confidence of the full council. Second, most important financial decisions require a qualified majority of two-thirds of the delegates present in plenary council (the same rule applies in Sweden) and this has prompted the development of a peculiarly consensual style of local policy-making. The parties engage in intensive preliminary talks

Table 5.2 Support for Communist parties at local elections in the
Nordic region, 1945–85

Finland		Norway*		Sweden†	
Year	Vote (%)	Year	Vote (%)	Year	Vote (%)
1950	23.0	1945	11.4	1946	11.2
1953	23.1	1947	10.0	1950	4.9
1956	21.2	1951	6.1	1954	4.8
1960	22.0	1955	5.3	1958	4.0
1964	21.9	1959	3.9	1962	3.8
1968	16.9	1963	1.9	1966	6.4
1972	17.5	1967	1.2	1970	4.3
1976	18.5	1971	0.7	1973	5.0
1980	16.6	1979	0.3	1976	4.7
1984	13.2	1983	0.4	1979	5.5
				1982	5.1
				1985	5.1

* In 1975 the Norwegian Communists ran candidates as part of the Socialist Electoral
Alliance.
† Landsting elections.

Table 5.3 Support for the main Finnish parties at local elections, 1950–84

Year	Party		Vote (%)	
	SKDL	SDP	Centre	Conservatives
1950	23.0	25.1	8.1	5.9
1953	23.1	25.5	16.0	7.6
1956	21.2	25.4	21.9	6.3
1960	22.0	21.1	20.4	14.0
1964	21.9	24.8	19.3	10.0
1968	16.9	23.9	18.9	16.1
1972	17.5	27.1	18.0	18.1
1976	18.5	24.8	18.4	.20.9
1980	16.6	25.5	18.7	22.9
1984	13.2	24.8	20.2	23.0

and in this way compromises are reached long before the formality of full council. In sum, whilst through the medium of inter-party bargaining the Communists are able to exert a degree of influence in about 80 per cent of Finnish communes, the Party has rarely managed to command the two-thirds of council seats necessary for outright control.

This chapter is divided into four sections. The first part sketches the main lines in the historical development of the Nordic Communist parties since the last war; the second outlines the institutional framework of local government in the region; the third concentrates on the ecology of support for the Nordic Communists; and, finally, there is an assessment of the goals and influence of the largest local Communist party in the region—the SKP in Finland.

A Short Profile of the Nordic Communists Since 1945

In any brief historical note on the Scandinavian Communist parties since 1945, it is important to contrast developments in the western and eastern halves of the region. In Denmark and Norway, extensive fragmentation has occurred on the radical left and the Communists have been eclipsed by parties embracing the ideas of the so-called 'new left'—the Socialist People's Party and Left-Socialists in Denmark and the Left-Socialists in Norway. In Finland and Sweden, the Communists continue to dominate the radical left—albeit in Finland within the umbrella organization, the Finnish People's Democratic League—and though, in line with the rest of the region, support for both parties has declined since the Second World War, the Finnish Communists remain one of the strongest parties of their kind in Western Europe.

The dramatic decline of communism in local elections in the western half of the region seems integrally bound up with the vicissitudes of parliamentary politics. Under the leadership of Axel Larsen, and having played a leading part in the Resistance movement during the Nazi occupation (1940-5), the Danish Communist Party (DKP) polled 12.5 per cent of the active electorate and gained eighteen Folketing seats in 1945. It disappeared from parliament altogether, however, in 1960 following Larsen's defection to form a new radical leftist group, the Socialist People's Party, but under its present Chairman, Jørgen Jensen, returned with six seats in 1973. This was at a general election held in the wake of a referendum on Denmark's affiliation to the European Community (EC) and reflected backing for the DKP's strongly anti-EC stance. Since then Communist support has fallen away badly: at the last three general elections in 1979, 1981 and 1984, the DKP has failed to cross the 2 per cent threshold necessary to qualify for Folketing seats. Indeed, with only 22,800 votes—a mere 0.7 per cent of the poll—1984 represented the Danish Communists' worst electoral perform-ance since the Second World War (*Politiken*, 12 January 1984). The radical leftist vote is nowadays shared by the Socialist People's Party with 11.5 per cent of the vote and twenty-one parliamentary seats in 1984 and the Left-Socialists with 2.7 per cent and five Folketing seats.

The parliamentary fortunes of the Norwegian Communists (NKP) have charted a similar course to their Danish sister party. The NKP achieved its best result in 1945—11.9 per cent of the poll and eleven Storting seats—but since 1961 it has failed to return a single delegate to the national assembly. In 1973 the Communists did form part of an anti-EC Socialist Electoral Alliance—along with the Socialist People's Party and Democratic Socialists—which polled a creditable 11.2 per cent of the vote. When confronted four years later by a merger of the two last-mentioned parties in the form of the Left-Socialists, however, the NKP contrived a meagre 0.4 per cent of the poll and this despite being able to run candidates in every constituency except Sogn and Fjordane in western Norway (Heidar, 1983, p. 150). At the last general election in 1985, the NKP plummeted to an all-time nadir of 0.2 per cent of the valid vote. Neither the Danish nor the Norwegian Communists have participated in national government.

The electoral base of the radical left in Sweden has been numerically weaker, at about 5 per cent of the vote, than elsewhere in post-war Scandinavia. Yet in contrast to developments in the western half of the region, the Swedish radical left has been monopolized by the Communists. Fragmentation in the Party's ranks was avoided in the early 1960s by accom-modating the non-dogmatic but innovatory socialism of the 'new left'—revisionism which in Denmark and Norway at this time had propelled the formation of splinter Socialist People's Parties—and under the vigorous leadership of C. H. Hermansson (1964-75) the Swedish Communist Party was given a revitalized, modern image. It explicitly committed itself to parlia-mentarism, rejected democratic centralism, took a more detached stance towards Moscow and in 1967 adopted the designation Left-Party Communists, Vpk. Unlike the Finnish party, Vpk has neither participated in government nor had a significant impact on government policy; it has not succeeded either in establishing a real foothold in the trade-union move-ment. None the less, under the leadership of Lars Werner since 1975, Vpk polled 5.4 per cent of the vote at the 1985 general election and 4.6 at the concurrent provincial and municipal elections. The Swedish Left-Party

Communists, in sum, have been a regular parliamentary party and have also contributed to local government policy-making.

The Finnish Communist Party has been *sui generis* in the region. The armistice with the Soviet Union in September 1944 brought with it the legalization of the Communists who soon became the dominant member of an electoral alliance known as the Finnish People's Democratic League (SKDL). Socialists of varying hues initially adhered to the League and for a time a number operated in leading positions within it. However, lacking sufficient ideological breathing-space under the same organizational roof as the Communists, their activities soon ceased. By the 1960s, SKDL became no more than a cover and support body for the Communists (*Helsingin Sanomat*, 30 September 1984) although the accession to the SKDL chairmanship of the long-serving Ele Alenius (1963–79) kindled debate about the future direction the radical leftist movement should take. Alenius and his supporters among the People's Democrats—the 'blue-and-white Finnish socialists'—canvassed the case for collaboration in government; the Communists remained more cautious and ambivalent.

As in a number of West European countries, the radical left participated in a broad post-war coalition between 1945 and 1948 and provided the Prime Minister, Mauno Pekkala, who is so far the only SKDL member to have held this post. The collapse of the Pekkala coalition was followed by eighteen years in the wilderness during which SKDL strengthened its constituency base, particularly in northern Finland, and also consolidated its poll. In 1958, SKDL became the largest parliamentary party and achieved the same status at the local elections two years later with 22 per cent of the active electorate. A combined-left victory at the general elections in 1966 coincided with a change in the Communist Party chairmanship and represented a watershed in the post-war history both of the radical left and Finnish policy-making as a whole. The Communists entered two centre-left 'Popular Front' governments led by Social Democratic prime ministers and these administrations had the numerical base to direct the economy in conjunction with the key labour-market organizations. A corporate policy channel emerged and quickly threatened the role of the parliamentary-electoral channel.

The Communist Party found itself divided by the Russian invasion of Czechoslovakia in 1968. The split into hardline and revisionist factions deepened during the 1970s and at intervals the Communists presented the unusual (and to many of the faithful, unedifying) spectacle of a party with one foot in government and the other in opposition. Talk of the minority defecting to form their own party gathered pace. The 1980s have witnessed intensified division and it was no surprise when at the general elections in

March 1983 SKDL registered its lowest post-war vote of 13.4 per cent. At present the hardliners control eight party districts, possess ten delegates—out of a total SKDL parliamentary group of twenty-six—and in *Tiedonantaja* have an organ for articulating their viewpoint. At the 1984 local elections, SKDL was more openly divided than ever before: in twelve of the 445 communes the majority revisionists and minority hardliners put up separate electoral lists.

The Institutional Framework of Local Government

In the unitary Scandinavian states, the implementation of central policies is vested in a nexus of independent administrative agencies and elected local authorities. In Denmark, Norway and Sweden, there are two elected tiers of local government in the form of county and district councils, whereas in Finland there is only a single level. The number of elected local authorities has tended to fall in recent years. In Denmark, for example, recent reforms have had the effect of substantially reducing the patchwork of historical units: the country is presently divided into fourteen counties, 275 districts, plus the cities of Copenhagen and Frederiksberg which have constitutions of their own. A universal principle throughout the region is that the number of council members is related to the size of the officially registered population in the area: thus in Finland it varies from seventeen for a commune of 2,000 to eight-five for a population of over 400,000. As to the division of powers between the upper and lower elected tiers, the county in Denmark is responsible for the hospital service and major roads, whilst the districts direct all the other local-authority services. In Sweden the county has powers to administer hospital and mental-health facilities, dental clinics, children's homes and a range of vocational provisions. The district authorities manage health, elementary and secondary education, housing, road construction and welfare services. Local government elections take place every four years in Denmark, Finland and Norway and every three in Sweden, a PR list system being deployed across the region.

The mobilization of the local electorate has been highest in Sweden where, since the constitutional reforms and the shift to unicameralism in 1970, general and local elections have been held on the same day. The turn-out at the Swedish local elections in September 1985 was 90 per cent, compared with 73.6 per cent in Finland in 1984 and 73.3 per cent in Denmark in 1981. In Norway, in particular, turn-out at local elections has been significantly lower than at elections to the national parliament (Storting). A differential of

10–15 per cent has been commonplace: a participation level of 82.0 per cent at the Storting elections of 1981 was followed two years later by a local election turn-out of 67.6 per cent, the lowest since the Second World War. It does not follow, of course, that the significantly higher turn-out in Sweden denotes any greater level of citizen involvement in local affairs. On the contrary, in October 1983 the Social Democratic Civil Affairs Minister set up a commission of inquiry to examine ways of activating interest in local democracy (Från Riksdag & Departement, 28 October 1983). The higher Swedish turn-out is plainly the product of holding simultaneous national and local elections, although ironically the status of the local elections has declined since the move to a single-chamber Riksdag. Before 1970, county councils functioned as electoral colleges for the election of delegates to the Upper House.

Paradoxically, Sweden boasts not only the highest but, among a section of voters, also the lowest turn-out at local elections in the region. In addition to all citizens of 18 years and over (the same local franchise qualification as elsewhere in Scandinavia), foreign citizens who have been resident in Sweden for the previous three years have since 1976 been entitled to vote in local elections. The numerically strong immigrant electorate in Sweden represents a distinctive feature of Scandinavian, indeed Western European, local government—a non-indigenous body of voters comparable in scale to the *gästarbeiter* in the German Federal Republic, albeit generally rather better assimilated socially and economically and, unlike the latter, enfranchised at all levels of government below the national. In 1982, no less than 2.8 per cent of the Swedish electorate comprised foreign citizens, rising to nearly 7 per cent in large cities like Stockholm and Gothenburg, and over 10 per cent in industrial centres elsewhere. Turn-out among this sizeable immigrant population, however, has been 30–35 per cent lower than that of Swedish citizens in the three local elections between 1976–82 and has declined—from 60 per cent in 1976 to only 52.5 per cent in 1982. True, in well over a quarter of all Swedish communes there is at least one full or deputy councillor who is not a Swedish citizen and nearly two-thirds of all these councillors and their deputies are Finns, easily the largest of the immigrant groups. None the less, turn-out among the Swedish *invandrare* is low: it ranged from 61 per cent in 1982 for Greeks and Turks to 49 per cent for Finns.

Just as in Sweden, a three-year residence qualification is required for foreign citizens to be eligible to vote in local elections in Denmark (*Bekendtgørelse af Lov*, 22 April 1981). In 1981, an estimated 55,515 foreigners, 1.45 per cent of the active electorate, were enfranchised for the first time, the majority of them situated in and around the cities of Copenhagen and

Frederiksberg (*Valgene til*, 1983, pp. 108–9). In Finland Nordic (but not other foreign) citizens, resident in the commune during the election year and registered in the two previous years, are entitled to vote in local elections. They numbered a mere 1,697 persons in 1980 of whom only 55.7 per cent troubled to vote (*Kunnallisvaalit*, 1980). Outside Sweden and Denmark, the size of the immigrant electorates in the region remains very small.

Local government elections in Scandinavia have become first and foremost party political elections: independents—environmentalists, feminists, peace candidates, etc.—invariably contest elections on the lists of established parties which in turn bear bland national slogans. In Copenhagen, to be sure, twenty-one lists contested the municipal elections in 1981 and they included two candidates for the 'Immigrant Minority' and three for the 'Party without a Name'; the fifty-five city council seats in the capital, however, were ultimately shared by delegates of nine political parties, all with the exception of the Communists, having representation in the national parliament (Folketing). Indeed, the local Scandinavian party systems mirror those operating at the parliamentary level. Issues tend to be national, the campaigns centrally directed, and local election results are interpreted as statements on the performance of the parties on the national stage. So much is, of course, true across the bulk of Western Europe as is the generally low level of voter familiarity with the structures of local government—where county assemblies meet, what powers are invested in them, etc. In the absence of an incompatibility rule, moreover, national politicians, MPs and ministers graduate from local politics, frequently continue to serve on local councils whilst members of parliament and return to local politics after their parliamentary career is over. For example, nearly half of the twenty Eduskunta delegates representing the capital city stood as candidates for the Helsinki city council in October 1984. Despite a heavy ministerial and parliamentary workload, candidacy at local elections provides the national politician with a means of gauging and maintaining his personal support base as well as giving him two career strings. The overlapping of national and local elites further contributes to eroding the local character of elections to the municipal and county councils in Scandinavia.

Consistently the largest group in the local multi-party systems of the region has been the Social Democratic–Labour Parties, with a poll presently varying from just over a quarter of the vote in Finland, to a third in Denmark, two-fifths in Norway and approaching half the active electorate in Sweden. Next have come the Conservatives, currently the strongest non-socialist party throughout Scandinavia with an average of about a quarter of the vote. They in turn are followed by the Centre (formerly Agrarian) Parties in

Finland and Sweden (the Centre is much weaker in Norway); the Agrarian Liberals (Venstre) in Denmark with approximately one-sixth of the poll; the radical left in Finland (the People's Democratic League) with 13.2 per cent in 1984; and, finally, a number of centre-based parties—*inter alia* Christians and Liberals—together with a number of protest groups, all with under 10 per cent of the poll. Interestingly, the Swedish Social Democrats' local election vote of 46.1 per cent in 1982 was slightly higher than the Party achieved at the simultaneous general election (45.6 per cent), despite a lower turn-out at the provincial and municipal elections. Doubtless this may partly be explained by the overwhelming supremacy of the Social Democrats among the large body of *invandrare*: between 1982 and 1985 no less than 86 per cent of those immigrants elected to serve on the municipal councils represented the Social Democrats. There is also evidence that at the general elections a number of Social Democrats, anticipating that a future Social Democratic government would need legislative allies from the radical left, voted tactically and supported the Left-Communists in their strongest areas so as to ensure that the latter achieved the 5 per cent threshold necessary to qualify for Riksdag seats.

The Ecology of Local Communism in Scandinavia

Consonant with a serious erosion in the electoral base of national communism since 1945 has gone a parallel collapse in Communist support in local elections in the west of the region. The Norwegian Communists polled 11.4 per cent at the local elections in 1945, 6.1 per cent in 1951, dropped below 2 per cent in 1963, and in 1983 obtained barely a quarter of that (see Table 5.2). Their decline has been equally accentuated in urban and rural districts. In 1979, for example, the NKP registered only 0.5 per cent of the active electorate in the larger towns of Oslo, Stavanger, Bergen, Trondheim and Tromsø, whereas in 1945 it had managed a substantial 26.4 per cent in Bergen alone. Only in the most northerly county of Finnmark, where the NKP gained 2.4 per cent, did the Party's vote exceed 1 per cent in 1979 (it had obtained 20.8 per cent in Finnmark in 1945). True, from a very low base NKP support rose at the county (*fylkesting*) and municipal (*kommunstyre*) elections in 1983: its 7,765 votes constituted 0.37 per cent of the valid poll—an increase of 16.4 per cent on the NKP's 1981 general election result (*Aftenposten*, 15 September 1983). At the same time, backing for another miniscule, radical leftist group, the Red Alliance, which polled 1.2 per cent in 1983, grew faster than the NKP and in one ward in the old working-class district of Oslo (*Lakkegaten skole*) it got 7.8 per cent of the electorate. Ironically, it was in this same ward that the radical rightist, anti-immigrant, anti-tax Progress Party did notably well. In this polarized situation, the NKP ws plainly unable to draw on the evident mood of working-class protest.

Plainly, too, with such a small vote, the NKP's influence in the council chambers of Norway has been at best minimal. Between 1975 and 1979, the NKP had only one county council seat, in North Trøndelag, but with a comfortable non-socialist majority and a Centre Party chairman (*Aftenposten*, 29 August 1979) there was no chance of exerting influence through holding the balance of power. Although the NKP managed two council seats in 1979–83, the position remained precisely as before.

Like the NKP, the local government vote of the Danish Communists (DKP) has deteriorated in recent elections. In November 1981 it gained 1.9 per cent of the poll for the district councils (*kommunale råd*) and 1.6 per cent for the county councils (*amtsråd*), compared with 3.3 per cent and 2.8 per cent for the districts and counties respectively in 1978. DKP support was greater in 1981 in the urban than in the rural communes—twice its national average in Copenhagen and higher than average in the Islands, but below its mean poll in the east and north. Unlike the other Scandinavian Communist parties, the DKP has not been strong in the outlying geographical areas: it ran lists of its own in only three of the twenty-seven communes in the most northerly county of North Jutland in 1981, averaged a meagre 1.1 per cent of the active electorate and claimed a council seat only in the main town of Ålborg. In the North Jutland county elections, the DKP obtained 1.2 per cent in 1981 and did not win a seat.

DKP gained its highest national vote in Slagelse in West Zealand where it polled 7.2 per cent in 1981 and won two council seats; a similar number accrued in Copenhagen, albeit with a lower vote of 4.2 per cent. Easily the best-known DKP representative in the capital has been Ivan Hansen, earlier the mayor of the city and currently chairman of the union of B&W Motors. At the last DKP Congress, Hansen lost his seat on the Central Committee, something which was widely seen as the result of his commitment to cooperating with the Social Democrats. Hansen, though, was not acting unilaterally with regard to this line: indeed, with an eye to strengthening its influence in the council chambers (Hans Kloster, 2 September 1984), the DKP has recently opted for a strategy of cooperation with the broad left appealing for a united stance against the Conservative-dominated Schlüter administration's proposed cuts in local-government support grants and the possible privatization of local services (Jørgen Jensen, August 1983). Without the support of the parties of the left, the DKP's influence in local government can at best be slight. In 1981 it won only twenty-two district seats, together with a further eleven elected on common socialist lists—about half the number it obtained three years earlier—and gained a seat on only one of the fourteen county councils.

In examining the electoral bases of Vpk support in Swedish local-government elections, it is necessary to emphasize that in none of the communes are the Communists currently the largest party or even the largest party of the left. Vpk is a minor party in terms of its local vote. None the less, marked ecological variations may be traced in the distribution of its support, notably between the northern and southern counties (provinces). Vpk's electoral centre of gravity has traditionally been located among the geographically isolated blue-collar workers in the mining districts in the most northerly county of Norrbotten. At the 1982 local elections, Vpk gained over 10 per cent of the vote in nearly half the Norrbotten communes and in Pajala *peripheral communism* was almost twice as strong. Norrbotten is a depressed region. In 1982 the Norrbotten executive was instructed by the Ministry of Industry to produce a development plan for Pajala, taking cognizance of the shifts occurring in the labour-force employed in the ore-fields (Från Riksdag & Departement, 22 October 1982), and the following year the Social Democratic government introduced a special Norrbotten bill with a three-year public investment programme designed to regenerate the infrastructure of the region (Från Riksdag & Departement, 25 March 1983). Industry in Norrbotten is run down and structural unemployment high. Interestingly, this type of peripheral communism is a cross-national manifestation: the Communists poll heavily in Finnish Lapland and achieve their highest proportional vote in Finnmark in the extreme north of Norway.

The balance between centre and periphery within the Vpk electorate has altered over the last two decades. At the local elections in 1962, Vpk polled only one-third more in absolute terms in Stockholm than Norrbotten, whereas in 1982 the Party gained two and a half times more votes in the capital. Vpk's support has varied between 15 and 20 per cent in a number of the old working-class areas of the capital and in Stockholm commune the Communists managed 8.8 per cent at the local elections in September 1985. The Party has also polled well in a number of small industrial communities in central and eastern Sweden—between two and three times its national average in Hällefors, Hofors, Norberg and Ludvika. Yet Vpk remains strongest in relative terms in the extreme north and weakest in the southern counties. Thus in contrast to over one-tenth of the poll in Norrbotten, Vpk's local election vote in 1982 fell below the 4 per cent required for parliamentary (though not local-government) representation in five of the twelve counties in the south.

In a social sense, though, Vpk has moved south—to recruit a greater proportion of the tertiary white-collar population in the central and southern towns. Undoubtedly the modernization of the Party in the 1960s and the incorporation of 'new left' ideas had ramifications for the socio-economic composition of Communist support. Two decades ago, Vpk was dominated by industrial workers and accordingly the average age of party supporters was relatively high. Thereafter, Vpk became increasingly favoured by young and highly educated voters as an intellectual alternative to social democracy and the monopoly capitalism it was charged with perpetrating. *White-collar communism* is nowadays an integral element in Vpk's support. It was estimated that in 1976 12 per cent of senior civil servants under 30 years of age supported the Party (Petersson, 1977, p. 4), and in a number of electoral districts of university towns like Lund, Uppsala and Umeå, Vpk gained 10 per cent of the vote at the 1982 local elections.

Positioned at the other end of the social continuum from its middle-class backing, local-government communism in Sweden has recently developed a sub-proletarian base, drawing a significant body of support from among immigrant voters. In many communes with a sizeable population of *invandrare*, Vpk was the third largest party in 1982. In the second Botkyrka ward, for example, a rather poor dormitory area serving Stockholm to the north and the town of Södertälje to the south and with an immigrant population numbering one-quarter of the electorate, Vpk got 10 per cent of the vote in 1982. In 1985 Vpk polled 8.3 per cent in Botkyrka commune, an advance of 0.6 per cent on its result there years earlier. Vpk moreover, is well represented among those immigrants elected to serve on local councils: 18.5 per cent of those non-Swedish delegates serving on Swedish councils in 1982-5 were elected to represent Vpk, second only to the body of Social Democratic representatives. The strength of Vpk support among immigrants, particularly Finns, makes it feasible to allude to a third type of communism and one, unlike the peripheral and white-collar varieties, exclusive to local elections, namely *imported communism*.

Obviously the cross-pressures faced by immigrant voters as part of resocialization in a new political environment can predispose them to abstain. Language difficulties, creating problems in following the campaign, will tend to have the same effect. Equally, lack of interest in a local election may well be related to the (short- or long-term) intention to return home. For Finns in particular the logistics of a move back are the most straightforward—their social benefits (pensions, etc.) are unaffected, the costs of the removal relatively small, and for younger Finns, many of whom find the process of settling in Sweden fraught with difficulties, the prospect of pulling out is distinctively attractive. Thus, as Tomas Hammar has observed: 'even if it is relatively easy for Finns to carry over their political allegiance into Sweden, this has not resulted in a high turn-out level simply because mobility rates are greatest among young immigrant Finns' (Hammar, 1984, p. 48). None the less, there can be no doubt that Sweden has imported a measure of Finnish communism. Certainly there were many Communists among the smallholders, agricultural and forestry workers, etc., in central and northern Finland who emigrated to Sweden in search of work in the 1960s and they were ready recruits to Vpk in the industrial villages of central Sweden where the bulk of them settled. The structural similarities in the multi-party systems of the two countries aided and abetted this transference of allegiance.

Like its Swedish sister party, SKDL in Finland has recruited the greatest share of its support (as a proportion of the active electorate) in the extreme north: peripheral communism, however, has been significantly stronger in Finland than Sweden. Thus, in the electoral period, 1980-4, SKDL was the largest party in almost 3 per cent of Finnish communes and nearly three-quarters of these were located in the three most northerly counties (provinces) of Kuopio, Oulu and Lapland. Aside from its greater numerical strength in Finland, there are a number of other differences between peripheral communism in Sweden and Finland.

First, in contrast to the marked intra-regional variation in Vpk support in northern Sweden—the Communists polled 10.2 per cent in Norrbotten, but only 5.2 per cent in neighbouring Västerbotten in 1982—there has been a notable consistency in the spatial distribution of SKDL support throughout its northern strongholds. It polled 21.6 per cent in Kuopio, 24.5 per cent in Oulu and 28.8 per cent in Lapland in 1980. (See table 5.3).

Next, whilst a strong Vpk vote in local elections in the far north has complemented rather than dented the Social Democratic vote, the Communists in northern Finland have consistently been the largest party on the left. SKDL was the best-supported party of the left in four-fifths of the communes in the far north in 1980 and in the vast majority of these the Social Democrats were the smallest of the four main parties. Unlike the Swedish situation, in short, peripheral communism in Finland has an ecological base distinct from social democracy. In fact, in two-fifths of the communes in Lapland and over two-thirds in Oulu, the farmer-based Centre Party has been comfortably the largest party and in several of these areas SKDL the only other party represented on the council. In northern Finland, it would be more accurate to speak of a two-party rather than a multi-party system at the local government level.

Finally, SKDL has penetrated some of the poorest agrarian districts since the Second World War: it polled over 40 per cent in Kittilä and Kolari, for example, in 1980 and in only six rural communes in the far north did SKDL's vote fall below 10 per cent. Despite SKDL's undoubted strength in the northern towns—in Kemi it gained nationally its highest vote of 44.2 per cent in 1980— the core Communist electorate in the non-urban areas has comprised smallholders, lumberjacks and fishermen. In Sweden, however, peripheral communism is predominantly a blue-collar rather than an agrarian and 'backwoods' phenomenon.

The bulwarks of blue-collar Communism in Finland have been in parts of the south west—in the former capital of Turku, for example, and industrial villages like Ruovesi, Ylöjärvi, Luopioinen, Pomarkku, Hämeenkyrö and Dragsfjärd. Indeed, it is necessary to identify a second-core Communist area concentrated on the three general-election constituencies of north Turku, south Turku and north Häme, where in 1980 SKDL averaged 20.2 per cent of the poll. The distribution of the total vote for the left in the south west demonstrates a different pattern from northern Finland: the combined left is generally stronger and the Social Democrats invariably the largest party of the left. The pattern is not dissimilar to that in Norrbotten in Sweden, except that in the small towns of Loimaa and Nokia and several rural districts, especially in north Turku, the Communists are the strongest party. In general, however, the ecological contours of this type of blue-collar communism are less distinct than the peripheral variety.

Communist Goals and Influence in Local Government: The Finnish SKDL

As one of the largest Communist parties in Western Europe, the Finnish Communist Party's objectives and achievements in the local government sphere are of particular interest. In point of fact, the designation SKP (Finnish Communist Party) is not used at local elections: the Party employs no local government secretary and their list of candidates bear the acronym SKDL (Finnish People's Democratic League) rather than SKP. However, to claim that SKP does not exist for local-election purposes, though technically correct, would be pedantic; rather, the Finnish Communists have viewed local politics as an important medium in their fight to improve the lot of working people. During the Party's long period in parliamentary opposition, especially over the years 1948–66, SKP laid much stress on the local arena, which it perceived as the most direct route to a measure of policy influence. In this last-mentioned era in the national political wilderness, SKP strove *inter alia* to equalize communal-housing conditions, develop local welfare provision and instil in the people a greater spirit of local democracy. SKP's intermittent participation in the series of broad centre–left governments since 1966, the deepening split on the radical left that this has exposed, and a period of economic retrenchment closely bound up with world recession, all have contributed to prompting SKP to re-examine its role and objectives in the local sector in recent years. As an opposition party since 1983, SKP has given renewed importance to communal affairs. Despite the development of a centralized welfare state in Finland in the 1960s, it has denounced the inadequacy of social and health-care standards in the large towns in the south of the country whilst urging the case for communes in the north hit by serious unemployment (over 20 per cent in parts of Lapland) to be encouraged to arrange work for inhabitants in their own locality.

In preparation for the forthcoming local elections, SKP expounded three main issues at its 20th Party Congress in 1984. First, against the background of cuts in central government funding, the Party expressed its determination to fight to maintain levels of local welfare provision and to ensure that resources are fairly distributed among the regions. There was unequivocal opposition to any proposal for raising the rates (*veroäyri*) and/or costs of basic communal services on the grounds that this would be unjust both from a social and regional standpoint. With a view to achieving work for everyone in their native area, the Communists urged the communes and municipalities to pursue programmes designed to achieve diversification in the local economy. In this last context, the onus was placed on fostering a conducive environment for small and medium-sized enterprises (*Tänään huomisen hyväksi*, 1984), a prima facie case of Communist backing for local capitalism (albeit democratically managed) at least as a middle-term expedient.

Second, the 20th Party Congress underlined the importance of promoting the opportunities for citizens to exert a direct influence on the management of local affairs. A variety of strategies was envisaged. In the light of research showing that communes exercise control over no more than 10–15 per cent of the decisions affecting the local sector, SKP urged the need to increase the policy authority of local councils. At the same time, influence was to be transferred from the local officials—inspectors, planners, advisers, etc.—to the elected representatives of the people in the executive committee of the council. Above all, it was argued that a centralized, bureaucratized state controlling the purse-strings constituted a serious threat to the basis of local government in Finland. More immediately, given the proximity of elections, SKP urged the need to mobilize more local government candidates. In 1980, the Party had put up 12,000 candidates for election, but this figure dropped by 2,000 four years later. In part this reflected a widespread public dis-affection with political parties; it was also related to the long-standing factionalization in the Party's ranks. Furthermore, it appears that at least some prospective SKDL candidates were deterred from revealing their party colours out of a fear of being blacklisted by their employers. Certainly in three Centre-dominated communes in the province of Central Finland where SKDL did not contest the local elections in 1984 (the Party had candi-dates in four-fifths of all communes nationally)—communes in which religious sects have exerted considerable influence—the Communist area organizer complained that people did not dare to become party candidates in case they subsequently lost their jobs (*Kansan Uutiset*, 4 September 1984, p. 14). All in all, the 20th Party Congress emphasized the need for residents to become more involved in the management of local affairs. Although a government commission is presently examining the role that local referen-dums (permitted in Sweden) might play in this respect, it was held that this was only scratching the surface. What was needed was to develop in the citizen a heightened sense of individual competence, to regenerate grassroots democracy in the local government arena.

Finally, the 20th Party Congress took as its third election theme the need for communes actively to be engaged in pursuing the cause of world peace. They should not be prevented from supporting the nation's foreign policy (it was assumed this had world peace as a paramount objective) by outdated constitutional prescription restricting the direction of foreign relations to the head of state. The communes, it was insisted, would only be following the lead of the President and central authorities. Moreover, in addition to activi-ties of their own, councils were encouraged to support the local events—marches, youth festivals, rallies, etc.—of the various peace organizations. They could also work to lower the international temperature by forging twinning arrangements with foreign towns with the goal of peace incorporated into their joint charter of friendship (*Suomen kunnallislehti*, August 1984, p. 6).

Because the local political process does not operate in accordance with the parliamentary principle in Finland, there are no government parties or opposition parties in the local councils. Opposition attitudes and dispositions, of course, develop: particularly if the balance between bourgeois and socialist blocs is tilted heavily in favour of the one, the minority assumes the role of opposition (Poukka in Larma, Eskola & Jokela, 1976, p. 74). But, just as in the case of the Swiss Federal Council, all the major parties are represented on the executive committee in relation to their strength in the plenary council. The three-weekly meetings of the full council in turn have become a complete formality: the spokesmen of the party groups intone on matters of lesser importance largely for press consumption and votes are virtually never taken. The real debate and negotiation takes place in preliminary inter-party talks, particularly so on matters requiring qualified majority support.

A two-thirds majority is necessary for the resolution of budget matters, a range of appointments, the disposal of property, the creation and termination of funds, raising and renewing grants, taking loans and securities, etc. The system of qualified majorities for significant monetary decisions in local government is distinctive in Finland in that it dates back to before independence—it has a parallel at the national level where, for example, tax changes designed to obtain for longer than one year require a two-thirds majority. This has, of course, dictated the need to achieve broad-based compromises in respect of most important local issues: the consensual policy style that has accordingly evolved has, however, made a precise calculus of Communist influence in local government extremely difficult. Thus in a number of the larger towns—Tampere is a case in point—the Social Democrats and Conservatives have cooperated to achieve the necessary two-thirds majorities; elsewhere, the two left-wing parties have worked as a bloc. Exceptionally, in a number of communes in the central and northern districts, the farmer-based Centre Party has contrived the qualified majority on its own. In general, though, it may be said that the Communist Party has deployed three channels of influence in local affairs.

First, SKP has been engaged in the (often extensive) preparatory talks that precede the proposals formally made in the council's executive committee and thereafter simply ratified in a plenary session of the council. In short, the Party has preferred to form part of the local consensus rather than adopting an anti-systemic stance on communal matters. The Communists have also been well represented on the committees (*lautakunnat*) set up by the full council to administer particularly policy areas. There are eight permanent committees required by law—schools, health, social policy, building, fire, roads, water and civic protection—and many more *ad hoc* bodies. Both the statutory and temporary committees are nominated on the basis of the relative strength of the parties in plenary council.

Second, although the movement naturally de-emphasizes personalities in the pursuit of collective goals and objectives, SKP has none the less profited from the exertions and individual appeal of a number of celebrated local figures: Ilkka Järvinen in Turku, Risto Hölttä and Taisto Johteinen in Kemi, and Veikko Saarto in Vantaa, to cite but a few. Saarto played a big part in getting the new town of Vantaa its own public-transport system (interview with SKDL's local government secretary, Ilja Koskinen, 1 October 1984). To this end, he was able to deploy the expertise built up as a former Minister of Transport; he has also brought to his position of local councillor the prestige and influence deriving from his chairmanship of SKDL's parliamentary group. Although only 50 years of age, Saarto can claim outstanding longevity of service on the Vantaa council—twenty years without a break.

Third, SKP has been adept at exercising a measure of influence through the direct mobilization of citizens bypassing the formal structures of local government. This it has done by means of organizing petitions, mass meetings, demonstrations and other 'extra-mural' activities. Residents have also been encouraged to attend council meetings to lobby a particular view. In rural districts, where an average of less than one person attends meetings of the plenary council, the impact of SKDL/SKP having ten present is likely to be considerable. In the 1960s, a proposed motorway planned to run through the centre of Turku was successfully prevented by mass petitioning orchestrated by the Communists. The same thing has happened with regard to raising taxi fares in the capital Helsinki.

In recent years, however, the influence of the radical left on Finnish local councils has been inevitably reduced as a result of lack of group cohesion—the more so after the October 1984 communal elections. In addition to the majority–minority split, any calculus of the balance of power within the Party has been complicated by the presence of so-called 'Third Liners', *kolmaslinjalaiset*, supporters of former Communist Chairman, Jouko Kajanoja. Whilst the minority wing ran lists of its own in twelve communes proclaiming the cause of unity and solidarity, the official SKDL lists of the majority wingers included Third Liners who also insisted that overriding priority should be given to unity. Furthermore, the first signs indicate that the 'forces of unity' (minority wing and Third Liners) possess a narrow plurality in the large towns of Helsinki and Turku over the 'Axe Men' (*kirveslinjalaiset*) in the majority who favour a final break with the hardliners led by Sinisalo. Although generally losing ground to the majority wing—in its three strongest constituencies of Helsinki, Uusimaa and Lapland, the Sinisalo faction polled 2.6, 2.0 and 1.0 per cent respectively—the minority did profit from a tactical concentration of votes on a few candidates. In the town of Oulu, for example, the minority gained five seats with less than 2,000 votes whereas the majority gained only eight places with 9,000 ballots, three of them going to Third Liners.

In 1980 there was almost a 2 per cent drop in SKDL support. The Conservatives got their best local-government result since the Second World

War and the Social Democrats, putting the Prime Minister, Mauno Koivisto, forward as their semi-official presidential candidate, achieved their second-best post-war result. The SKDL cause during the campaign was not aided by an unofficial strike in the Communist-controlled Metalworkers' Union and remarks by Communist Chairman, Aarne Saarinen, in which he came out cautiously in favour of Kekkonen continuing as head of state after 1984. Saarinen also criticized Koivisto for not working to improve relations between the Social Democrats and the majority-wing Communists in government (*Helsingin Sanomat*, 21 September 1980, p. 31). Above all, however, the long-standing split in the Party took its toll. In Helsinki, for example, SKDL lost 2.0 per cent of its vote and though a plurality of those elected belonged to the majority wing—eight majority faction, five minority and one People's Democrat—the three most successful candidates were all Sinisalo supporters. At the polls on 21-22 October 1984, the SKDL's election slogan, '[Vote] Today for the Sake of Tomorrow', was not taken up by Finnish voters in the manner intended. There was a 3.4 per cent drop in the radical leftist poll compared with 1980 and a drop, too, on its performance at the 1983 general elections. SKDL appeared to suffer in three ways from an evidently widespread mood of protest among voters.

First, the Greens, who were contesting local elections nationally for the first time, succeeded in gaining representation on over 100 of the 445 communes and in several they now hold the balance between socialists and non-socialists. The evidence suggests that the Greens took votes off SKDL in particular and articulated best the hostility towards politicians that was felt widely among the electorate, especially by young voters. Next, the low turn-out at the 1984 local elections (73.6 per cent)—young voters and voters in the large towns were especially apathetic—also detracted from the performance of the radical left. Finally, the split in the Party again proved damaging: in Helsinki, for instance, the two lists contrived three seats less than the single SKDL slate obtained in 1980. In Vantaa, where there has been a left-wing majority since 1945, both radical leftist lists did poorly and once more the Communists lost three seats compared with 1980. In its heyday in 1964, the combined left possessed absolute control with thirty-four of the forty-seven seats on the Vantaa council. In contrast, the Greens presently hold the balance between socialists and non-socialists. On the brighter side, SKDL did better than the opinion polls had indicated—as much as 2 per cent better in one case—and lost only 30,000 votes compared with its general-election performance the previous year. In Varsinais-Suomi in the south west, Kuopio and Oulu in the north and Kymi in the south east, it even registered modest gains.

Local Communism in Scandinavia: Future Prospects

Overall, however, local–government communism in Finland appears to be on the retreat and the road ahead long and hard. Interviewed in the minority-wing organ, *Tiedonantaja*, after the October 1984 local elections, a successful Sinisalo candidate in Oulu, asked about the Party's post-election agenda, replied that first there must be maximum participation on a peace march arranged for the following day and then an all–out effort to collect signatures for the 'party solidarity' petition—inspired, it might be added, by the minority wing (*Tiedonantja*, 24 October 1984, p. 2). The main *Tiedonantja* editorial, too, emphasized the need for unity that was to be achieved by convening an extraordinary party conference to rescind those decisions taken at the 20th Party Congress. Unity on the minority-wing's terms is out of the question; unity, indeed, on any terms, will be extremely difficult to achieve given the long-standing and deep-seated nature of the party divisions. Suspicion between the two sides remains intense and on the majority wing there exists considerable bitterness over continuing Soviet interference into what is felt to be the internal affairs of the Finnish Communist Party. This was well reflected in the (majority-wing) leadership's rejection of a highly critical letter to the Finnish Communist Party delivered by a Soviet delegation under Central Committee Secretary, Grigory Romanov, shortly before the local elections (*Tiedonantaja*, 24 October 1984, p. 15).

True, the Finnish Communists have probably reached the bedrock of their electoral constituency and now rest on a relatively stable body of voters, albeit comprising relatively few younger elements. Yet if the Party is unlikely to decline much further in the short term, the challenge is plainly to claw a way back at a time when the electoral climate is treacherous and characterized by continuing voter volatility. Particularly in view of the prevalent anti-establishment mood of Finnish citizens, the Communists will be required to demonstrate the relevance of their Party to the needs of ordinary people. Obviously this will demand hard work, *concertation*, within its ranks and effective leadership. A number of radical and attractive policies exist—the premium will be on their successful projection to voters.

Moreover, in Finland, as throughout the Scandinavian region, the core blue-collar constituency of communism is being eroded, whilst the proportion of the electorate engaged in white-collar and white-blouse occupations, particularly in the tertiary sector, has expanded since the 1960s. The Scandinavian Communist parties will need to respond to the structural demands of this post-industrialization process, refurbish traditional programmatic tenets and develop forward-looking scenarios with which to attract a new generation of electors. Social and economic change, however, cannot be allowed to prejudice the quality of life, but rather must inform and enhance it. The deployment of resources to the end of technological modernization must be counterbalanced by an unflinching concern on the part of the Communists to protect human and individual values in increasingly state-centred, machine-orientated and leisure-based societies. Communism, in sum, cannot afford to lose sight of the people. Equally, the crucial fissures in advanced capitalism must be identified and exposed: the problems of depressed regions with high levels of structural unemployment, the plight of non-integrated immigrant workers, the care of the elderly and infirm, etc. Above all, in the context of this chapter, the institutions of local government must be used to renew and regenerate democracy—to forge a link with the grassroots and to offset the widespread feeling of low competence among electors. In complex, mass societies, the local political arena affords the Scandinavian Communist parties possibly the best opportunity for experimentation and the generation of new models of worker self-government. Without the necessary vision, the auguries for all the parties look bleak.

Bibliography

Publications

Aftenposten, 29 August 1979, 'Sp. i teten blant de borgerlige'.

Aftenposten, 15 September 1983, 'Velgerflukt fra de fleste partier'.

Bekendtgørelse af Lov om kommunale valg, Kap 1:1. Indenrigsministeriets lovbekendtgørelse nr 196 af 22 April 1981.

Från Riksdag & Departement, 28 October 1983, 'Fördjupad kommunal demokrati'.

Från Riksdag & Departement, 22 October 1982, 'Pajala kommun'.

Från Riksdag & Departement, 25 March 1983, 'Stöd på både lång och kort sikt'.

Hammar, Tomas, 'Röstberättigade utländska medborgares valdeltagande i de kommunala valen 1976–1982 och i folkomröstningen 1980', *Rösträtt och medborgarskap*, Bilaga 2. Stockholm, SOU, 12, p. 48.

Heidar, Knut, 1983. *Norske politiske fakta 1884–1982*. Universitetsforlaget, Oslo–Bergen–Stavanger–Tromsø, p. 150.

Helsingin Sanomat, 30 September 1984, Ele Alenius, 'Nyt on aika miettiä Skdl:lle omaa linjaa', pp. 29–30.

Helsingin Sanomat, 4 September 1984, 'Kommunistien riidat hajottivat Skdl:n listat 12 kunnassa'.

Helsingin Sanomat, 21 September 1980, 'Presidenttipeli heiluttaa hallitusta', p. 31.

Helsingin Sanomat, 4 September 1984, 'Skdl maksaa Skp:n riitoja'.

Jensen, Jørgen, 1983. *Til kommunalbestyrelsesmedlemmer* valgt af S, SF, VS og socialistiske fælleslister, August.

Kansan Uutiset, 4 September 1984, 'Keski-Suomessa yhteiset listat', p. 14.

Kunnallisvaalit 1980. *Suomen virallinen tilasto XX1XB:6.* Helsinki, Tilasto, 1981, p. 116.

Petersson, Olof, 1977. *Den Svenske Väljaren. Några data från 1976 års valundersökning.* Statsvetenskapliga institutionen i Uppsala universitet, Örebro, p. 4.

Politiken, 12 January 1984, 'Kommunisternes dårligste valg'.

Poukka, Pentti, 1976. 'Kunnalliselämä ja puoluepolitiikka', in Otto Larma, Aarne Eskola ja Mikko Jokela (eds), *Kunnallismiehenkirja.* Helsinki, Kirjayhtymä, p. 74.

Suomen kunnallislehti, August 1984, Kalevi Kivistö, 'Millaisin eväin . . . Palvelujen, kehittäminen ja turvaaminen', p. 6.

Saarinen, Aarne, 1984. *Suomen kommunistin kokemuksia.* Helsinki, Tammi, Cited in Janne Virkkunen, 'Kommunisti ja veljespuolue', *Helsingin Sanomat*, 30 September 1984.

Sinisalo, Taisto, 1980. *Vastaus on vasemmistopolitiikka.* Helsinki, Kursiivi, pp. 119–21.

Tiedonantaja, 24 October 1984, 'NKP: n kirje SKP:lle', p. 15.

Tiedonantaja, 24 October 1984, 'Vaalit ja oppositiopolitiikaa', p. 2.

Tänään huomisen hyväksi, 1984. SKP:n 20 edustajakokous, *SKDL:n kunnallispoliittinen asiakirja.*

Valgene til de kommunale og amtskommunale råd, 17 November 1984, Hæfte 2. Kobenhavn, Danmarks Statistik, 1983, pp. 108–9.

Virolainen, Johannes, 1969. *Pääministerinä Suomessa.* Helsinki, Kirjayhtymä, p. 21.

Interviews and Correspondence

SKDL:n kunnallispoliittinen sihteeri, Ilja Koskinen, 1 October 1984.

Hans Kloster, Danmarks Kommunistiske Parti, Centralkomiteens Sekretariat, 2 September 1984.

6 A Receding Tide: France's Communist Municipalities

Andrew F. Knapp

It was a boast of the French Communist Party (PCF) after the 1977 municipal elections that nine million French people lived under a Communist mayor. Of France's 36,422 communes (more local government units than in all the rest of the European Community), only some 1,500 had a Communist-led municipality. But Communist mayors headed a ruling left-wing coalition in a third of towns of over 30,000 inhabitants. While the biggest cities remained in the hands of the right (Paris, Lyon, Bordeaux, Toulouse) or the Socialists (Lille and Marseille), the PCF had seven municipalities of over 100,000 inhabitants (Argenteuil, Le Havre, Nîmes, Amiens, Le Mans, Reims and Saint-Étienne).

'Municipal Communism' was thus far from a marginal phenomenon in France. Largely confined for four decades after the Party's creation in 1920 to the 'Red belt' of Paris suburbs won between the wars (Saint-Denis, Ivry, Vitry, Aubervilliers, Montreuil, Gennevilliers, Bagnolet and others) and to a handful of other large communes, it spread rapidly after the establishment of the Fifth Republic in 1958. No major Communist muncipality was lost in the elections of 1965, 1971 and 1977. Many of the gains of these years were not working–class suburbs but more socially varied provincial cities. They were made in alliance with the Socialists, who shared power on the council, an arrangement most Socialist mayors reciprocated (cf. Maps 6.1 and 6.2).

At a time when the national Communist vote was stagnating at about 20 per cent, when the Socialists were overtaking the PCF as the leading left-wing party, and the Communist-led union federation, the CGT, was facing a strong challenge from its Socialist-led rival, the CFDT, in the aftermath of May 1968, local government became the PCF's major area of success of the 1960s and 1970s. Only the 1983 municipal elections broke the pattern. The PCF lost eight major provincial towns and seven big Paris suburbs; even some Red belt bastions looked vulnerable as the Communist vote fell by 10 per cent or more; and more municipalities fell in by-elections after the Council of State had upheld allegations of electoral fraud (Table 6.1).

Like the Socialists (and the right in 1977), the PCF suffered in 1983 from being in power nationally (four Communist ministers—the first since 1947—were appointed after the left's 1981 election victory). This is, however, an

Table 6.1 Number of French towns of over 30,000 inhabitants held by left-wing mayors, 1959–85

	1959	1965	1971	1977	1983	1985*
Communist (PCF)	25	34	45	72	56	51
Socialist (PS/MRG)	41	33	40	83	68	68
Various left	17	14	9	8	0	0
(centre and right)	(75)	(77)	(98)	(58)	(93)	(98)
Total†	158	158	192	221	217	217

  * Following by-elections.
  † The total number of cities of over 30,000 inhabitants grew steadily between 1965 and 1977. Between 1977 and 1983, six (of which two held by the PS, two held by the PCF, one held by the right, and one won by the right from the PCF) passed below the threshold, while two (one PS, one PCF) rose above it.

  Source: *Le Monde*, 1983; Schain, 1985, p. 29.

insufficient explanation of the Communists' varying municipal fortunes. We also need to examine the performance of Communist local elected officials and to relate it both to the PCF's national strategy and—given the centralized nature of Communist policy-making—to the evolution of official party policy on local government.

I shall argue in this chapter that the Communists' municipal successes up to 1977 owed much to a convincing fit between national party strategy and the opportunities local office offered the PCF in a period of fast urban growth. Conversely, after 1977, national and local strategies became much less easy to articulate and the evolution of French society began to work against rather than for the PCF at local level. We shall look first at the evolution of the official line before considering the PCF's local policy outputs. The conclusion will relate the PCF's local set-backs to its national decline and assess prospects for recovery or further losses.

The PCF Approach to Local Government

From the start, the PCF has faced a choice between using municipalities as centres of 'revolutionary activity'—if necessary in defiance of the tight legal controls of the unitary French state—or aiming at more moderate, impartial administration at the price of class compromises. The Party's handling of this central problem has varied over time.

Up to 1977, the official PCF approach underwent a more or less continuous evolution, well summarized by Jerome Milch (1977, pp. 340-52),
from a 'hard' to a 'soft' line. The change had six main elements: a rallying to
France's patchwork of local institutions (in the 1920s the PCF had called for
their replacement by workers' Soviets); a broadening of appeal from 'the
working class', both to other non-class categories in need (the old, the young,
the handicapped) and more generally to the 'whole population' of municipalities; attempts to mobilize voters on cross-class urban and environmental
issues, supplementing more traditional support for working-class struggle; an
insistence that local party sections and federations, though entitled to the
same loyalty from PCF mayors and councillors as from any other activists,
should not interfere in day-to-day municipal affairs; a new stress on administrative skills like medium-term budget and land-use planning, even within a
capitalist context; and the municipal alliance with the PS (a national agreement provided for joint left-wing lists in 92 per cent of large cities for the
1977 elections).

These developments were structured by transformations both in national
PCF strategy and in French city politics. From 1946 to 1958, the PCF used the
Fourth Republic's ground rules—the concentration of power in a National
Assembly elected by proportional representation—to play a largely 'tribunician' role. It 'defended' the working class (or channelled its grievances into
institutional forms), praised the Soviet Union (under a Secretary General,
Maurice Thorez, whom Stalin had picked for the job), equated getting into
government with the distant goal of revolution, and avoided serious attempts
at alliances with the Socialists. The Fifth Republic, however, penalized such
isolation, both tactically (in the two-ballot, single-member-constituency
parliamentary electoral system) and strategically (the presidential regime
marginalized parties that did not join a close alliance aimed at winning
power). The PCF had to adapt its strategy to these new conditions, a process
that culminated in the signing of the Common Programme of Government
with the Socialists in 1972.

The 1964 law for municipal elections in cities of over 30,000 inhabitants
also favoured inter-party alliances, replacing PR (proportional representation) with a two-ballot system under which no lists of candidates could
merge between ballots and winning lists took all the council seats. The new
system required the PCF to prise the Socialists away from their old centre-
right local alignments—as was done progressively from 1965 to 1977. The
municipal Union of the Left, a necessary complement to the national union,
demanded lengthy negotiations on the composition of each list—on who was
to lead it, and on the distribution both of council seats and of posts of assistant

mayor (*maires adjoints*, or senior councillors delegated specific tasks—not to be confused with *députés maires*, or mayors who also hold parliamentary seats). The successful conclusion of such negotiations, however, offered the Communists the chance to win majority positions in cities where they had hitherto been in opposition. Given their slight ministerial record (in 1944-7), that also meant the opportunity for Communists to prove their governmental credentials to a wider section of the population than the working class. The policy modifications described by Milch should be seen in this light. Subordination of local elected officials to the party hierarchy, to the support of working-class struggles, or to distant perspectives of workers' soviets, was incompatible both with the Socialist alliance and with the image of a party of government in the Fifth Republic context.

If the 1964 law helped to polarize and politicize local government, France's post-war urbanization raised the stakes. Fast growth forced many provincial cities into headlong programmes of construction—of housing and basic utilities as well as social amenities—for which many were ill prepared. Electorates grew rapidly, and demanded more facilities and better access to local decision-making. The PCF was well placed to take advantage of this. It offered advancement in any case to competent organization men, and its Red-belt mayors had acquired useful experience as innovators, using 'methods that recall Joseph Chamberlain in Birmingham more than Lenin in Petrograd' (Brogan, 1967, p. 638). Like the Socialists but unlike the right, the PCF could blame local set-backs on the government. For Communist mayors and councillors, presenting themselves as capable administrators pushing against the arbitrary limits imposed by an interfering and predatory state could prove a winning formula that struck many chords in the French municipal tradition.

The 1977 election crowned the PCF's local strategy with a major success, but also confirmed the Socialists' leadership on the left, and faced the Communists with the unacceptable prospect of becoming junior partners in a social-democratic government after the following year's parliamentary elections. By proposing to 'update' the Common Programme on terms the PS would refuse, the Communists effectively ensured that the left would fight the 1978 elections in disarray and would lose. The aftermath of the defeat and the leadership's decision to restate the PCF's revolutionary, working-class credentials at the expense of the previous decade's more open line inevitably affected the official approach to local government—but in a way that makes clear the Communists' reluctance to sacrifice local positions to the new national line.

Administration on behalf of 'the whole population' and broad cross-class struggles were largely replaced in the post-1977 literature by renewed references to the working class. Thus for one commentator cities were 'the patrimony of the working class' and town planning 'wholly subordinate to the need to produce massive quantities of high-quality low-cost housing' (Arnaud, 1981, p. 39). Similarly, Secretary-General Georges Marchais encouraged mayors and councillors to 'pursue their struggles in close liaison with workers organized at the workplace' (Marchais, 1979, p. 23). The 'new' discourse did not, however, simply put the clock back. Far from proposing the replacement of communes by Soviets, the PCF defended them more intensely than ever against the other parties' 'anti-democratic' projects of reform (Rosette, 1979, p. 5). Direct control of local elected officials by the party apparatus was not reinforced, though it is probable that the creation of the *Association Nationale des Élus Communistes et Républicains* (ANECR) under the presidency of Marcel Rosette, senator and former mayor of Vitry, was an indirect step in this direction (Pronier, 1983, pp. 89–92). The PCF still claimed that it could run cities as well as other parties—pointing out, for example, on the occasion of Marchais's campaign visit to Le Havre that port traffic had doubled there under Communist rule (*L'Humanité-Dimanche*, 24 October 1980). Finally, Rosette claimed that 'Communist local elected officials do not intend to transfer to the local level the serious divergences that exist nationally' with the PS. Wholesale splits on left-wing councils were avoided, though the Communists' insistence on 'holding the Socialists to the agreements of 1977' provided fuel for the local conflicts that did occur (Rosette, 1979, p. 13).

The sectarian line of 1977–81 was thus modulated by the PCF's local government spokesmen so as to pose no immediate threat to gains made through the successful pre-1977 strategy. The question of how to fight the next municipal elections without an alliance with the PS was, however, avoided by the events of 1981 and the rebirth of the Union of the Left. As a presidential candidate, Marchais campaigned vigorously against Mitterrand right up to the first ballot in April 1981 (when he won 15.5 per cent of the vote to Mitterrand's 26.1). Communist voters, motivated more by their own desire for a left-wing victory than by their leadership's unenthusiastic declaration for the Socialist candidate, contributed to Mitterrand's election at the second ballot in May: four Communist ministers duly took office after the June parliamentary elections.

The events of 1981 had four main effects on the PCF's local government policy. The problem of maintaining local alliances with the PS at a time of national polemic disappeared; the right-wing government could no longer serve as an alibi for the insufficiencies of the Communists' local performance; the Communists had a chance to prove their governmental credentials nationally as well as at a local level; and the PCF's overall credibility diminished with its share of the vote. Between June 1981 and March 1983, the PCF line on local government thus suffered from as many uncertainties as the Communists' national political discourse.

On the one hand, Communist spokesmen stressed the left-wing government's positive effects on local authorities. These included the 1982 Decentralization Act, an element of PR in the new local electoral law, solidarity contracts between government and employers (including local authorities) aimed at more jobs through shorter hours, new vocational training provisions (under a Communist minister), and local employment committees including representatives from the state, local authorities and industry. Ministerial visits to Communist municipalities received maximum publicity, and parallels were drawn between the achievements of Communist mayors, ministers, and heads of nationalized industries. PCF spokesmen even talked of the need to improve the 'productivity' of municipal services (Trigon, 1982, p. 46).

At the same time Communists argued that the changes effected 'did not go far enough'. The left's victory, they said, had ended neither the crisis of capitalism nor the class struggle, at a time when companies were sabotaging France's economic recovery by exporting capital, while the right attempted to 'politicize' the coming municipal elections (a charge formerly laid against the PCF itself). Mayors were encouraged to monitor companies' use of government subsidies, and voters to 'take matters into their own hands in order to strengthen the forces of change' and to 'further the march towards socialism'. As a bogeyman for use by mayors, though, the right in opposition was far less handy than the right in government.

The PCF's departure from government in July 1984 and the subsequent renewal in earnest of attacks on the PS produced a similar situation to that of 1977–81 (open enmity at the summit, but Union of the Left in the town halls, the difference being that for twenty-one months the Socialist enemy was in government) and a similar official party line. Communist elected officials were invited to denounce government policies (such as cuts in subsidies to local authorities) in the run-up to the 1986 parliamentary elections: PCF authors argued that local authorities were testing-grounds for the Socialists' plans to govern nationally with the right, and denounced the 'worrying attitude' of Socialist mayors and councillors in some municipalities. At the same time, Rosette stressed that Communist local officials would continue to work on the basis of the 1983 election platforms worked out with the

Socialists in each municipality, and would not attempt to carry the national rupture to local level (*L'Élu d'Aujourd'hui*, June 1985, pp. 46–7; Clement, 1985, p. 47; Rosette, 1986, p. 12). And, indeed, between 1983 and 1986 the most serious splits were not on the left but in newly-elected municipalities of the right such as Brest and Louviers.

The success of the PCF's approach to local government before 1977 rested on two conditions: a resolute opposition to national government, presented, in a centralized state, as the source of all municipal ills, and a credible strategy for winning power and carrying out far-reaching changes in alliance with the Socialists. The first condition was absent in 1981–4, and the second in 1977–81 and again since 1984. The credibility of the Communists' local discourse suffered accordingly. Even at the official level, however, local policy did not merely reproduce every change in national strategy. The national polemics with the PS have not been systematically carried into every municipality. That local policy has, at least in part, its own dynamic is confirmed by an examination of Communist policy outputs on the ground.

The Policy Outputs of Communist Municipalities

Detailed research on Communist municipal policy outputs remains rare, though more is available than when Milch wrote his 1977 article (cf. Ducros, 1966; Hoss, 1969; Milch, 1973, 1974 and 1977; Montaldo, 1977 and 1978; Harris & de Sédouy, 1978; Lacorne, 1980; Schain, 1980 and 1985; Knapp, 1983; Pronier, 1983). These studies both confirm some of Milch's general statements and reveal diversity between municipalities. This section will analyse these variations as well as considering outputs common to all munici- palities and how they have changed over time.

Resource Transfer Policies

Communist mayors have consistently used the (often limited) possibilities open to them to practise classic left-wing resource transfer policies, visible in municipal budgets. Both Ducros's comparison of two Paris suburbs (Villejuif and Montrouge) and Milch's of two southern cities (Nîmes and Montpellier) show that Communists in Villejuif and Nîmes relied more for current receipts on direct taxation, and less on payments for services, than their conservative neighbours (Ducros, 1966, p. 105; Milch, 1974, pp. 148–9). The evolution of Le Havre's budgets from 1965 (when a PCF mayor was elected) to 1980 confirm these tendencies. Moreover, Le Havre's municipality made ready use of the slight opportunities available to weight business taxes against domestic rates in the overall fiscal burden, charging a maximum 1 per cent levy on company wage bills to subsidize public transport (Knapp, 1983, pp. 174–6). Communists have also been more ready than many right-wing mayors to pay for investments with state subsidies and loans rather than self-financing from the current budget surplus. Milch found that conservative Montpellier self-financed far more of its investments than Communist Nîmes: Schain noted a marked shift away from self-financing in five Paris suburbs won by Communists in 1977 (Milch, 1974, pp. 66–9; Schain, 1980, p. 249, 1985, p. 65). This use of state funds by communist municipalities indicates an ability to establish a working relationship, financially necessary for the application of high-spending social policies, with a government bureaucracy that was unlikely before 1981 to do them favours.

On the spending side, both Milch and Schain find that Communist municipalities give greater priority to social and educational programmes than to 'economic' services like roads, car-parks and street-lighting (Milch, 1973, pp. 110–15; Schain, 1980, p. 247). In Le Havre, current spending on education, culture and sport grew 50 per cent faster than the overall current budget between 1965 and 1980, and investments over twice as fast as the total capital budget (Knapp, pp. 184–7). In the post-war generation, much of this type of investment spending went into basic amenities. Since the early 1960s, however, some of France's major theatres and *maisons de la culture* (provincial cultural centres, launched by de Gaulle's minister André Malraux) have been built in Communist towns like Nanterre, Aubervilliers, Le Havre and Le Mans.

Municipal control of housing policy is indirect. Low-cost housing units (*Habitations à Loyer Modéré*, or HLMs) are built by public offices or private associations using low-interest government loans. However, municipalities can subsidize land purchase, infrastructure or green spaces; their representatives on HLM boards may influence construction policy and rent levels; and they may choose to guarantee loans raised by private HLM developers. During the housing crisis of the post-war generation, Communist municipalities used these opportunities to maximize HLM building (Milch, 1973, pp. 122–4; Schain, 1980, pp. 250–2; Pronier, pp. 243–5). This was particularly true in Red belt bastions like Ivry or Vitry: but even in Le Havre, rented HLMs represented over half of total housing construction between 1965 and 1980, compared with a quarter nationally (Knapp, pp. 416, 421). Massive HLM construction met an urgent social need, and providing for working-class tenants helped to consolidate the PCF's electoral base as well as according with basic PCF priorities. Until the mid-1970s, Communists were also, however, more ready than right-wing mayors to accept an influx of immigrants, who provided no electoral pay-off.

By the late 1970s, HLMs had become a mixed electoral asset for the PCF, being associated with shoddy building, delinquency and immigrants (the right-wing press equated the last two). Communist mayors responded by engaging better architects like Jean Renaudie, and by mixing more middle-income housing with HLM developments (Schain, 1985, pp. 76–8). They also became reluctant to accept more immigrants and in one dramatic move the mayor of Vitry helped to vandalize a brand-new immigrant hostel (*Le Monde*, 26 December 1980). Rosette's presence on this occasion indicated the backing of the party leadership in the middle of Marchais's presidential campaign and the extent to which the PCF was prepared to sacrifice a tradition of social solidarity for an apparent electoral advantage (cf. Schain, 1985, pp. 78–80).

Redistributive policies have been a hallmark of Communist mayors since the inter-war years, when their record in the Paris suburbs stood out in the indifferent annals of French municipal administration. But their radicalism has been limited, both absolutely and relatively. Early Communist mayors often contrasted their own financial probity with the practices of their right-wing counterparts: aside from gestures such as drawing up budgets to include 'state subsidies to compensate for inflation' that were rejected by the prefect, they have excluded fiscal profligacy ever since. In *Le Point*'s 1979 list of indebtedness per head of population in France's thirty-nine biggest cities, only Saint-Étienne (second, but Communist only since 1977) and Le Havre (twentieth) came into the top twenty (*Le Point*, 19 November 1979). Communist mayors have never attempted the head-on attacks on government financial constraints made by British Labour councillors at Claycross or Liverpool. And they have not been above privatizing municipally-run services (such as the abattoirs at Amiens) when the financial advantages of doing so have been clear (*Le Monde*, 8 June 1984). Budgetary limits have also shaped Communist housing policy, obliging provincial cities to site HLMs on cheap peripheral land, and thus to participate in the removal of lower-income groups from city centres.

The relative radicalism of the Communists' local policy outputs has been limited by greater involvement of all municipalities in social service provision. Thus while the Communist-run Paris suburb of Fontenay-sous-Bois counted two crèches in 1982, the Giscardian mayor of neighbouring Vincennes had built five for a comparable population. Communist mayors claim, with some justification, that their competitors have merely stolen their clothes in this respect, but admit that differences have narrowed. Moreover, the cost of running municipal services has grown fast and the share of investments in local budgets has tended to decline. The provision of municipal amenities, a radical innovation in the inter-war years, became a norm during the post-war generation and has now lost some of its earlier urgency. The new priority of big municipalities right across the political spectrum, running existing services efficiently through such techniques as computerization, has reduced the scope for distinctively left-wing outputs—or at least if the scope exists, the Communists have not used it with the same originality they brought to the inter-war Paris suburbs (Pronier, pp. 243–6; *Le Monde*, 26 June 1980). Indeed, municipal 'radicalism' is now most noticeable in some of the town halls won by the right in 1983, where programmes of privatization, cuts in services and subsidies, and (in the case of Nantes) massive expulsions of HLM tenants with rent arrears have been applied with varying degrees of success. It could thus be argued that Communist municipalities are now characterized rather by their refusal to apply downright reactionary policies than by their capacity to go on producing particularly left-wing ones.

Relations with the State and with Business

French legal texts before the 1982 Decentralization Act spelt out a hierarchy of authority between prefects, ministerial field services like the *Directions Departementales d'Équipment* (DDEs), and mayors. Research over the past twenty years has established that this centralized model is misleading and that relations between actors in the local decision-making process have formed a complex pattern of interdependence in which city mayors have enjoyed considerable powers to exert pressures in their own interests and even to by-pass their hierarchical 'superiors' (Schain, 1980, p. 234; Wright, 1978, pp. 212–25).

This does not, however, exclude the need for close working relationships between mayors and the state (and now regional) officials whose cooperation they need to receive government money. Simple projects, like a single primary school, may only need a well-prepared dossier for approval: a major housing estate, though, requires lengthy negotiations with the DDE and the prefecture. If the 1982 Act has now replaced many subsidies with an overall investment grant (the *Dotation Globale d'Équipement*), relations still need to be close. Moreover, urban structure plans and land-use regulations are still jointly elaborated by state and municipal representatives under the 1967 *Loi d'Orientation Foncière*. There is also a clear need for close contacts with business to protect jobs in a recession.

Unable, outside of the 1981–4 period, to expect favours from the state,

Communists emphasized the importance of 'struggle'—petitions and demonstrations organized from the town hall—in attracting state funds (recently they have complained that the uncoupling of subsidies from specific projects has made it far more difficult to mobilize the people in this way). Even if the immediate objectives of 'struggle' were not achieved, it would, the argument ran, sensitize the electorate to broader PCF policies (Rosette, 1977, pp. 64–6). Such methods have at times succeeded. Colette Privat used them to renegotiate an extravagant redevelopment plan bequeathed by her centrist predecessor as mayor of the Rouen suburb of Maromme. Louis Bayeurte rallied a broad movement (including the local Gaullist deputy) to get the Fontenay-sous-Bois section of the regional metro network covered over. Joseph Sanguedolce successfully prevented the closure of Saint-Étienne's main industry, Manufrance. But a working relationship with the state authorities was of more lasting importance than such spectacular actions. Thus Daniel Colliard, Le Havre's first assistant mayor, invariably engaged in informal talks with the DDE long before submitting major projects: the DDE's respect for his competence helped him to head off politically-motivated interventions from the prefecture. It also allowed him to avoid serious confrontation with state field services in the 'joint elaboration' of planning documents. Mayors Dupuy (of Choisy-le-Roi) and Canacos (of Sarcelles) also stress their partnership with state representatives, and Milch notes that in Nîmes the 'alternative' left (*Parti Socialiste Unifié*) councillors criticized the Communists' preference for orthodox negotiating tactics as against mass mobilization (Knapp, pp. 208–10; Dupuy, 1975, pp. 93–4; Canacos, 1979, pp. 242–6; Milch, 1973, pp. 227–33).

The instrumental reasons for such collaboration are clear: it usually attracted more money than 'struggle', which can rarely be a continuous process in any case. There were also more symbolic motives at work: the PCF was trying to extend its audience and prove its governmental credentials. Colliard claimed that the municipality's role in producing Le Havre's planning documents had 'given the PCF the image of a party of government', and stressed the importance of his monthly tripartite meetings with the port authority and the chamber of commerce. Canacos claimed to have one of the Paris region's fastest-selling industrial zones in Sarcelles, and the Nîmes municipal bulletin vaunted the town hall's role in attracting a German biscuit factory to the city (Knapp, pp. 101, 212, 263; Canacos, pp. 235–7).

The hardening of PCF policy from 1977 to 1981 led to no systematic deterioration in municipal relations with the state and with business, despite the renewed official emphasis on work-place struggles. After 1981, relations with the state were understandably better—at least until the break with the

Socialists in July 1984. As employers, Communist mayors were quick to sign solidarity contracts providing for government help to shorten working hours and hire more staff. They also took advantage of new vocational training credits, probably with special help from Marcel Rigout, the Communist minister responsible (Jeambar, 1984, pp. 86-7). The softening of relations with business was more indirect. Nationally, the PCF has denounced the 'bosses' for investing abroad and sabotaging growth. Locally, though, Communists have had to face redundancies and closures in traditional industries without the alibi of a right-wing government. This has obliged them to limit rate increases and to seek understandings with local businesses under the (slightly) greater competences granted to them within the new local employment committees.

The Party and its Local Elected Officials

In other French parties, the office of mayor may be a step in the *cursus honorum* leading to ministerial posts, as for Prime Minister Pierre Mauroy, mayor of Lille, or Interior Minister Gaston Defferre of Marseille. Or established politicians may use it to put down local roots, as did Georges Pompidou, Valery Giscard d'Estaing and Francois Mitterrand (all before becoming President) as well as Jacques Chirac. In the PCF, however, ever since Thorez's main rival for the leadership, Jacques Doriot, left the Party and took his fief of Saint-Denis with him in 1934, mayors have tended to stay mayors, or possibly *députés maires*, but no more. Unlike a Defferre or a Mauroy, they cannot use their strong local positions to swing votes at party congresses. Only one, Roger Fajnzylberg of Sèvres, openly opposed the line of 1977-81: he was excluded from the Party and defeated in 1983. Rosette resigned as mayor of Vitry before becoming head of ANECR, Jack Ralite as assistant mayor in Aubervilliers when appointed Health Minister. Six mayors sit on the 144-member Central Committee, none on the Politbureau.

This subordination of Communist mayors reflects the PCF's hierarchical structure. Typically, they regard the job as a task assigned by the Party—'like sticking up posters', according to Colette Privat—whereas other mayors mention their personal notability as a factor in their rise to office (Lacorne, 1980, pp. 67-70). Party loyalty is thus crucial in the selection of mayors by PCF federations in the *départements*. Between the wars this often took the form of working-class activism (Doriot's predecessor in Saint-Denis still worked full time in the Hotchkiss factory). Post-war Communist mayors were often recruited among the Party's Resistance leaders, but this generation is near the end of its active life. At present, mayors and their top assistants in big PCF municipalities are almost all full-time party activists, since the PCF redistributes the pay of its deputies and top mayors to give a wider circle of elected officials the equivalent of a skilled steelworker's wage. Such men and women have often been party members for ten years—twenty in the case of mayors. However, while full-time status usually follows accession to high positions in the provinces, it frequently precedes it in the Red belt.

In the provinces, local roots and length of time in either union or party activism are vital. Émile Jourdan of Nîmes, Jacques Rimbault of Bourges, and Robert Jarry of Le Mans are good examples. Working-class origins are useful but not essential: ten of Le Havre's twenty-six Communist councillors in 1977 had been workers, while the PCF chose a doctor for Thionville and a teacher for Reims in the same year. Mayors of long-standing provincial municipalities have usually served a long apprenticeship on the council, like André Duroméa of Le Havre. By contrast, in the Paris suburbs where the PCF's organization and vote are stronger, federations tend to 'parachute' their own full-time activists from one municipality to another. This may serve to reinforce the Party's control in a particular commune, to offer consolation posts to federal secretaries who fail to reach the Central Committee, or—as in the case of Léo Figuères of Malakoff, a pro-Soviet ultra whose ideas accorded ill with the 'liberalism' of the 1970s—to put potentially embarrassing party leaders out to grass (Pronier, pp. 50–68).

Communist mayors and their top assistants thus depend on their Party for their recruitment and often for their livelihood. That they are not openly insubordinate is understandable. A Communist mayor is expected, at least, not to distance himself publicly from party positions; to support them at vital moments (such as Marchais' presidential campaign); to participate in the 'canal' of confidential orders passed to activists by the leadership (for example, not to further the official call to vote for Mitterrand in May 1981 with too much zeal); and to maintain the Party's municipal positions. These requirements may conflict. Many provincial Communist mayors owe their success to administrative ability more than to Party affiliations, and thus tended to mute even their calls to vote for Marchais in April 1981 (Pronier, pp. 416–17). The reality of relations between the PCF's elected officials and its apparatus is thus complex.

We have seen that a too-flagrant subordination of Communist mayors and councillors to the local Party section would damage both relations with their PS partners and attempts to broaden the PCF electorate. These political constraints are strongest in recently-won provincial cities where the PCF's implantation is still vulnerable. They may be reinforced by the Party's organizational weakness. Le Havre in 1979, for example, counted 1,600 members—of whom maybe 160 were active—for 200,000 inhabitants. The Party itself had just two full-time workers, but the mayor and seven of his assistants were full time, not to speak of political advisers on the municipal payroll. The PCF's centre of gravity was thus the town hall, not party head-quarters. True, the local party boss (himself a councillor for the *département*) was kept informed by his colleagues, remarking after his election as assistant mayor in 1983 that council work was nothing new to him 'since I always followed municipal affairs very closely anyway'. Detailed supervision of a town hall counting over 3,000 employees by just two party workers was still impossible. Another possibility is that the town hall establishment in such cities may split into 'activists', keen to impose the latest party line, and 'managers'. It is not certain that the 'activists' are necessarily stronger in such cases.

In the Red belt, though, constraints on control of municipalities by the apparatus are weaker and party organization stronger. National PCF leaders like Pierre Juquin (in Essonne), Jack Ralite (in Seine-Saint-Denis), Liliane Marchais (in her husband's suburb of Champigny) or Marcel Rosette (after stepping down as mayor of Vitry) may subject Communist councils to their effective tutelage (though in the first two cases this did not survive criticisms by Ralite, and especially by Juquin, of the party leadership after 1984). The most flagrant example was party treasurer Georges Gosnat, whose role in Ivry's affairs was such that at his funeral the Communist weekly *Révolution* spoke of 'the town of which he was mayor for many years' although he had never (officially) been mayor in his life (Pronier, p. 95). Such municipalities are far more likely to dance to the latest party tune than provincial ones. It was in Vitry in the 'open' 1970s that Rosette pioneered the '*assises communales*'—municipally-led neighbourhood discussions on different aspects of local life. And it was in Vitry that Rosette, with his 'successor' Paul Mercieca, led the 1980 attack on the immigrant hostel. Both were pilot applications of a new line, approved by the party leadership, which a provincial mayor would not have attempted on his own initiative. The control of municipalities by the party apparatus, then, depends on the relative local strengths of the two. The Paris–provinces dichotomy is important in this respect, though an oversimplification in itself: some Red-belt mayors have still been able to maintain a measure of independence that belies the right's stereotype of their subordination to obscure—and non-elected—bureaucrats (cf. Montaldo, 1977, pp. 89–93).

Patronage

French local authority investments in the 1970s regularly exceeded those of central government, and current spending exceeded investments. Inevitably some of this money finds its way into private purses or party coffers. Given the PCF's tight organization, we would expect such transfers to benefit the party rather than individuals. The truth about this murky area of research probably lies between the right's allegations of Communist milking of municipal resources (Montaldo, 1977, pp. 86-136) and the PCF's own claims of its snow-white record. The PCF does transfer human and financial resources, probably more systematically than other parties, but to a degree that varies between municipalities and is tightly limited by several constraints.

Such transfers may be effected by letting property to the PCF or the CGT at peppercorn rents; by big municipal subscriptions to the Communist press; by supplying municipal labour, and municipal food and drink, for Party events like the local *Fêtes de l'Humanité*; and by hiring Communist-run companies (which plough profits into the party) to undertake municipal services such as town-planning studies, vocational training, and group purchase of office equipment, though never building. The constraints are twofold. Bulges of *ex gratia* payments will be noticed by Socialist councillors and by the Finance Ministry officials who audit municipal budgets. Moreover, rules on tendering for big municipal contracts are strict, so that Communist companies working for Communist municipalities have to maintain broadly competitive rates. These constraints will be weakest in Red-belt suburbs where Communists face small minorities on the council and have had time to mould the budget structure. Pronier suggests that 1 per cent of total spending in such municipalities may reach the Party—an appreciable addition to flagging receipts but hardly a crippling burden on ratepayers. Where PCF control is weaker, the proportion will be much less (Pronier, pp. 116-20).

Housing and jobs are other important forms of municipal patronage. The 'popular conviction' reproduced by Montaldo (1978, pp. 165-6) that a party card is necessary to rent an HLM flat in a Communist municipality has a limited basis in fact. Municipalities can name tenants to a proportion—generally some 15 per cent—of the HLM flats whose construction loans they underwrite. Thus Le Havre's town hall holds the keys to over 2,000 HLMs—but not all the city's 1,600 party members live in them. Pronier argues that Communist municipalities use this form of patronage to tie in and reward key activists and to place them in strategic neighbourhoods. The overall effect on tenancy of the HLM stock (over 20,000 units in Le Havre in 1980) is slight (Pronier, pp. 355-7).

A party card no more guarantees a town hall job than it does an HLM flat. Well-qualified senior municipal managers are recruited by competitive regional examination and are not always to be found among Communist ranks, while manual grades have often been poorly paid and thus unattractive compared to similar non-municipal jobs. Even many well-established town halls keep a non-Communist in the top post of *secrétaire général*. Equally, though, Communist cities were certainly among the thirty-two major French municipalities that changed their *secrétaire général* in the two years after the left's 1977 victory (Dion, 1984, pp. 147-9, 419). And it would be surprising if Communist municipalities did not try to recruit suitably loyal advisers or, more crudely, to get full-time activists on to the payroll.

These ends can be achieved in three ways. First, promising candidates may be helped to qualify for top jobs. Le Havre's first Communist *secrétaire général* owed his appointment (in 1983 at the age of 37) in part to a doctoral thesis on the city's electoral sociology, written largely on the town hall's time. Second, the municipality may create a 'parallel hierarchy' in the town hall, for example, by giving a Communist *secrétaire général adjoint* more real power and better access to the mayor than are enjoyed by his hierarchical superior. Third, contractual employees may be recruited without the restrictions that apply to permanent staff and used to man particularly sensitive posts such as the mayor's secretariat. Such contract employees may simply be party activists. This was the case of Jean-François Le Barth, a PCF section secretary from Orléans who drew a salary from the Montargis municipality without ever having been seen at the town hall. His discovery (by PS councillors in Montargis) illustrates the risks of such abuse of contract hire, which are similar to those of financial transfers and likely to be less serious in Red-belt bastions than in smaller or less secure provincial municipalities (Pronier, p. 111).

Below the administrative grades, manual workers may be used occasionally for Party tasks like bill-posting. Most employees of Communist municipalities are CGT members. Since the local CGT secretary is often a councillor, this creates something of a bosses' union. Communist municipalities have also allowed their workers to strike on full pay to supply troops for CGT 'days of action', though this was stopped in many cases during 1980 (Dion, 1984, p. 131). The impossibility of ensuring that the employees concerned use their time off in the correct way prevents municipalities from using the CGT as a mere cipher, however: the risk of demobilization among workers who found it impossible to express work-place demands through their union would be too great.

Relations between many Communist town halls and their employees have deteriorated after 1981. The alibi of a right-wing government no longer served to refuse demands on pay or conditions: more and more town halls have tried to withhold pay for 'days of action': and the new concern with improving efficiency has entailed negotiations on new working practices that have not always gone smoothly. In Le Mans, indeed, they reached a point in November 1983 where union activists locked the mayor and his colleagues in the council chamber (*Le Monde*, 17 November 1983). In Le Havre, senior municipal administrators have used their own CGT membership to try and explain the need for rationalized working arrangements to sceptical junior colleagues at union meetings.

Communist mayors and councillors do not line their own pockets with municipal funds—though at least one employee in Le Havre has been convicted of doing so. Rather they use municipal positions and posts for the benefit of their Party more systematically than other elected officials. In relation to municipal budgets, the sums are small. In relation to the PCF's own receipts, hard hit by drops in membership and press sales, municipalities constitute a major asset and their loss a material blow.

Democracy and Relations with the Electorate

Rosette argues that Communist municipalities are distinguished 'above all by their high level of democracy', and other party spokesmen have both pointed out the Socialists' shortcomings in this respect and claimed that right-wing municipalities are incapable of democratic practices as they necessarily act in the interests of a tiny minority (Rosette, 1977, p. 80; *Cahiers du Communisme*, February–March 1976, p. 339, June 1970, p. 123). Right-wing critics, on the other hand, see the PCF's municipal advances of the 1970s as part of a plot to establish a people's democracy in France (Montaldo, 1978, p. 133). Even between parties of the left, local elected officials have often been highly mistrustful of each other's democratic credentials (Lacorne, 1980, p. 102).

Socialist mayors range from authoritarians like Tony Larue of Sotteville or Joseph Franceschi (Mitterrand's Police and Security Secretary) of Alfortville, to Michel Rocard of Conflans-Sainte-Honorine or Hubert Dubedout, who made Grenoble a byword for democratic innovation for over a decade. Variations between Communist municipalities are narrower, but still exist. Milch (1973, pp. 185–95) contrasts the high-handed style of Montpellier's right-wing mayor with Jourdan of Nîmes, who was merely 'first among equals' on the council. Pronier (pp. 325–7) notes that in Bourges Jacques Rimbault reversed his Gaullist predecessor's autocratic practices and applied the PCF's democratic discourse inside and outside the town hall. These were both recently-won municipalities with a strong Socialist minority. In long-held bastions where the PCF conceded a handful of council seats to its allies in 1965 or 1971, such openness is rare (Pronier, pp. 127–9).

Detailed research on decision-making has been done in few Communist municipalities. Le Havre, a big provincial city with a weak party organization, where the Communists won the town hall in 1965, joined a full alliance with the Socialists in 1971, but maintained their overall council majority till 1983, may be taken as an 'average' example. The forms of democracy were respected: eleven committees met fairly regularly, Socialists had seats on them (and three chairmanships) as well as positions as assistant mayors proportionate to their electoral strength, and PS and PCF councillors maintained working relationships over the period 1977–81. Three factors, however, limited fully democratic decision-making.

First, while Socialist assistant mayors had some electorally 'profitable' areas of responsibility such as social assistance and senior citizens, strategic sectors were kept in Communist hands. Thus Daniel Colliard, the first assistant, handled finance, economic affairs, town planning, land policy, employment, inter-communal cooperation and computerization. Second, within the *conseil des adjoints*, which discussed committee agendas, was an 'inner cabinet' of the mayor and the full-time assistants, or seven Communists to one Socialist. Third, not only were council meetings a rubber stamp, as in most munici-palities elected under the 1964 winner-takes-all system: committee meetings often were, too (Dion also characterizes committees he encountered in five socialist and Communist Paris suburbs as 'deliquescent' (Dion, 1984, p. 175)). Le Havre's Town Planning Committee rejected just one motion from the chair in fifteen years (and the two Communists who opposed Colliard were dropped from the council in 1977). Real discussion of different planning options took place in Colliard's meetings with other interested parties like the port authority, the DDE and the chamber of commerce—all of whom valued Colliard's ability to get the council to stick to his agreements. The situation has changed since the Communists lost their majority in 1983: democracy in Le Havre depends more on power relations in the town hall than on the Communists' commitment to the fruitful confrontation of ideas (Knapp, pp. 166–72).

Communists have also stressed their democratic approach to relations with associations and the public generally, and Milch (1973, pp. 80–3) points out the openness of Nîmes in this respect compared with conservative-run Montpellier. Such liaison with associations may serve the purpose of 'struggle' in line with Rosette's triad of 'Information, Consultation and

Action' (Rosette, 1977, pp. 80–3). In Le Havre, the municipality formed an association to save the liner *France* (a source of civic pride and several hundred jobs) and used it to publicize PCF opposition to the Giscardian government's industrial policy. Elsewhere, groups like parents' associations may be colonized by the PCF, subsidized by the municipality, and enlisted in struggles on government social spending. At the same time, however, maintaining links with groups led by non-political or even right-wing personalities (such as Le Havre's thirty *comités de quartier* which group small traders), may help to demonstrate the town hall's even-handedness and to neutralize potential opposition. Liaison with associations may also allow a municipality to take soundings before committing itself to controversial projects, as when Le Havre's municipality abandoned plans for a multi-storey car-park on advice from the local *comité de quartier*. The limits of political tolerance are reached with associations tainted by Trotskyism, threatening as they do to mobilize dissent among Communist supporters. Propositions from one such group to alter the layout of an HLM estate in Le Havre were listened to politely before being gently stifled by the municipal bureaucracy.

Within these limits, the balance between the three ends of relations with associations ('struggles' behind party objectives, heading off opposition, and sounding out opinion) varies between municipalities. Colonization and struggle' will generally be more frequent in the Red-belt bastions. However, the Paris suburbs' greater permeability to the Party line of the moment also led them to be most 'open' and experimental in the mid-1970s, and most sectarian thereafter. In the provinces there has been greater evenness over time, with variations according to personalities in each city. Le Havre has taken few risks, limiting consultation to general pre-election questionnaires and liaison with tenants on housing improvement schemes. Jacques Rimbault in Bourges, on the other hand, continued to organize *assises communales* long after they ceased to be a major party priority (Pronier, pp. 325–34).

French town halls also produce municipal bulletins, which tend everywhere to be propaganda sheets. The expression, in Nîmes, of different views by the PCF, PS and PSU council groups on plans for a new town hall is exceptional—most bulletins present councils as working in unity for the common good. They are thus seldom overtly partisan. A Communist municipality's bulletin may thus refer to cuts in government social spending (before 1981) or the resistance of capitalists to change (after the left's victory). But references to the PCF as such are usually confined to crucial moments, with some mayors even managing to avoid mentioning Marchais's name in their editorials for April 1981 (Pronier, pp. 416–18).

As it appears in municipal bulletins, the relationship that PCF mayors and councillors sought to establish with their electorate may be termed the 'tribunician consensus'. French municipal rhetoric is steeped in the notion of the 'defence of local interests' (taken to be a consensual whole) against a central government that is viewed with suspicion (Kesselman, 1967, Chap. 1). Communist elected officials have tried to couple this rhetoric with the PCF's 'tribunician' discourse as the 'defender' of the working class. They thus presented themselves as responsible civic leaders representing the vast majority of their electorate apart from monopoly capitalists and striving constantly against the limits on their freedom imposed by Paris. The balance between 'responsibility' (and thus good relations with state officials) and 'struggle' was not always easy to strike, and it varied between municipalities: Ivry's concentration of partisan references, from the bulletin to street names, is characteristic of many Paris bastions but not reproduced in Nîmes or even Le Havre. By and large, though, the 'tribunician consensus' brought electoral dividends during the 1970s. Systematic comparisons with national elections are all but impossible, but some right-wing voters almost certainly supported Communist-led lists in 1971 and 1977 (Hayward & Wright, 1977, p. 449). Le Havre's results (Table 6.2) show, first, that the left achieved its best Fifth

Table 6.2 PCF and left-wing percentage of votes cast:
France and Le Havre 1946–86

Election	France PCF vote	Commune of Le Havre	
		PCF vote	Total left vote
1946 (Nov.) parliamentary	28.6	41.9	60.5
1958 parliamentary, first ballot	19.2	31.0	45.9
1965 municipal, second ballot	–	–	51.4
1971 municipal, first ballot	–	–	59.8
1973 parliamentary, first ballot	21.4	39.7	56.3
1974 presidential, second ballot	–	–	57.0
1977 municipal, first ballot	–	–	60.9
1978 parliamentary, first ballot	20.7	41.6	59.6
1979 European	20.6	34.4	57.3
1981 presidential, first ballot	15.6	26.5	56.7
1981 presidential, second ballot	–	–	60.3
1981 parliamentary, first ballot	16.1	39.9	65.4
1983 municipal, first ballot	–	–	56.8
1984 European	11.2	21.6	44.8
1986 parliamentary	9.8	29.3	53.7

Republic totals (aside from the June 1981 landslide) in municipal elections. Second, while the PCF's national decline was reflected in local results for presidential and European elections, it was attenuated by a 'favourite son' effect in parliamentary elections, where well-known municipal figures were candidates. In June 1981, the PCF vote in Le Havre ran within two points of the 1946 record, compared with a twelve-point drop nationally. The 1986 results, as in most, though not all, Communist towns, conform far more to the 'presidential' pattern: with the adoption of PR using *départements* as constituencies, voters who wanted to support Le Havre's mayor also had to vote for Roland Leroy, leader of the Communist list in Seine-Maritime and handicapped in Le Havre both by his origins in the rival city of Rouen and by his close identification with the hardline wing of the party leadership.

In any case, the 'tribunician consensus' proved less convincing after 1981. References to the 'pressures of the right and the bosses' and oblique criticisms of the government's record were a poor substitute for a right-wing administration in Paris to explain higher rates, poor housing or services, or redundancies in local industry. This contributed to the losses sustained in 1983.

National Policy, Local Outputs

The PCF's mayors and councillors are more accountable than those of the PS or the right to their party organization and thus in theory more responsive to national policy changes. However, the relationship between national policy and local outputs is a complex one, as the refracted effect at local level of the changes of 1977–8 and 1981 illustrate. The variables that affect it include the difference between the Paris suburbs—with the proximity of national leaders—and the provinces; the length of occupancy of the town hall by a Communist mayor; the PCF's strength on the council; its organizational solidity; and the proportion of its most solid clientele, the working class, in the population. The extremes are old Red-belt bastions and provincial cities won with Socialist help in 1977, but in many communes the variables do not cumulate so neatly. Moreover, the mayor's personality may still have an effect. An unreconstructed Stalinist like Léo Figuères and a modernizing technocrat like Marcel Rosette, although both in Paris bastions, may apply different policies.

The redistributive policies that distinguished inter-war Communist municipalities appear less remarkable in a period where extensive social and educational provision is expected of all municipalities, and Communists admit the narrowing of differences. Moreover, Rosette's claims for the PCF's superior democratic credentials are exaggerated. Communist experiments with popular consultation have been no more convincing than those of the Socialists, and ultimately conflict with the traditional Leninist conception of the Party's vanguard role.

The widespread weakening of the PCF's organization, the conquest of cities where it was never very strong anyway, and the growth of local service provision, and with it bureaucracy, have increased both the opportunities for patronage and the PCF's dependence on local office. To this extent the Party has become 'municipalized' like the Radicals and the pre-1971 Socialists before it, if in a somewhat different way. By 1983 self-preservation and civic achievement had become as important as aims for many Communist mayors and councillors as the application of radical policies of distribution or of popular consultation.

The 1983 Elections

Conservatism and defensiveness thus marked much of the Communists' election campaign. In 1925 and 1929 the PCF had run women municipal candidates against the law and the weight of public opinion: in 1982 it, like the right, rejected Socialist proposals to give the local vote to immigrants (the Party's position on this later changed—after the elections were over). The agreed basis of negotiations with the PS on the composition of lists for 1977 had been the two parties' votes since 1971: in 1982 the PCF proposed that incumbent mayors should head lists in all left-wing municipalities, a response to local Socialist sections anxious to capitalize on gains made against their 'allies' in 1981. Faced by a right-wing opposition poised to recover lost ground and united for the first ballot in many cities, the PS leadership shared little of the local activists' optimism and proved receptive to the Communists' arguments. Separate Socialist lists ran against Communist incumbents at the first ballot in just fourteen major communes.

The PCF drew frequent attention during the campaign to the right's 'thirst for revenge' and its plans to 'use municipalities as centres of opposition to a government elected by universal suffrage' (Salini, 1983, p. 6)—as the PCF had done before 1981. Calls to 'reinforce the Union of the Left' with a display of electoral strength were not backed by a comprehensive statement of municipal policy like the 'communal contracts' or 1971 and 1977. If this absence was officially explained as being 'in the spirit of the 1982 Decentralization Act' (Trigon, 1982, p. 42), it still reflected the uncertainty of the PCF's municipal discourse. Communist mayors were thus largely left to campaign on their local records against opponents running with the national political tide.

The left suffered in 1983 from the simultaneous defection of left-wing supporters (often through first-ballot abstention) and of centre voters who had supported Mitterrand in 1981 and who now returned to the right. A major reason for both was the government's poor economic results. The PCF, despite attempts to distance itself (often through the CGT) from unpopular measures like the wage freeze of summer 1982, suffered worse losses than the PS. Compared to Mitterrand's percentage in May 1981, the left's vote in major towns fell by 5.1 per cent (from 59.1 to 54 per cent) where the incumbent mayor was a Communist, against 3.1 per cent where he was a Socialist (losses in right-wing towns were between 13 and 16 per cent). And the Communists lost sixteen out of seventy-two major town halls compared with the Socialists' fifteen out of eighty-three.

Two general explanations may be given for the drop in the PCF vote. The first was the secular decline of the traditional working class: the 1982 census found half a million fewer workers than in 1975. Schain (1985, pp. 46–50) has noted the impact of this in municipalities run by the PCF since 1965: it was especially marked in the Red belt, where de-industrialization was rapid. The shrinkage of the French working class and the influx of voteless immigrants to the bad jobs does not of itself explain PCF losses: the Communists also signally failed to hold their working-class clientele or to win solid support among other social groups.

The second cause of the decline of municipal communism cannot be shown in figures. Communist councils were widely regarded as determined and effective in dealing with the main urban problems of the post-war generation—providing more low-cost housing, hospitals, schools, and social amenities both for new and for long-standing but ill-supplied city-dwellers. They often proved less able when tackling problems that surfaced in the 1970s—running services economically, cleaning up the environmental mess left by urban programmes of the 1950s and 1960s, retaining existing businesses and attracting new ones, facing a rising crime rate, and decentralizing decision-making. HLMs, for example, were still cited by many Communists as the main solution to a continuing housing shortage at a time when their consumer image (and often their physical structure) was fast deteriorating; when over half the population (by 1982) lived in owner-occupied housing and many of the rest aspired to; and when a generation that had barely known the post-war housing crisis (and thus refused to see HLMs as an improvement on anything) was reaching voting age. That many of the new problems were accentuated in PCF municipalities was not always the Communists' fault: their municipal image had none the less suffered by 1983.

Communist losses were not, however, evenly spread. Three factors help to explain local differences. First, as the Communists hastened to point out, disunity cost the left votes. True, the PCF held off the Socialists' first-ballot challenge in every town where a 'primary' took place, except Reims; but it lost seven of these fourteen towns (Reims, Poissy, Nîmes, Sète, Chelles, Athis-Mons and Gagny). Second, nine of the sixteen towns lost in 1983 had elected a Communist mayor for the first time in 1977. Five of these were provincial municipalities (Grasse, Reims, Saint-Quentin, Béziers, and Saint-Étienne), the remainder being Paris suburbs. On the other hand, thirty-seven of the forty-two PCF municipalities re-elected at the first ballot had had a Communist mayor since 1965 or before. The Party thus had a better chance of resisting defeat where it had had time to put down roots. Third, the Paris region tends to amplify national voting tendencies. This was especially true in a municipal election that was also a vote on the left-wing government's record: in the mosaic of communes surrounding the capital the sense of local identity, and thus the advantage of incumbent mayors, is diminished. The PCF's long-standing implantation led to losses of town halls being proportionally lower in Paris suburbs (seven out of forty-two) than in provincial cities or suburbs (nine out of thirty). The vote, though, often dropped very heavily against 1977: by 10.7 per cent in Aubervilliers, 13.4 per cent in Argenteuil, and 14 per cent in Vitry.

These tendencies do not, however, explain the PCF's showing in every municipality. If Reims was lost decisively and Saint-Étienne narrowly, Robert Jarry kept Le Mans (won in 1977) with a drop of just half a percentage point, despite the Socialists' first-ballot opposition. Jacques Rimbault lost fewer than two points in Bourges. Colette Privat, having successfully renegotiated Maromme's redevelopment plan, saw her list's percentage jump from 54 to 60. All of these were communes where Marchais' 1981 vote had shown a big drop against earlier PCF results. Some scope thus remained for innovative municipalities to resist the PCF's decline by appealing to their local record.

The 1983 elections had a long drawn-out postscript, as the Council of State upheld the right's allegations of fraud and found the Communists guilty of ballot-stuffing in five major municipalities. The resulting autumn by-elections in Sarcelles, Antony and Aulnay-sous-Bois were all lost by the PCF (the poll in Sarcelles, which defeated one of the Party's most able mayors, Henry Canacos, showed a particularly strong swing away from the PCF in polling stations where the fraud had taken place). Prolonged litigation in a fourth Paris suburb, Noisy-le-Grand, and in La Seyne-sur-Mer, also ended in right-wing by-election victories in 1985. Only in Houilles and Thionville, where the Communists were condemned for 'unfair propaganda' not fraud, were PCF mayors re-elected. Neither the frauds themselves nor the Communists' claims that the Council of State was acting out of partisan motives did much to lay the foundations for a recovery of municipal communism.

Conclusion

The weakening of the PCF's local positions is clearly related to its national crisis, the most visible symptom of which is the collapse of the Communist vote (Table 6.2). The 1986 figure of 9.8 per cent represents the lowest score since 1928 and is barely higher than that of the far-right National Front: European comparisons place the PCF closer to the deliquescent Spanish Communist Party than to the still-powerful if frustrated Italian PCI. Jean Ranger (1986) has diagnosed competently the organization and sociological weakening that preceded the electoral decline. But another important element of it is the PCF's failure to find answers to the fundamental questions about its identity and goals that have been posed since 1956–8. Despite its stated commitment to pluralism and to democracy and its recent sharing of responsibility in a far-from-extreme left-wing government, the PCF retains a public image and a self-image (reinforced since the move into opposition in summer 1984) as a working-class, revolutionary and pro-Soviet party. In the long term this was bound to lose votes at a time when the working class is in numerical decline; when workers have become more integrated than ever into the norms and aspirations of the rest of French society (despite facing an attack on living standards and jobs without precedent since the Liberation); and when only a small hard core still believe in the Soviet Union as the 'motherland of socialism'. The PCF has failed either to achieve the broader cross-class alliance it sought in the 1970s or to present a convincing left-wing alternative to social democracy. Withdrawal from government, the stifling of 'liberal' dissent (notably from former Politbureau member Pierre Juquin, former Minister Marcel Rigout, and Lucien Lanternier, mayor of Gennevilliers), and the consolidation of Georges Marchais's leadership at the 25th Congress, may have deflected the risk of 'fractionalism' but did little to point a way forward. The same is true of the marginalization of dissidents at the Central Committee meeting that followed the March 1986 elections.

Local and national decline have not, however, gone hand in hand. The pattern of the 1970s was of national stagnation but local growth. The articulation between national strategy and local policy outputs is, as we have seen, complex. The losses of 1983-4 were inevitably related to the Communists' role in an increasingly unpopular national government, but they should also be seen as a delayed repercussion of the PCF's secular shrinkage. As the Party's apparatus weakened, and as its 'most dynamic elements were drained into the municipal system' even in some Paris suburbs (Dion, 1984, p. 132), municipalities increasingly became organizational and financial props for its flagging position in the country. Just as not losing—adopting low-risk consensus policies and using patronage to offset organizational weakness—became a central preoccupation of Communist elected officials, so one of their biggest earlier assets, their originality and dynamism, wasted away.

How important for the PCF is the possibility of losing more town halls in 1989? March 1986 was admittedly a very party-political contest, with PR based on *département*-wide lists being used for the simultaneous parliamentary and regional elections (the Chirac government has promised to restore a single-member constituency system). Notability proved to be a rather ineffective shield against electoral decline. Fourteen Communist mayors headed lists for the parliamentary elections and nine for the regional ballot. Of these, only Jacques Rimbault of Bourges (who improved on the PCF's 1981 percentage in Cher) and Robert Jarry of Le Mans (whose regional list in Sarthe did 5 per cent better than his parliamentary running-mate) showed substantially different results from the national tendency. Both are city mayors whose standing in their *départements* owes little or nothing to the party apparatus. But if municipal notability is in general an unreliable barrier to national electoral collapse, it remains organizationally and financially important: Ranger illustrates the point perfectly with the budget of a medium-sized party federation north of Paris which draws over half of its receipts from payments made by elected officials (Ranger, 1986, p. 60).

The PCF faces a dilemma if it wishes to retain such assets. The municipal Union of the Left, rendered indispensable by the 1964 electoral law, is only marginally less necessary under the system adopted in 1982. But the current state of open hostility with the PS looks set to continue at least until the next presidential election (in 1988 at the latest). In this context it is hard to imagine a national PS–PCF agreement like those of 1977 and 1983 providing for common municipal lists in major cities. Without such an agreement, the PCF could easily lose another twenty town halls (including Le Havre, the biggest of all). It is not hard to see why local elected officials (albeit not the most powerful of them as yet) have been prominent in the renewed opposition to the leadership that surfaced in March 1986.

ap 6.1 French municipalities of over 30,000 inhabitants held by Communist mayors, 1986 (brackets indicate municipalities *lost* between 1983 and 1985)

(Inner-belt Paris suburbs are shown on Map 6.2)

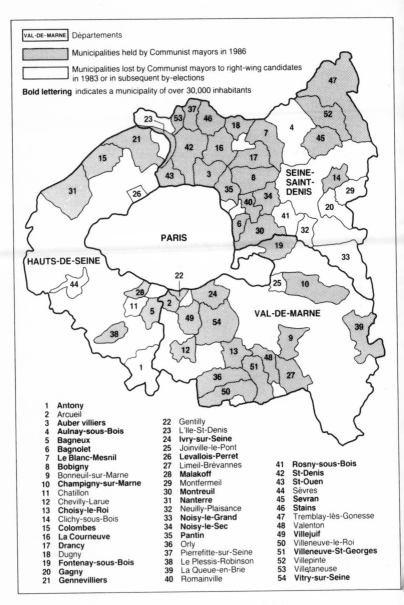

		VAL-DE-MARNE	Départements
		▨	Municipalities held by Communist mayors in 1986
		▢	Municipalities lost by Communist mayors to right-wing candidates in 1983 or in subsequent by-elections

Bold lettering indicates a municipality of over 30,000 inhabitants

1	**Antony**		
2	Arcueil	22	Gentilly
3	**Auber villiers**	23	L'Ile-St-Denis
4	**Aulnay-sous-Bois**	24	**Ivry-sur-Seine**
5	**Bagneux**	25	Joinville-le-Pont
6	**Bagnolet**	26	**Levallois-Perret**
7	**Le Blanc-Mesnil**	27	Limeil-Brévannes	41	**Rosny-sous-Bois**
8	**Bobigny**	28	**Malakoff**	42	**St-Denis**
9	Bonneuil-sur-Marne	29	Montfermeil	43	**St-Ouen**
10	**Champigny-sur-Marne**	30	**Montreuil**	44	**Sèvres**
11	Chatillon	31	**Nanterre**	45	**Sevran**
12	Chevilly-Larue	32	Neuilly-Plaisance	46	**Stains**
13	**Choisy-le-Roi**	33	**Noisy-le-Grand**	47	Tremblay-lès-Gonesse
14	Clichy-sous-Bois	34	**Noisy-le-Sec**	48	Valenton
15	**Colombes**	35	**Pantin**	49	**Villejuif**
16	**La Courneuve**	36	Orly	50	Villeneuve-le-Roi
17	**Drancy**	37	Pierrefitte-sur-Seine	51	**Villeneuve-St-Georges**
18	Dugny	38	Le Plessis-Robinson	52	Villepinte
19	**Fontenay-sous-Bois**	39	La Queue-en-Brie	53	Villetaneuse
20	Gagny	40	Romainville	54	**Vitry-sur-Seine**
21	**Gennevilliers**				

Map 6.2 Inner suburbs of Paris: municipalities held by Communist mayors in 1986, and municipalities lost between 1983 and 1985

Yet even if PS–PCF relations improve sufficiently for such a national agreement to be possible, the PCF would be negotiating from very weak positions. In March 1986, the PS ran ahead of the PCF in over thirty of the fifty-one large Communist-run municipalities (Table 6.3). The PCF vote in towns with a Socialist mayor, on the other hand, exceeded 15 per cent in only one case out of sixty-eight, while it was below 10 per cent in over fifty, and in only one of these municipalities was the Socialist lead on the PCF less than 20 per cent. In this context, for the PS to allow what it allowed in 1983—a clear run for almost all incumbent Communist mayors—seems unthinkable.

For a long period in opposition under the Fifth Republic, the PCF attempted to finesse the question of what kind of party it was, and it did this most successfully at municipal level, where it could play its tribunician and government roles simultaneously. Maintaining the ambiguity became much more difficult after 1982, and July 1984 marked what could well be a prolonged return to a tribunician 'strategy' in isolation from the PS. This is likely to be highly dangerous from the Communists' municipal positions: even if the line is reversed, it will be too late for some PCF mayors. And the loss of more town halls will, in turn, represent a further body-blow to the Party itself.

Bibliography

Arnaud, Christian, 1981. 'Reconquérir le Droit à la Ville', *Cahiers du Communisme*, no. 3, March, pp. 32–8.

Blackmer, Donald L. M. and Tarrow, Sidney, 1977. *Communism in Italy and France*, Princeton, Princeton University Press, paperback edn.

Brogan, D. W., 1967. *The Development of Modern France*, 2nd edn., London, Hamish Hamilton.

Cahiers du Communisme, no. 6, June 1970. Resolution of the PCF Central Committee, Drancy, 21 May 1970, pp. 116–24, no. 2–3, February–March 1976, special 22nd Congress number.

Canacos, Henry, 1979. *Sarcelles, ou le Béton Apprivoisé*. Paris, Éditions Sociales.

Cerny, Philip G. and Schain Martin (eds), 1980. *French Politics and Public Policy*. London, Methuen.

Clément, Robert, 1985. 'Des Élus Communistes Engagés', *Cahiers du Communisme*. November, pp. 44–8.

Dion, Stephane, 1984. 'La politicisation des Administrations Publiques: l'Exemple de l'Administration Communale Française', unpublished doctoral thesis, Paris, Institut d'Études Politiques.

Duclos, Jacques, 1956. 'Les Municipalités au Service des Masses', *Cahiers du Communisme*, 14th Congress number, July–August, pp. 69–107.

Ducros, Jean-Claude, 1966. 'Politique et Finances Locales', *Analyse et Prévision*, no. 2, pp. 499–520.

Dupuy, Fernand, 1975. *Être Maire Communiste*. Paris, Calmann-Levy.

L'Élu d'Aujourd'hui (monthly of ANECR). June 1985.

Fajon, Étienne, 1953. 'Pour la Victoire aux Élections Municipales', *Cahiers du Communisme*, no. 3, March, pp. 373–86.

Harris, André and de Sédouy Alain, 1974. *Voyage à l'Intérieur du Parti Communiste*. Paris, Seuil.

— —, 1978. *Qui N'est Pas de Droite?* Paris, Seuil.

Hayward, Jack, and Wright, Vincent, 1971. 'The 37,708 Microcosms of an Indivisible Republic: The French Local Elections of March 1971', *Parliamentary Affairs*, summer, pp. 284–311.

— —, 1977. 'Governing from the Centre: The 1977 French Local Elections', *Government and Opposition*, vol. 12, no. 4, Autumn, pp. 433–54.

Hoss, Jean-Pierre, 1969. *Communes en Banlieue: Argenteuil et Bezons*. Paris, Armand Colin.

Jeambar, Denis, 1984. *Le PC dans la Maison*. Paris, Calmann-Levy.

Kesselman, Mark, 1967. *The Ambiguous Consensus*. New York, Knopf.

Knapp, A. F., 1983. 'Revolutionaries or Technocrats? Communists and Town Planning in Le Havre, 1965–1980', unpublished D.Phil thesis, Oxford.

Lacorne, Denis, 1977. 'Left-Wing Unity at the Grass Roots: Picardy and Languedoc' in Blackmer and Tarrow, op. cit., pp. 305–39.

Lacorne, Denis, 1980. *Les Notables Rouges*. Paris, Fondation Nationale des Sciences Politiques.

Lancelot, Alain, 1983. 'Vue sur le Gauche à Marée Basse: Les Élections Municipales des 6 et 13 mars', *Projet*, no. 175, May, pp. 437–53.

Machin, Howard (ed.), 1983. *National Communism in Western Europe*. London, Methuen University Paperbacks.

Marchais, Georges, 1979. Speech to 1st ANECR Congress, *L'Élu d'Aujourd'hui*, December, pp. 17–24.

Marty, André, 1947. 'Les Elus Municipaux Communistes dans le Grande Bataille pour le Pain et la Liberté', *Cahiers du Communisme*, no. 12, December, pp. 1245–68.

Milch, Jerome, 1973. 'Paris is Not France: Policy Outputs and Political Values in Two French Cities', unpublished Ph.D. thesis, MIT.

—, 1974. 'Influence as Power: French Local Government Reconsidered', *British Journal of Political Science*, vol. 4, no. 2, pp. 211–29.

—, 1977. 'The PCF and Local Government: Continuity and Change' in Blackmer and Tarrow, op. cit., pp. 340–69.

Le Monde, 1983. *Les Élections Municipales de Mars 1983: L'Avertissement à La Gauche*. Supplément aux Dossiers et Documents du *Monde*, mars 1983.

—, 1986. *Les Élections Législatives de 1986: Le Retour de la Droite*. Supplement aux Dossiers et Documents du *Monde*, mars 1986.

Montaldo, Jean, 1977. *Les Finances du PCF*. Paris, Albin Michel.

—, 1978. *La France Communiste*. Paris, Albin Michel.

Platone, Francois, 1967. 'L'Implantation du Parti Communiste dans la Seine et sa Conception de l'Administration Locale', unpublished dissertation, Paris, Institut d'Études Politiques.

Le Point, 1979. 'Grandes Villes: 1,000 Milliards de Dettes', no. 374, 19 November, pp. 91–5.

Pronier, Raymond, 1983. *Les Municipalités Communistes: Bilan de 30 Années de Gestion*. Paris, Balland.

Ranger, Jean, 1986. 'Le Déclin du PCF', *Revue Française de Science Politique*, vol. 36, no. 1, pp. 46–63.

Rosette, Marcel, 1970. 'Collectivités Locales et Démocratie Politique', *Cahiers du Communisme*, no. 1, January, pp. 30–42.

—, 1971. 'Pourquoi un Contrat Communal?', *Cahiers du Communisme*, no. 1, January, pp. 21–7.

—, 1972. 'Une Gestion Sociale au Service des Travailleurs', *Cahiers du Communisme*, no. 7–8, July–August, pp. 33–9.

—, 1977. *La Gestion Communale dans l'Action*. Paris, Éditions Sociales.

—, 1979. Speech to 1st ANECR Congress, *L'Élu d'Aujourd'hui*, December, p. 4–16 (excerpts in *Cahiers du Communisme*, no. 1, January 1980, pp. 70–75).

—, 1982. 'Les Élections Municipales et la Stratégie du 24ᵉ Congrès', *Cahiers du Communisme*, no. 9, September, pp. 24–33.

—, 1986. Speech to 4th ANECR Congress, *L'Élu d'Aujourd'hui*, January, pp. 12–16.

Salini, Laurent, 1983. 'Élections Municipales: Deux Attitudes Significatives', *Cahiers du Communisme*, no. 3, March, pp. 4–8.

Schain, Martin, 1980. 'Communist Control of Municipal Councils and Urban Political Change', in Cerny and Schain, op. cit., pp. 243–6.

—, 1985. *French Communism and Local Power*. London, Frances Pinter.

Trigon, Marcel, 1982. 'Programmes d'Action Municipale: Démarche Novatrice et Autogestionnaire', *Cahiers du Communisme*, no. 10, October, pp. 42–8.

Wright, Vincent, 1978. *The Government and Politics of France*. London, Hutchinson.

Table 6.3 France's Communist municipalities (over 30,000 inhabitants), 1986: recent election results*

Communist mayor since	Municipality	Municipal elections, first ballot, 15 March 1977		Presidential elections, first ballot, 26 April 1981				Parliamentary elections, first ballot, 14 June 1981				Municipal elections, first ballot, 6 March 1983		European elections, 17 June 1984				Parliamentary elections, 16 March 1986[a]			
		Union of the left lists		Marchais (PCF)		Mitterrand (PS)		PCF candidates		PS candidates		Union of the left lists		Marchais list (PCF)		Jospin list (PS)		PCF lists		PS lists	
		no. votes	% of votes cast	no. votes	% of votes cast	no. votes	% of votes cast	no. votes	% of votes cast	no. votes	% of votes cast	no. votes	% of votes cast	no. votes	% of votes cast	no. votes	% of votes cast	no. votes	% of votes cast	no. votes	% of votes cast
	Suburbs of Paris																				
1935	Argenteuil	24,396	70.3	14,148	32.4	10,115	23.2		46.3		26.0	18,955	56.9	7,248	28.4	4,165	16.3	10,446	29.5	8,318	23.5
1945	Aubervilliers	14,804	71.7	9,976	39.0	5,322	20.8		54.0		22.6	11,907	61.0	4,991	33.7	2,289	15.5	6,290	30.5	5,030	24.4
1935	Bagneux	10,701	71.6	5,665	29.2	4,730	24.4		42.6		24.4	8,988	62.2	3,157	28.3	2,158	19.3	3,690	23.8	4,872	31.4
1925	Bagnolet	7,594	64.2	5,217	36.1	3,258	22.6		46.6		25.6	6,919	62.2	3,500	27.1	1,972	15.3	3,227	27.9	3,040	26.3
1935	Le Blanc-Mesnil	11,439	66.3	6,813	30.8	5,199	23.5		40.5		28.8	9,834	58.1	2,929	33.7	1,402	16.2	4,182	23.7	4,392	24.9
1920	Bobigny	9,179	70.5	6,232	34.8	4,230	23.6		49.9		29.4	8,010	61.8	3,041	31.6	1,402	15.1	3,583	25.9	3,597	26.0
1950	Champigny	15,508	58.0	10,602	30.5	7,691	22.1		34.5		25.8	15,245	54.7	6,161	28.1	3,409	15.5	7,138	24.8	7,252	25.0
1959	Choisy-le-Roi	9,721	66.9	4,412	26.0	3,989	23.6		35.4		30.2	6,835	50.1	2,514	23.1	2,006	18.5	3,488	24.2	3,787	26.3
1965	Colombes	20,878	63.8	8,696	22.1	9,368	23.9		37.3		22.5	17,551	52.5	4,707	18.0	4,562	17.5	7,231	21.7	8,071	24.2
1959	Corbeil-Essonnes	9,687	65.2	4,444	26.6	3,971	23.8		45.7		19.8	7,597	53.0	2,064	21.05	1,665	17.0	4,038	28.1	2,948	20.5
1953	La Courneuve	8,791	74.7	5,602	39.2	3,114	21.8		53.8		23.7	7,406	70.5	2,707	35.2	1,136	14.8	3,095	29.2	2,672	25.2
1935	Drancy	19,951	79.4	12,312	39.8	6,355	20.5		63.4		17.9	15,824	66.9	5,263	30.2	2,893	16.6	7,625	30.8	5,711	23.1
1965	Fontenay-sous-Bois	11,247	54.1	5,819	23.2	5,661	22.6		36.3		20.2	10,189	48.2	3,357	20.5	2,662	16.3	5,441	24.1	5,306	23.1
1945	Garges-les-Gonesse	6,286	65.6	3,226	24.8	3,956	30.4		36.2		32.8	5,060	54.3	1,482	21.6	1,316	19.2	n.a.	n.a.	n.a.	n.a.
1934	Gennevilliers	11,694	77.7	7,694	44.0	3,625	20.7		59.9		20.6	8,626	62.5	3,563	35.1	1,567	15.4	5,516	39.6	2,802	20.1
1977	Houilles[1]	6,557	52.5	2,753	18.7	3,511	23.8		21.3		33.9	5,647	43.5	n.a.	n.a.	n.a.	n.a.	n.a.	n.a.	n.a.	n.a.
1925	Ivry-sur-Seine	20,058	100.0	11,966	44.7	5,246	20.4		59.4		19.5	18,659	77.4	9,661	55.1	2,299	13.1	9,423	42.4	4,970	22.4
1935	Malakoff	11,887	81.7	6,450	37.9	3,489	20.5		45.5		22.7	8,238	61.1	3,653	34.1	1,708	15.8	4,829	33.5	3,429	23.8
1935	Montreuil	22,521	66.0	13,413	31.2	9,869	23.0		42.7		26.1	16,977	53.8	6,385	25.8	4,338	17.5	7,853	22.9	9,930	28.9
1935	Nanterre	19,103	75.0	10,636	30.7	7,811	22.5		41.7		28.4	15,243	56.4	5,424	26.3	3,692	17.9	6,898	24.2	7,725	27.1
1959	Noisy-le-Sec	8,565	62.7	4,399	25.9	4,256	25.0		40.5		25.3	7,974	57.6	2,413	22.8	1,855	17.6	2,988	20.8	3,972	27.6
1959	Pantin	9,618	62.2	4,373	22.6	4,992	25.8		28.7		29.3	7,547	50.0	2,327	19.9	2,229	19.1	2,595	15.9	5,202	31.9
1945	St-Denis	20,515	75.5	12,289	36.6	7,564	22.5		48.7		27.4	16,290	64.8	5,676	31.0	3,176	17.3	6,535	25.2	7,327	28.2
1965	Ste-Geneviève	7,909	62.8	3,066	20.6	3,787	25.4		32.2		30.7	7,412	58.0	1,557	16.5	1,895	20.1	2,092	15.8	4,062	30.6
1935	St-Ouen	12,575	90.5	5,892	34.0	3,815	22.0		46.3		25.7	7,243	53.8	2,864	28.3	1,697	16.8	3,551	25.6	3,680	26.5
1959	Sarrouville	9,551	59.6	4,299	21.5	4,939	24.7		25.1	n.a.[3]	33.0	10,287[3]	58.9	2,208	16.7	2,462	18.6	2,575	13.6	5,928	31.4
1977	Sevran	5,726	51.4	3,890	23.5	4,493	27.1		31.9		36.5	9,294[4]	67.3	1,725	18.2	1,824	19.3	2,654	18.3	4,140	28.5
1935	Stains	9,817	100.0	5,835	39.5	3,141	21.6		54.0		24.0	7,408	64.5	2,909	33.7	1,321	15.3	n.a.	n.a.	n.a.	n.a.
	Villejuif	14,156	75.5	9,216	39.3	4,999	21.3		50.2		23.4	11,848	64.2	5,922	40.0	3,515	23.7	6,992	35.6	4,617	23.5

Year	Town																		
1977	Villeneuve-St-Georges[1]	6,885	52.2	3,562	25.3	3,585	25.5	33.8	30.1	5,024	42.3	n.a.	n.a.	n.a.	n.a.	n.a.	n.a.	n.a.	n.a.
1925	Vitry-sur-Seine	23,440	74.0	13,057	34.2	9,160	24.0	43.6	29.7	18,306	60.5	7,151	31.3	4,225	18.5	9,427	30.2	8,259	26.5
	Suburbs of Grenoble																		
1945	Echirolles	9,239	100.0	3,922	27.4	4,335	30.3	31.1	41.2	8,217	68.1	2,327	24.9	1,939	20.8	2,945	21.3	4,870	35.3
1947	St-Martin-d'Hères	6,042	67.4	3,219	27.0	3,588	30.1	37.3	34.3	5,543	59.1	1,691	23.4	1,786	24.7	2,206	19.9	4,226	38.2
	Suburbs of Lyon																		
1945	Vaulx-en-Velin	6,328	70.2	4,139	30.3	4,114	30.2	36.3	41.3	4,902	48.1	1,754	25.2	1,393	20.0	2,303	20.5	3,216	28.6
1945	Vénissieux	14,308	70.2	8,373	32.3	7,423	28.6	47.1	30.7	10,532	59.0	4,077	29.0	2,943	20.9	5,050	24.7	6,023	29.4
	Suburbs of Rouen																		
1959	St-Étienne-du-Rouvray	9,233	68.9	5,125	32.2	4,698	29.5	43.3	32.2	8,066	65.5	2,734	30.2	2,062	22.8	3,175	24.7	4,902	38.1
	Provincial towns																		
1965	Alès	13,919	64.8	8,151	34.9	4,420	18.9	42.4	25.7	11,748	55.6	5,262	31.5	2,539	15.2	5,496	25.9	4,775	22.5
1971	Amiens	32,925	56.2	14,376	21.9	15,568	23.7	27.0	35.0	26,894	46.9	6,786	16.1	7,357	17.5	7,895	14.3	16,643	30.2
1959	Aubagne	10,515	69.6	6,362	32.7	3,275	16.8	46.8	19.1	10,234	56.1	3,944	27.7	1,706	12.0	5,021	26.5	3,089	16.3
1977	Bourges	14,246	45.9	6,753	18.0	9,100	24.3	29.4	24.9	18,537	54.0	4,669	18.9	4,249	17.2	11,284	32.9	6,066	17.7
1971	Calais	25,943	68.1	12,533	30.3	9,419	22.8	49.6	21.3	18,954	51.8	6,320	26.0	4,099	16.9	10,475	29.8	7,466	21.3
1977	Chalons-sur-Marne	11,707	58.0	3,974	16.7	5,670	24.9	29.3	24.8	10,955	51.0	2,089	15.0	2,321	16.8	4,198	21.5	4,404	22.6
1977	La Ciotat	7,181	50.3	5,148	29.3	3,615	20.6	36.4	27.9	8,360	49.2	3,090	24.3	1,760	13.8	3,287	19.6	3,418	20.3
1971	Dieppe[2]	7,837	57.9	5,132	23.9	5,010	23.3	25.3	33.9	11,637[3]	59.8	2,678	20.2	2,510	19.0	3,603	19.3	5,996	32.2
1977	Évreux	9,691[4]	57.8	2,710	12.6	6,041	28.0	19.8	33.4	10,043	52.9	1,501	11.4	2,805	21.4	2,360	12.9	5,710	31.3
1965	Le Havre	62,285	60.9	27,893	26.5	25,482	24.2	39.9	23.5	48,015	53.4	13,513	21.6	11,894	19.0	19,413	22.1	25,644	26.2
1977	Le Mans	32,847	48.1	13,705	17.6	21,159	27.1	22.5	36.5	41,216[5]	58.3	7,070	14.9	10,240	21.6	13,034	18.7	21,862	31.4
1959	Martigues	10,677	74.5	6,515	33.3	4,531	23.2	44.5	27.4	11,008	61.5	3,708	27.9	2,334	17.5	4,813	24.4	4,807	24.4
1977	Montluçon	15,194	53.3	7,872	27.4	6,747	23.5	35.7	45.7	19,355[5]	72.6	5,093	27.4	3,336	17.9	7,048	24.7	6,015	24.7
1971	St-Dizier	7,580	55.6	3,138	20.3	4,198	27.1	29.1	33.0	8,131	58.1	1,610	17.1	1,515	16.1	2,004	15.1	4,135	31.2
1977	Tarbes	11,148	50.6	5,668	23.5	6,562	27.2	27.5	36.5	13,145[5]	61.9	3,518	21.4	3,455	21.0	4,312	19.3	5,850	26.1
1977	Thionville	9,002	49.1	2,628	13.1	5,045	25.1	14.8	38.6	10,180	51.3	1,493	11.4	2,562	19.5	1,828	9.5	5,389	28.0
1959	Vierzon	9,227	55.0	5,809	31.2	3,995	21.4	39.0	26.7	8,962	54.9	3,142	28.9	1,930	17.6	5,023	32.2	3,972	25.4

Notes

[1] Houilles and Villeneuve-St-Georges had over 30,000 inhabitants in 1977, fewer than 30,000 in 1983.

[2] Dieppe had fewer than 30,000 inhabitants in 1977, but over 30,000 in 1983.

[3] Figures given in Le Monde are based on constituencies which do not coincide with municipal boundaries. (Percentages from Pronier).

[4] Evreux 1977: combined total of two Left lists—PCF 6,081 (36.3%); PS 3,610 (21.5%).

[5] Sartrouville 1983: combined total of two Left lists—PCF 6,511 (37.3%); PS 3,776 (21.6%).
Sevran 1983: combined total of two Left lists—PCF 5,144 (37.2%); PS 4,150 (30.0%).
Dieppe 1983: combined total of two Left lists—PCF 6,088 (31.3%); PS 5,549 (28.5%).
Le Mans 1983: combined total of two Left lists—PCF 25,077 (35.5%); PS 16,139 (22.8%).
Moutluçon 1983: combined total of two Left lists—PCF 12,194 (45.8%); PS 7,141 (26.8%).
Tarbes 1983: combined total of two Left lists—PCF 9,142 (43.5%); PS 4,003 (18.5%).

[6] With the adoption of PR and the abolition of the old constituencies, municipal-level figures became available for the 1986 parliamentary elections.

* Figures for Union of the Left lists at municipal elections, unless otherwise stated; and for Communist lists of candidates at national or European elections, with comparisons with Socialist party strength.

Sources: Pronier, 1983, pp. 433–36; Le Monde, Les Élections Municipales de 1983; Le Monde, 28 April 1981, 19 June 1984, 18 March 1986.

7 The Communist Party of Great Britain and Local Politics

John Callaghan

When measured against most indices of political potency the Communist Party of Great Britain (CPGB) has been in decline since the first few years after the Second World War. The high point of its experience in local politics was in 1945–6, when the Party benefited from the general swing to the left in the British electorate and when Soviet prestige was at its greatest in the immediate aftermath of the war and before the onset of the Cold War. Table 7.1 illustrates the Communist Party performance in local government since 1945.

Between the First and Second World Wars the CPGB set little store in local politics as it pursued a Leninist strategy that envisaged a transition to socialism based on the spontaneous creation of soviets. These catastrophist perspectives served to focus party politics on the industrial struggle and the creation of factory cells rather than specifically political arenas of struggle. This did not prevent, however, the emergence of Communist strongholds in certain communities, such as Mardy, the Vale of Leven and Lumphinnans—the 'Little Moscows' as they were known (MacIntyre, 1975, 1980). In these areas the CP vote was slightly more or less than that of the Labour Party in local politics. In the Vale of Leven it was even possible for a Communist, Hugh MacIntyre, to get elected as convener of the county council's key housing committee by a Conservative majority—such was the experience and ability of the Party's elected representatives in these areas. In the Communist strongholds of Wales, Scotland and parts of England, such as the East End of London, the CPGB was invariably able to conclude electoral pacts with the local Labour Party whereas nationally this was not always possible. Generally such agreements prevailed up to 1927, when commonly supported candidates usually won, while the period of Communist sectarianism that followed (the notorious Third Period) resulted in acrimonious relations between the two parties, damaging the CP's local electoral performances up to 1935. None the less, the party was occasionally able to achieve respectable results such as those obtained in the London Councy Council elections of 1928, which saw twenty-two 'left-wing' candidates average 40 per cent of the Labour vote in the areas contested.

However, it was not until the 19th Congress of the Party in 1946 that this work was deemed sufficiently important to warrant the creation of a Local Government and Parliamentary Department Sub-committee of the Executive. By now the CPGB had virtually ceased altogether its traditional 'soviet power' rhetoric and had begun to think in terms of a specifically *British* road to socialism. The change in thinking—though not yet coherently formulated (Chester, 1979)—had gone far enough to give a new and higher priority to the Party's electoral work. Of course, the proximate cause of this new emphasis was the Party's performance in the elections of 1945.

In the general election the Party re-elected W. Gallacher to West Fife and won Mile End for P. Paratin. Although the CP's aggregate vote represented only 0.4 per cent of the turn-out, in the areas it contested its 102,780 supporters amounted to 31 per cent of the Labour vote. Its performance in the municipal elections was even more impressive: by April 1946 the Party had elected 215 councillors (CPGB Executive Committee, 1946). So, having begun this cycle of elections with one MP and eighty-one councillors, the CPGB began to think of itself as an electoral force, having succeeded with about 25 per cent of its 840 local candidates. Of these, 352 had stood for the parish councils—an arena not yet systematically contested by the major parties—and ninety-five were elected. In Wales twenty-one CP councillors were returned with an aggregate vote of 76,266 as against 118,698 Labour votes in the same wards. Generally, the Party's biggest advances were made in the rural areas and of these the East Anglia District proved the most rewarding with twenty-eight Communist councillors. Otherwise the Communist performance can be seen as indicated in Table 7.2.

The Party's urban performance was less impressive. In the borough council elections of November 1945, Labour took 1,250 seats from the Tories. In London CP candidates averaged 27.5 per cent of the poll and over 50 per cent in some wards. This is more signficant when it is remembered that the turn-out in these elections was about 50 and 60 per cent, that is, high by present standards. Communist representation was highest in Stepney and Westminster where the Party returned nine and three councillors respectively.

In the county council elections of spring 1946, the CP fielded eighty-six candidates, electing two in London, one each for East Anglia, the Midlands and the North East Coast and three in Wales. The twenty Communist candidates in Wales secured 57 per cent of the Labour vote in the areas they contested, that is 22,257 as against 39,155. In all types of council election the CPGB performance was best in the cycle completed by the spring of 1946, but it will perhaps set this performance in some kind of context to note that at

Table 7.1 Communist Party performance in local elections since 1945

Year	No. of candidates	Total votes	% of Labour vote	% total vote	No. of councillors
1945	356 of whom:				42
	133 London	95,199	47	27	18
	14 Wales	11,249	40	18	2
1946	86 (county)	50,676	48		
Total 1945–6	820	500,000			206
1948	40 (Urban and rural District)				
1951	220	37,433			
1952	165 (May)	50,543			16
	15 (April)	10,859			
1953	151	35,577			
1954	189	40,846			
1955	330	80,000			17
1955	17 (LCC)	11,473	10	6	0

Year		Votes	%	Elected
1956	321 of whom:	58,500		10
	6 Rhondda	3,885	37	4
1957	109	23,102		21 (11 Scot, 6 Wales)
1958	245	72,000		4
1960	238	45,000		1 (Glamorgan)
1961	27 (county)	16,066		28
	420	100,000		7
1962	489	90,000		0
1964	36 (LCC)	92,000		22
	570	100,000		28
1967	520 of whom:	101,000		
	6 Rhondda	4,884	25 Rhondda	
	6 Clydebank	4,725	75	10
1968	615	103,929		5
1969	368	56,547		20 Scotland
1973	306	75,000		4
1977	273	52,000		2 (Fife, Cowdenbeath)
1982	147 (i.e. 5% of (the contests)	16,495	2.7 UK / 4.1 Scotland	

Table 7.2 Communist Party performance in local government, 1945–46

	Communist vote	% of Labour vote
General election	102,780	31
Borough councils (Nov. 1945)	227,597	47
County councils	64,850	45
Urban district, rural district parish council	133,538	45

Source: *World News*, 27 April 1946.

this time there were sixty-two administrative counties, 309 non-county boroughs, eighty-three county boroughs, 572 urban districts, 475 rural districts, 7,000 parish councils and, in Scotland, thirty-three county councils, 196 burghs and 201 districts: tens of thousands of seats were involved of which the CP held 215. It is also relevant to observe that the Party's unprecedented successes took place at a time when ballot papers for local elections did not stipulate the candidate's Party affiliation. Moreover, seven years had elapsed since the last local elections, thus producing an unusually high backlog of contests. None of the major parties was particularly well organized in local politics anyway, so that a great number of contests were not fought by the dominant organizations. In the rural areas in particular it was possible for CP candidates to stand unopposed.

The CPGB campaigns in local elections were not based on any special characterization of this field of activity. Of course, it was recognized that the municipalities were centres of growing powers of expenditure. But beyond this there was no Communist variant of 'community politics' or 'municipal socialism' other than the practical work conscientiously carried out by the best of the Communist councillors. Communist literature merely argued that with Communist councils there would be more houses constructed, more health centres, schools and hospitals. Apart from the demands for a 2 per cent interest ceiling on past housing loans and a local income tax to replace the rates, the CPGB apparently felt able to compete with the Labour Party within the latter's conceptual framework. In other words, the Communists, like the Labour Party, regarded local authorities as providers of services and regarded Communist councillors as militant champions of greater provision. So if the CP had a distinctive local profile it was merely a question of a more militant economic style than that of its rivals, though this did not prevent it from spreading propaganda that tried to link the allegedly poor Labour performance in the area of public expenditure with its support for the Marshall Aid programme.

Despite the CPGB's growing alarm at what it perceived as an increasingly pro-American, anti-Soviet foreign policy, its political positions in the immediate post-war years were still informed by the spirit of 'national unity' pursued by the Party since 1941. The Party's response to the economic crisis can be seen from its attempt to take credit for the Sunday work which Rhondda miners initiated as an emergency measure during the first years of austerity under Labour. The lesson was clear: 'The sense of responsibility shown by the Communists during this crisis proves that they serve the people and the country and that they will show equal responsibility to the community when elected to local Councils.' (*World News*, 22 March 1947, p. 112). None of this, however, prevented the decimation of the Party's councillors during the municipal elections of 1947 and 1948. These results were sufficiently bad to prevent the Executive Committee reports to the 20th and 21st Congresses from mentioning any figures, though the Tory successes were said to represent 'a grave crisis to the whole movement'. The continued deterioration of the CP's local government performance was signalled by the decision to drop the Local Government Sub-committee of the Party's Executive in 1948. Its work was supposedly transferred to the Organization Department, but this could not disguise the actual demotion of local politics as a party objective which followed its municipal defeats in the elections of May 1949 when it fielded a record number of candidates.

Thereafter the number of Communist candidates fell from its peak numbers in the years 1945-9. While the Communist vote increased in parts of Lancashire, Yorkshire and London, a decline was registered in the North East, Teesside and the East Midlands and 'a serious decline in votes in Glasgow and the Rhondda was recorded' in the local elections of May 1951. The following year the Party only contested 165 wards and divisions for the borough and district councils and a mere fifteen in the April county elections. Only sixteen Communists were elected, yet this was an increase of three on the previous record. The best CP results were in Clydebank where A. Henderson retained his seat with a 582 majority over Labour, and in Leiston where Paxton Chadwick scored 497. In Cwmbran, W. Waters topped a list of twenty candidates with 2,209 votes and the Party won its first seat on Wrexham rural district council. Overall, the fifteen prospective county councillors received a total of 10,859 votes, while the 165 Communists who contested in May gained 50,543. But this poor showing was still an improvement on the Party's performance in the general election of 1951 when 220 party candidates totalled a mere 37,433 votes.

In the spring of 1953, despite further gains for Labour, the CPGB lost its six seats in Stepney and one in Hackney and by comparison with 1952 the trend for Communist voting was down. The best results for the Party were in the Darranlan ward of Mountain Ash (South Wales) where J. Lewis increased his majority over Labour by 400 and in traditional bastions of Communist support such as Clydebank and Greenock. But the fact that even the Red strongholds were on the wane was illustrated by the rout in Stepney and by the results from the Rhondda where six CP candidates amassed 3,048 votes but registered only one success (*World News*, 9 June 1951, and 16 May 1953).

The demise of the Little Moscows may well be attributable to a combination of relatively full employment, the effects of the Cold War and industrial diversification (as Stuart MacIntyre has argued, 1975 and 1980). Such factors were of course especially evident in the 1950s, yet it is noteworthy that as late as the elections of 1956 the CP did particularly well in Stepney, where it recaptured four of the lost seats, and Whitburn in Scotland where it won two. On the Rhondda, six party candidates obtained 37 per cent of the Labour vote in the areas fought for but only Annie Powell was elected. Other gains were also in the old strongholds: two on Cowdenbeath town council and one on Fife county council. Communist councillors were also returned on Clydebank, Aberdare and Greenock. While the Party's results in the big cities were generally (and typically) bad, above-average performances were recorded in five wards of St. Pancras, five in Islington and four in Wandsworth. In all, 321 Communist candidates contested 280 wards with an aggregate vote of 58,500.

In the spring of 1957 the CP vote generally fell and it is significant that in the wake of the invasion of Hungary by Soviet troops the Party even lost Annie Powell's seat on Rhondda council as well as its positions in Greenock, Clydebank and Whitburn. Though the election was a good one for Labour, which gained 328 seats, this usually beneficient trend did not work for the CP on this occasion. Only five old faithfuls—Cowdenbeath, Cleveden, Aberdare, Leiston and Trowbridge—survived the traumas inflicted on the Party in the previous year. In all, 109 Communist candidates mustered a mere 23,102 votes—the first time ever that the party vote was less than the party membership (*World News*, 25 May 1957).

Ironically the Party had been committed since 1951 to the 'British Road to Socialism'—a programme that envisaged a democratic and parliamentary route to power. Thus, at a time when party membership had fallen to 35,124 (from 60,000 in 1945), the CPGB formally announced its conviction that it could play a leading role in the construction of a 'broad anti-monopoly' alliance. Though the extension of democracy was held to be a central part of this strategy, this did not stop the CP from enforcing rigid Stalinist internal norms to silence dissident members aroused by the revelations about Stalin and the Kremlin's crushing of the Hungarian Revolution. As many as 10,000 members were lost in 1956-7 because of these upheavals.

Beyond vague reference to the decentralization of the machinery of government, the party programme had little to say about local government. There is some evidence, however, that in the late 1950s that CP began to think seriously about the implications of its strategy. Even *The Economist*, for example, recognized the thoughtful and considered nature of the Party's contribution to the inquiry on the reorganization of London local government. But paradoxically as the CPGB gave more thought to such issues its actual standing in local politics continued to decline.

In 1958 it marginally improved on its 1955 figures (the last relevant round) by taking Communist representation from fifteen to twenty-one councillors. In all, 245 Communists had stood—fifty of them miners (of whom eight were successful)—collecting 72,000 votes. Eleven of the elected were in Scotland, six in Wales, with others in Thorne (Yorkshire), Sevenoaks (Kent), Chesterfield and Houghton-le-Spring (Durham). By 1962—despite fielding 489 candidates, the largest number for years—only seven were successful, among them the old faithfuls of Stepney (three), Rhondda and Trowbridge. The Party fought the new GLC elections in 1964 in every one of the authority's thirty-two boroughs on a platform which emphasized houses and comprehensive education. None was elected and the 92,000 votes obtained averaged 2,840 in the inner London boroughs and 2,900 in outer London. It is noteworthy that only five of the CP candidates were women even though women held 20 per cent of GLC seats at this time. Party candidates were still overwhelmingly male manual workers (*Comment*, 4 April 1964).

Party councillors by now were more often than not old campaigners with a record of consistent community work in Welsh and Scottish areas with a long history of Communist support. Annie Powell, for example, was first elected to the Rhondda Borough Council in 1955 after thirteen previous attempts; in 1980 she completed her term of office as mayor of Rhondda. Likewise, the long history of Communist representation in Leiston (Suffolk) enabled men like Paxton Chadwick to make an enduring mark on local politics (in recognition of his services to the town an estate built for retired people is named after him) and to enable the Communist tradition to stretch into the 1980s there. Today its two Communist councillors are products of nearby Somerville School. Elsewhere in England Communist councillors only make fleeting appearances and then only after many previous attempts. Henry Suss fought Swinton and Pendlebury ten times before his election in

1964. Yet in these elections the Party elected only twenty-four of its members from a field of 900 candidates (who shared 250,000 votes) in a context of leftward swing just prior to the general election. By now the breakdown of CP representation was as follows (*Comment*, 23 May 1964):

2 county councillors	5 rural district
4 borough councillors	3 scottish burgh
5 urban district	5 scottish county

The Party was obviously increasing its efforts in local politics and reaping diminishing returns. In January 1966 it set up an electoral department and nominated 398 candidates to fight the spring elections: only three were successful and the aggregate vote dropped to 61,000. Later that year Norman le Brocq was elected for the CP in the Jersey States elections and in 1967 all county and borough elections and most district and parish contests saw a field of 590 Communists result in twenty-eight successes. All told, the Party then had thirty-seven seats (CPGB Executive Committee, 1967).

By the early 1970s the number of CP councillors in England had shrunk to four and these were confined to parishes. In Scotland the party had about thirty seats—nine of them in Central Fife—and a further six could be found in Wales. In 1976 a local-government bill that had originated with the Wheatley Commission introduced community councils throughout Scotland. In Glasgow alone ninety-seven were set up of varying sizes (the largest, at Drumchapel, covered 34,000 people). For a time this gave a much-needed stimulus to CP local politics. In the first elections to the new bodies over eighty Communists served in Glasgow alone. However, the Party made little of its opportunities, failing even to coordinate the work of its representatives. After the first year this potential field of community action fell into decline as did the numbers of Communist community councillors (*Comment*, 7 February 1981). By 1980 the CPGB lost in every area of Glasgow it contested in the district elections and only five of its thirty-one candidates there achieved treble figures.

As the CP entered the 1980s it could reckon its council representation on one hand, with seats on Fife borough council, Rhondda borough council, Leiston district council, Gwent county council (lost in 1981) and in Cowdenbeath. Of its 149 candidates in 1982 only twenty-five were women and three black—figures that illustrate the inertia which apparently prevents it from beating its rivals for the 'progressive' image (in the same elections 25 per cent of Labour's candidates in London were women and 6 per cent black). Significantly its best result in England was achieved by Vishnu Sharma in Southall who obtained 17 per cent of the poll with 668 votes. Throughout the 1970s,

CP performances in local politics were already so bad that the Party was regularly beaten by even smaller organizations of the political fringe. In 1978, for example, the Fascist National Front did better than the Communists in twenty-six out of twenty-nine contests in which they were both involved. Likewise, the Trotskyist 'Socialist Unity' candidates surpassed the CP in five out of seven contests, while the newly emerged ecology movement eclipsed the CP in three out of five. So in a period when it has had to contend with a growing list of left-wing rivals such as Socialist Unity, the Militant Tendency candidates of the Labour Party, the Workers' Revolutionary Party, etc., the CPs' local vote has fallen to around 2 per cent of the English poll in the wards it contests and 4 per cent of the Scottish vote. Although the Party has come to regard this work as a very important part of its activity and, by comparison with its 1945 perspectives, has a far more sophisticated understanding of the local political scene's potential, the initiative lies elsewhere and revivals of 'municipal socialism' will take place without its involvement. The evidence afforded by the successes of Militant in Liverpool and elsewhere suggests that there is scope for the far Left in local politics but only under certain conditions. The first of these seems to be a close association with the Labour Party, organizationally and ideologically.[1] The second is patient and systematic local political work. By its very nature the CP is excluded from the first of these conditions and, except in the traditional strongholds, was unable to fulfil the second because of the notorious zigzags of its Moscow-directed policy. That is why the CP today starts from square one in local politics in spite of sixty-five years' existence.

Note

1. I have argued elsewhere (Callaghan, 1984) that Militant's relative success owes a great deal to its ideological borrowings from the Labour Party and the low profile it gives to specifically Marxist, Leninist or Trotskyist ideas.

Bibliography

Callaghan, J. T., 1984. *British Trotskyism: Theory and Practice*. Oxford, Blackwell.
Chester, A., 1979. 'Communist Strategy from the 1940s to the 1970s', *Marxism Today*, September.
Comment, 4 April 1964; 23 May 1964; 7 February 1981.
CPBG Executive Committee, 1946. Report to the 19th Congress.

—— 1967. Report to the 30th Congress, August 1965–July 1967.

MacIntyre, S., 1975. 'Red Strongholds Between the Wars', *Marxism Today*, March.

—— 1980. *Little Moscows*. Cambridge, Cambridge University Press.

World News, 27 April 1946; 22 March 1947, p. 112; 9 June 1951; 16 May 1953; 25 May 1957.

8 Communist Mayors in Greece

D. G. Kousoulas

The involvement of Greek Communists in the country's politics on a sub-national level is a novel subject even among Greek political scientists. In order that an English-speaking reader can follow the complexities of Greece's political system and the Communists' role in it, it seems appropriate first of all to sketch the structure of the local administration in Greece.

The Republic of Greece is divided administratively into fifty-two *nomoi* (prefectures); within these there are 264 *demoi* (municipalities) and 5,774 *koinotites* (communities) (see Table 8.1). The highest official in each *nomos* is the nomarch who is appointed by the Minister of the Interior. The nomarch oversees the work of the various governmental services (ministries, agencies, etc.) which have branches within the *nomos*. Currently, each *nomos* has a council elected by the *nomos* voters. This council has limited functions, mostly of an advisory nature. The nomarch may be dimissed or transferred to another *nomos* by the Minister of the Interior. By contrast, the members of the council can be replaced only by the *nomos* voters at election time.

Table 8.1 Administrative divisions in Greece

	Prefectures (*nomoi*)	Municipalities (*demoi*)	Communities (*koinotites*)
Athens metropolitan region	1	41	16
Sterea Ellas and Evia (Central Gr.)	7	49	880
Peloponesus	7	34	1,321
Ionian Islands	4	6	273
Epirus	4	12	556
Thessaly	4	18	518
Macedonia	13	50	1,117
Thrace	3	8	151
Aegean Islands	5	35	373
Crete	4	11	560

The larger urban centres within a *nomos* (cities and towns) are designated as *demoi* (municipalities). The municipality is governed by a mayor elected for a four-year term by the voters residing in the municipality. Day-to-day decisions are under the authority of the mayor. Long-term decisions involving major projects or significant monetary outlays require the approval of the city council, which is elected by the city voters at the same time as the mayor. The election of the council members is based on a proportional system, which usually results in a majority closely connected with the mayor. The electoral system, however, allows the presence of minorities on the council.

Villages in Greece are organized in the form of *koinotites* (communities), with a village president and a village council elected by the voters of the village. The present government has increased the authority of the village president and the council so that small projects of concern to the village (roads, water supply, etc.) can be decided by the village officials and financed with funds provided by the central government through the nomarch. Such decisions, however, seldom fall outside the jurisdiction of the nomarch who is the conduit of the state funds and who can block the implementation of a decision if, in his view, it happens to conflict with state policies or with the broader interests of the *nomos*.

The past record

The Communist Party of Greece (Kommunistikon Komma Ellados—KKE) evolved from the Socialist Workers' Party of Greece, founded in November 1918 by a small group of leftist intellectuals. The Party has had a rather chequered history, dominated by factionalism and internal struggles almost from its foundation. In the inter-war period the KKE's membership and influence grew rapidly during the years of depression. In the November 1926 parliamentary elections, ten KKE candidates were elected and by 1935 the number of KKE members had increased to fifteen. The Party was banned in August 1936 and remained illegal under the Metaxas dictatorship. During the Second World War the KKE organized a strong resistance movement and after the Nazi retreat it unsuccessfully attempted to seize power by force in December 1944. It was outlawed in December 1947 but conducted a guerrilla campaign which was crushed in August 1949. During the next two decades, from 1951, it operated through a front organization, the United Democratic Left (EDA). This substitute organization had only minor success in the municipal elections conducted in those years. EDA commanded a following of only 10 per cent nation-wide, while coalitions with other parties were uncommon. The union was banned after the imposition of the military dictatorship in April 1967.

During the colonels' rule (when, of course, no elections were held), the KKE split into two factions: KKE (Exterior), organized by activists residing outside Greece in Eastern Europe and the Soviet Union, and KKE (Interior), organized by some of those who remained in the country. After the collapse of the dictatorship in July 1974 and the return to democratic rule the two factions have remained separate organizations with distinct policies and structures. The KKE (Exterior), which has policies in line with the CPSU and which enjoys the support of the ruling Communist parties is now referred to by its original name without any additives. In contrast, the KKE (Interior), which follows a more moderate, Eurocommunist line, is not accorded any legitimacy by the Soviet Union or the other East European Communist parties with the exception of that in Romania. In the parliamentary elections of 1974, 1977, 1981 and 1984, the KKE (Exterior) has not shown any dramatic increase in its following, which ranges between 10 and 12 per cent.

The Communists and Sub-national Politics

The last municipal election in Greece was held on 17 October 1982 and the next is scheduled for October 1986. There is no reason to expect that the number of municipalities having Communist mayors will then change substantially, although the Communist Party (KKE) suffered some losses in the parliamentary election of 2 June 1985 (for details see Chapter 1 in this volume).

The success of Communist mayoral candidates is owed in part to the electoral system, in part to the concentration of pro-Communist voters in certain areas (primarily working districts around Athens), and in part to the careful selection of attractive candidates.

Under the present electoral system only the candidate who receives over 50 per cent of the total vote within the municipal electoral district is elected during the first round. If no candidate receives such a clear majority the election is repeated a week later. The two candidates with the largest percentages of votes participate and whoever receives over 50% is elected. By contrast, the members of the municipal councils are elected on a modified proportional system which allows the representation of most major groupings on the council.

The electoral system favours the election of Communist candidates, especially during the second round. The reason is simple. The two major left-wing parties, the Panhellenic Socialist Movement (PASOK) and the

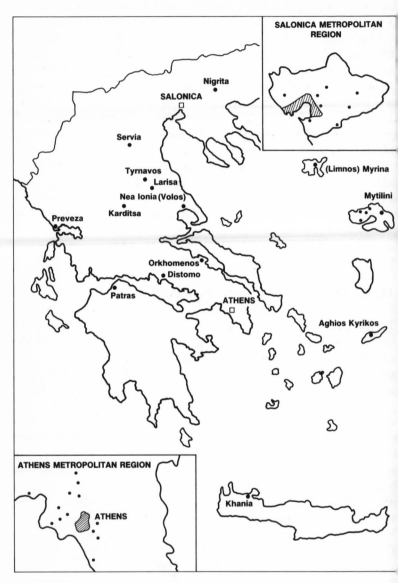

Map 8.1 Communist mayors in Greek municipalities

Communist Party, in several municipalities offer common tickets; in others they 'swap' support for mayoral candidates, each withdrawing its candidate in the municipality where the candidate of the other has shown relatively greater strength during the first round. As a result, candidates supported by the conservative New Democracy Party (ND) may receive a plurality during the first round while both PASOK and KKE candidates may be in the minority. During the second round, the ND candidate may lose to the combined strength of the two leftist parties.

In the 1982 municipal elections, candidates supported by ND received over 50 per cent in thirty-four municipalities. They had a plurality in another thirty-eight. However, during the second round of the thirty-eight munici-pality elections, only fifteen elected ND candidates. The rest went to either PASOK or KKE, or to candidates supported by both, as the voters of these two parties pooled their votes to elect a candidate representing the left. In the end, PASOK elected mayors in 167 municipalities, KKE in thirty-eight, and ND in forty-nine. Ten were won by independents, while three went to the KKE (Interior) (the Eurocommunist Party), and four to EDA (a leftist party which in the two decades 1950 and 1960 stood for the outlawed KKE).

To illustrate the effects of the electoral system, we may use the case of Salonica, Greece's second-largest city. During the first round, the ND candidate received 40.84 per cent, the PASOK candidate 34.09 per cent, the KKE candiate 23.59 per cent and one independent 1.49 per cent. During the second round, however, the PASOK candidate was elected with a very sub-stantial majority since he received the support of most of those voters who in the first round had voted for the KKE candidate.

No less important is the fact that in the first round of the 1982 municipal election, PASOK candidates supported by KKE were elected mayors in sixty-six municipalities, with majorities ranging from 53 to 54 per cent (much higher than the 48.06 per cent PASOK had received in the 18 October 1981 parliamentary election), and in four cases as high as 76 per cent. In those municipalities KKE had not run separate candidates for mayor. Only twenty-three PASOK candidates were elected in the first round without Communist support. The effect of the Communist Party on the outcome of the municipal elections in Greece is thus quite obvious.

Table 8.2 Municipalities with KKE mayors*

	Percentage of KKE Vote†	Population
Athens metropolitan region		
Keratsini (1st round)	53.70	74,179
Kesariani (1st round)	52.06	28,972
Nikaia (1st round)	74.58	90,368
Petroupolis (1st round)	50.69	27,902
Kamatero (1st round)	53.12	15,593
Vyronas (KKE vs. PASOK, 2nd r.)	60.30	57,880
Nea Ionia (KKE vs. PASOK, 2nd r.)	50.15	59,204
Nea Philadelphia (KKE vs. PASOK)	56.06	25,320
Kifisia (1st round)	53.02	31,876
Glyfada (KKE vs. PASOK)	61.12	44,018
Korydalos (KKE vs. PASOK, 2nd r.)	50.06	61,313
Ano Liosia	50.70	16,862
Ilioupolis (KKE vs. PASOK, 2nd r.)	53.55	69,560
Salonica metropolitan region		
Ambelokipoi	61.15	40,033
Sykies	62.11	33,789
Triandria	58.13	10,637
Pylaia	54.6	12,015
Menemeni	59.0	12,141
Neapolis	57.88	31,464
Stavroupolis	66.78	32,225
Evosmos	57.32	26,528
Nomos Khanion		
Khania (capital) (KKE vs. PASOK, 2nd r.)	55.31	47,338
Nomos Prevezis		
Preveza (cap.) (KKE vs. PASOK, 2nd r.)	52.75	13,624
Nomos Larisis		
Larisa (cap.) (KKE vs. PASOK, 2nd r.)	54.89	102,426
Tyrnavos (1st round)	54.48	11,118
Nomos Akhaias		
Patras (cap.) (KKE vs. PASOK, 2nd r.)	52.28	142,163
Nomos Lesvou		
Mytilini (cap.) (KKE vs. PASOK, 2nd r.)	54.70	24,991

Eresos (1st round)	55.61	1,494
Mithymna (1st round)	67.40	1,427
Ayiasos (1st round)	52.30	3,427
Nomos Fthiotidos		
Orkhomenos (KKE vs. PASOK, 2nd r.)	65.38	5,369
Nomos Magnisias		
N. Ionia Volou (not reported)		24,433
Nomos Kozanis		
Servia (1st round)	56.39	3,934
Nomos Karditsis		
Karditsa (cap.) (KKE vs. PASOK, 2nd r.)	51.21	27,532
Nomos Viotias		
Distomo (not reported)		5,604
Nomos Serron		
Nigrita	54.23	6,531
Island of Lemnos, Myrina (not reported)		3,744
Nomos Attikis		
Elevsis (KKE vs. PASOK, 2nd r.)	54.20	20,320

* In several other cases, the KKE supported PASOK candidates or joint candidates with PASOK. Because of the electoral system, which requires an absolute majority for the election of a mayor, a second round is necessary in most municipalities. In the second round, held on the following Sunday, the two candidates who have received the largest number of votes in the first round compete and whoever receives over 50 per cent is elected. Both in the 1978 and 1982 municipal elections, PASOK and KKE (and KKE (Interior)) supported the leftist candidate who was in the running during the second round. This resulted in a significant increase in the number of municipalities controlled by either PASOK or KKE. In several municipalities a KKE and a PASOK candidate competed during the second round. It is difficult to identify precisely the number of municipalities having KKE mayors because a large number of candidates received the endorsement of KKE, PASOK and KKE (Interior) jointly. In one Communist publication no less than fifty-three municipalities were identified as having elected mayors supported by KKE' (*Rizos tis Devteras*, 19 October 1982). In the municipalities listed above, the KKE affiliation of the candidates was more clearly identifiable.

† The percentages received by the Communist candidates in no way reflect the actual following of the Communist party which has ranged in the parliamentary elections since 1974 between 10 and 12 per cent. During the second round, whenever KKE was competing with PASOK, the voter abstention was very high, often over 40 per cent.

The Financing of Municipalities

In Greece the municipal authorities depend heavily on the national budget. Subsidies from the national treasury are given to each municipality at the ratio of approximately 3,000 drachmas (approximately $US20 at the current exchange rate) per capita annually. However, since these funds are distributed through the nomarchs who are government-appointed, the distribution is occasionally slanted in favour of municipalities having mayors with political ties to the governing party (PASOK) or to the KKE, depending on its relations with PASOK at any given moment. Moreover, certain large municipalities such as Athens enjoy services which are paid for directly by the central government. This leaves a higher portion of the state subsidy for other purposes.

A second source of income for municipalities is the payment by residents for services rendered by municipal agencies. Residents pay proportionate charges for the use of fresh water, the collection of garbage, the maintenance of the sewage system, the maintenance of cemeteries, and similar services. For the most part, the municipalities establish the respective charges on the basis of actual cost.

The third major source is the income a municipality obtains from the operation of municipal enterprises. Some municipalities operate a city bus system, others bottle and market drinking water (or mineral water) from natural springs within their jursidiction. Other municipalities operate annual 'bazaars', the income actually coming from the rental of space to local or visiting merchants. Others have wine festivals, municipal theatres, or eating establishments and refreshment stands within municipal parks. Several municipalities maintain public parking areas.

Finally, through a special law, municipalities are authorized to levy a special tax on vacant sites.

What the Municipalities Can and Cannot Do

Greek cities in 1986 are cluttered with automobiles parked wherever their drivers find an empty space, even on pavements. The municipalities have no police of their own to enforce parking regulations. In fact, their ability to enforce any orders regulating traffic, curtailing noise level, limiting the covering of walls with posters, or preventing the littering of streets, is almost non-existent. They have to rely on the local branch of the state police, which is under the jurisdiction of the nomarch. The mayor has no authority to press the state police for action.

The law clearly provides that all decisions of the municipal councils must be sent for review and ratification to the nomarch who may also modify a decision. Municipal employees are prohibited by law from implementing any decision that has been rejected by the nomarch.

Exerting Influence

In spite of their limited jurisdiction, the mayors are free to decide on a number of issues that have a direct impact on the lives of local residents. One such area is patronage. The mayors have a great deal of leeway in the manner in which they actually spend the state subsidy. The hiring of workers or the selection of contractors or suppliers can be determined by political criteria. In this regard, a Communist mayor may use his authority to reward electoral supporters, attract new followers, or discriminate (subtly) against opponents.

No special study has been made to evaluate the extent of politically motivated patronage by mayors. However, we may safely assume that within certain limits mayors use patronage for political purposes and that the use of patronage by Communist mayors is used to expand Communist influence in a municipality. However, we must also note that areas that have elected Communist mayors with substantial majorities, especially in the first round, traditionally have Marxist majorities for historical or other reasons not directly related to the activities of the Communist mayor. On balance, the patronage activities used politically by a Communist mayor tend to reinforce and perpetuate the pro-Communist orientation of the voters.

Another area that is open to a Communist mayor is the organization of cultural activities. Marxist-orientated cultural festivals, plays, lectures, the celebration of anniversaries, marches for peace and the like, can be promoted and even financed by the municipal budget. Due to budget limitations, however, the mayor's support may consist merely of permission for the use of municipal space (squares, parks, cultural centres) by leftist groups organizing such politically-motivated cultural activities.

The ability of a mayor to use funds for patronage or to give permission for leftist activities on municipal space may be curtailed to some extent by the opposition members within the municipal council. As mentioned earlier, the election of the council members is based on a proportional system; therefore, in most cases the councils contain members from other parties. However, the opposition members, being in the minority, cannot prevent a decision supported by the mayor and the majority in the council. The most they can do is play the role of watchdog and publicize any serious offences.

The most important implications of there being Communist mayors within a municipal setting is the aura of political legitimacy their presence imparts to the Communist Party. Communist mayors are 'living proof' that KKE is a national party fully integrated into the national family.

Bibliography

Epikentra, November 1982, Centre for Political Research.
The Greek Municipal Code.
Interviews with mayors and members of municipal councils.

9 The Japanese Communist Party in Local Government*

Richard Boyd

Any discussion of the role of political parties in the local government of Japan must recognize at the outset that local government in Japan is now, and has been since 1947, the all but perfect monopoly of independent notables, men who owe allegiance to no political party and who do not depend on a party machine to secure, maintain and discharge the positions and responsibilities of local government.

With this firmly in mind, it can be noted that when and if a local politician decides to join a political party, perhaps because of ambitions for higher office or because of an invitation from a party, or a faction within a party that is seeking to expand its links at the periphery, his first port of call will be the ruling Liberal Democratic Party (LDP). He goes there in pursuit of access to the goods and services dispensed by the administration—access which is the pivot of his brokerage role (his constituents preferring not to deal directly with the bureaucracy) and both an element in and a consequence of his notability (the administration preferring to deal with known and trustworthy men rather than with unknown and impersonal clients). A detailed awareness of rank order that guides his quest for status, and hence for a reinforced notability, serves only to sharpen his sense of direction.

The LDP is the natural home of the local notable turned councillor: there ideology is implicit, understood but not articulated; goals may well be fixed and rigid but the means to their attainment is not; hence an image of pragmatism and flexibility, of a politically neutral, efficient government by men of good character who know 'the problems', which mirror core elements in the local rhetoric of apoliticism. There is, too, an organizational as well as an ideological fit between the LDP and local notables: in both worlds there is a preference for particularism, for reliance on informal, carefully nurtured personal ties over universal, formalistic, impersonal and instrumental modes of organization and ways of doing things.

There is no such obvious cohesion between the organization and the ideology of the Japanese Communist Party (JCP) and the world of the local

* The research upon which this article is based was financed in part by the School of Oriental and African Studies, University of London, and by the Japan Foundation Endowment Committee.

notable. Indeed, the opposite seems to be the case. The JCP is a mass party, organized on precisely articulated principles of democratic centralism, and congenitally unsympathetic to particularism. It suffers by association with a clearly defined and well-publicized ideology—bad enough in itself at the local level—but still worse, it is burdened with a history and reputation of, and continuing ideological commitment to, 'conflict', and the transformation of those social conditions to which the local councillor owes his notability, and hence his office.

Notwithstanding these considerable disadvantages, the Party has claimed a representation in the local councils second only to the LDP amongst the six major political parties, and despite recent reverses continues to be well represented. In the most recent nation-wide local elections in 1983, the LDP won 3,896 of the 38,776 seats contested, the Socialists 2,316 seats, the Clean Government Party, 2,248 seats, the Democratic Socialists 699, the New Liberal Club seventy-nine, while the JCP won 2,023 seats. The ubiquitous independents secured no less than 27,492 seats.

The institutional context of these elections is defined by a much-amended Local Autonomy Law, promulgated in May 1947 (Ministry of Home Affairs, 1984, pp. 87–107). This distinguished basic local public entities, the *shi* (cities), *chō* (towns) and *son* (village), which are 'general and pervasive in terms of organization, function and other factors', and intermediary local public entities, namely, the *To* (Tōkyō metropolitan government), *Do* (Hokkaidō Island), *Fu* (Osaka and Kyōto prefectures), and *Ken* (the remaining forty-three prefectures), which perform similar functions, many of them on behalf of central government. An additional local entity is the special ward, which is the basic administrative unit of the Tōkyō metropolitan government. The *shi* is a city of at least 50,000 inhabitants, at least 60 per cent of its total work-force is engaged in urban industrial or commercial activities, and 60 per cent or more of the houses are concentrated in its urban area. *Shi*, with a population in excess of 500,000, acquire a special administrative status as a 'designated city' (Ministry of Home Affairs, 1984, pp. 89–901).

Each of these bodies elects an assembly and a chief executive officer by direct popular vote in accordance with Article 93 of the Japanese constitution. Elections are held every four years and under the present system of 'unified local elections' all local public entities of a certain type hold their elections on the same day.

Communist Participation in Local Government in International Perspective

The Parliamentary Road Versus Armed Struggle

The post-war history of Communist interest in local elections has been highly variable and has been inextricably linked with the post-war history of the international Communist movement. The story opens in October 1945, when the prisons of Imperial Japan disgorged hundreds of half-starved, long-imprisoned Communists intent no doubt on freedom, but at the same time convinced that a number of decisive factors had created a situation whereby the Party and its policies might prove popular: the defeat of the 'fascist' forces; the return of key leaders from Yenan; and the presence of the agency of the American occupation forces whose reforms (adumbrated, it has been suggested, under the influence of the Japanese Communists themselves (William, 1979, pp. 16–17)) were, in their view, to complete the bourgeois revolution begun in 1868. Any consequent success at the polls would create a genuine possibility for the revolutionary transformation of Japan. This analysis was adopted as the official party programme at the 4th National Congress in 1945, and on this basis the Party contested the national elections of 1949. The outcome was a real, if limited, success: 3,000,000 votes were polled (10 per cent of the total) and thirty-five Communists took their seats in the House of Representatives (Scalapino, 1967, pp. 50–52; Pohl, 1976; JCP Central Committee, 1984).

The Communists attributed even less significance to local government and politics at this time than did the other political parties, specifically because the object of the new programme was 'peaceful revolution', not 'mere parliamentarianism', and so the preferred means were the key levers of power, namely, the Diet. As for local government, it was characterized by a degree of central control which in the pre-war period extended to the appointment of local chief executives and, in the post-war period, to a control of local finances, which justifies the use of the expression 'one-third local autonomy' (Steiner, 1965). Indeed, it seems more appropriate to talk of local administration than local self-government (Samuels, 1983). To this general distinction there can be added the absence of an effective organization in the localities (the Party had been driven underground and abroad by the 'Thought Police' (officially, the Special Higher Police) and the military police, and its organization dismantled piecemeal (Beckman & Okubo, 1969; Scalapino, 1967; Swearingen & Langer, 1952) or any pre-existing social foundation, with the inevitable result that the Party made a very poor showing in the first post-war local elections in 1947 (Table 9.1). The cities, towns and villages of Japan were looking for 191,391 councillors: they chose 383 Communists, 0.2 per cent of the total; they also elected 10,441 mayors of whom eleven (0.1 per cent) were Communists. The pattern was repeated at the prefectural level in the same year when four (0.2 per cent) of the 2,490 places in the prefectural assemblies were filled by members of the JCP (Steiner, 1965, pp. 398–9, Zenkoku Senkyokanriiinkai, 1952, pp. 11–13).

Table 9.1 Results of the local government elections, 1947

Political party	Councillors (cities, towns and villages)	Councillors (prefectural)	Mayors
Communists	383 (0.2%)	4 (0.2%)	11 (0.1%)
Democrats	5,551 (2.9%)	604 (24.3%)	405 (3.9%)
Liberals	4,785 (2.5%)	491 (19.7%)	383 (3.7%)
Socialists	5,549 (2.9%)	411 (16.5%)	264 (2.5%)
Independents	173,209 (90.5%)	803 (32.2%)	9,273 (88.8%)
Others	1,914 (1.0%)	177 (7.1%)	105 (1.0%)
Total	191,391 (100%)	2,490 (100%)	10,441 (100%)

Commitment to peaceful revolution was affirmed at the 6th Party Congress in 1947 (Scalapino, 1967, pp. 57–60) and it might have been anticipated that the next elections in 1951 would witness renewed efforts by the JCP to win seats and secure a foothold in local government. This was not to be. On 6 January 1950 the Cominform, at Stalin's instigation, published a withering critique of the JCP programme and castigated the 'peaceful transition to socialism' and 'the naturalization of Marxism–Leninism' as both 'anti-Marxist and anti-socialist'. Any realistic chance of withstanding the icy blast from Moscow disappeared a fortnight later when cold winds began to blow from Peking. The dominant 'mainstream' faction in the Party, authors of the programme and closely associated with the Communist Party of China, capitulated. Nosaka Sanzō, a leader of the 'Mainstream' faction and principal architect of the new road, issued an abject self-criticism which was endorsed by the full Central Committee. The peaceful line went out of the window and with it, necessarily, continued participation in local and national government. Henceforth 'armed struggle' was to be the watchword (Scalapino, 1967, pp. 60–7).

The consequences were immediate, predictable, enduring and cata-strophic: Japan in 1951 bore little resemblance to revolutionary China in 1949; there was no social foundation for armed struggle since revolutionary tensions in the villages had been assuaged by land reform, and much the same could be said of the cities and towns whose workers were the beneficiaries of unprecedented and perhaps unparalleled freedoms. Peasantry and proletariat had a stake in the new order and, thanks to the American-inspired reforms, the prospect of a ready, painless, constitutional redress of grievances. In such a context the new political arrangements were seen as gains to be defended, not obstacles to be overcome. The state had the means and the will to defend itself and the ring was held by the occupation forces, mindful of the recent history of China and in no sense indifferent to the fate of a regime they had been instrumental in creating.

The upshot was the death, imprisonment, exile and pursuit abroad of Communist leaders and their organizations shattered or driven under-ground. The electoral consequences of the new 'New Programme' (less confusingly, the '1951 thesis') were inevitable. At the end of 1951 there were no Communists in the House of Representatives (there had been thirty-five in 1949), there were no mayors (there had been eleven in 1949) and party membership slumped from a peak of 150,000 in 1949 to about 20,000 in 1955. The masses turned their backs on a party that had become a byword for tragic and violent futility. The vote collapsed: from 3,000,000 in 1949 to 897,000 in 1952 (Scalapino, 1967, pp. 86–7; Pohl, 1976, pp. 53–69; Steiner, 1965, pp. 401–2).

For a full ten years the Party was politically and electorally moribund, incapacitated by bitter internal divisions, occasioned in part at least and certainly exacerbated by the intervention in Japanese Communist Party affairs of the Soviet Union and China in 1951. Intra-party factions flourished in the fissures opened by that crisis and guaranteed that conflicts within the international communist world would be articulated within the Party, thereby fuelling factional strife. There could be no revision of the disastrous 1951 thesis' without a prior or parallel resolution of factional competition within the Party, which would in turn draw the JCP further into the hazardous waters of the Sino-Soviet split and ultimately necessitate a settle-ment of accounts by the JCP with the two Communist superpowers.

A full account of these difficult years cannot be given here; suffice it to say that Miyamoto Kenji, a champion of 'Left-wing Adventurism' and chief critic of the Mainstream faction, in 1951 joined and came to dominate the Mainstream faction and championed efforts to return to the parliamentary road. His major success was in decoupling, for a time at least, the domestic international aspects of conflict, so that by the 8th Party Congress in 1961 he had managed to crush or oust factional opposition to the Mainstream group which henceforth dominated the Party, to redefine the Japanese revolution in terms compatible with the winning of elections, and to maintain an international posture of scrupulous neutralism and thereby avoid an open break with either Moscow or Peking (Fukui, 1978; Hakamada, 1978; Iizuka, 1974; Kim, 1976).

If consolidation of the Miyamoto line created the conditions for renewed efforts at the local level, the rapid collapse of the campaign against the United States–Japan Security Treaty (the famous 'Ampō' struggle of 1960–1— Packard, 1966; Scalapino & Masumi, 1971, pp. 125–53) argued the necessity of establishing a strong local foundation to underpin and substantiate mass movements at the national level. In short, participation was once more in order, and an energetic and detailed cultivation of united-front alliances with the Socialists (recent partners in the Ampō struggle) contributed to the capture of twenty-two seats in city and prefectural assemblies and 699 seats in town and village assemblies—almost double the 1959 total of 376 seats.

The JCP's commitment to the new line was subject to serious examination shortly after the 1963 local elections. Despite the efforts of the Party to walk the tightrope of neutralism, espousal of a national solution to the problems of revolution branded the Party as pro-Peking, which in the harsh, confrontational logic of the age meant anti-Soviet. Certainly there was much sympathy for China within the JCP, not least because of the shelter and training afforded there to Japanese Communists in the war years and in the armed struggle period of 1951–3, the continuing financial aid, channelled to the Party through Japan–Chinese trading companies and, less prosaically, because China was Asian and lessons born of the Chinese revolution seemed more relevant.

By 1964 the Soviet Union, its patience exhausted and no longer persuaded that it could woo back the JCP, launched an all-out attack on the Party in general and the new line in particular. But circumstances had changed: it was no longer 1951; the JCP retained the support of the Chinese; within the Party the 'China lobby' built around Miyamoto, Hakamada and Nosaka had a stranglehold on leadership positions, while pro-Soviet elements constituted little more than a fragment of the whole Party; moreover, and this the Chinese themselves were to discover shortly, the Party had tried blind reliance on the leadership of the international Communist movement, it had sampled one alternative to its national, peaceful line and vividly recalled its bitterness. There was no collapse. Pro-Moscow elements were expelled from the Party. Miyamoto announced at the 9th Party Congress in 1964 that an immediate task was the defence and expansion of the democracy won by the Japanese people since the Second World War—an essential means of doing this was an extensive participation of the Communist Party of Japan in local and prefectural assemblies (JCP Central Committee, 1964). To drive home this point, new advances in local elections were noted—votes up by 78 per cent and the number of candidates up from 818 to 1,096, clear evidence of renewed efforts to establish a presence and to develop the party organization in the localities. Indeed, the Miyamoto leadership was predicated on this basis, namely, the reconstruction and orderly development of party organization and finances.

This policy, and so inevitably Miyamoto's position, together with the autonomy of the Japanese Communist Party, was challenged again in the mid-1960s. Mao Zedong, rather than Joseph Stalin, now sought to redefine the task of Japan's Communists in terms of world rather than national revolution. The return to militancy was to be justified by reference to attempts to open fresh fronts against the United States, already heavily committed in Vietnam. The natural reluctance of the Party to exchange one hard master for another was only reinforced by the desperate experience of the Indonesian Communist Party which was not only a close ally of the JCP, but in the view of the altter a victim of the decision of an armchair general to send the revolutionary troops 'over the top'. The Party leadership was further chastened and any lingering doubts about resisting demands from the Soviet Union were removed when Mao Zedong proved refractory to JCP efforts to promote Sino-Soviet cooperation over Vietnam, opposition that was considered explicable only in terms of national calculations of interest (Kojima, 1980).

The Chinese were no more prepared to accept the pursuit of an independent line by the JCP than the Russians had been two years earlier. The national and peaceful strategy favoured by Miyamoto was no longer compatible with the requirements of world revolution as seen from Peking: consequently the strategy must be changed. When the JCP refused to kowtow, the Chinese, like the Russians in 1964, sought to bully the Party into compliance and when that failed an attempt was made to undermine the Party by stopping the flow of funds, discrediting the leadership (Miyamoto was branded as one of China's four arch-enemies), and encouraging intra-party factionalism. When that failed, Peking looked for sympathetic elements outside the JCP that might be promoted as an alternative to the recalcitrant Communists (Pohl, 1976, pp. 219–23; Nihonkyōsantō, 1975).

The Party withstood the challenge: pro-Peking elements were expelled and fraternal ties were ended. The Communist Party of Japan had formally espoused the parliamentary road at its 8th Party Congress in 1961. It stuck to that road despite a formidable challenge from the leaders of the Communist world and at the price of considerable isolation within that world. That commitment has endured to the present and was recently formally renewed in the partly-revised Party Constitution of 1982 (JCP Central Committee Publications Bureau, 1982; Fukai, 1977).

Communists in Local Government: Current Practice

The Representative Role of the Communist Councillor

Survey data (Hayase, 1981; Kansai Daigaku Seiji Keizai Kenkyūjo, 1982, 1984; Chihōjichi Kenkyū Centa, 1982; Itō 1981, Muramatsu & Itō, 1980; Yoda, 1980) confirm that the Communist councillor is the least likely of all councillors to view his task as representing an 'areal' interest. Certainly he recognizes a responsibility—which will be considered in detail later—to his constituency which he, like his peers, construes as 'the locality' or, with little shade of meaning, 'local society', but he is much more sensitive to the interests of his party than his colleagues are to their respective parties. One survey suggests that 40 per cent of Communists see themselves as in the council to represent the Party, a view endorsed by only a fraction of other councillors (7 per cent of Socialist councillors, for example).

This does not mean that the Communist councillor neglects 'local residents'—a favourite expression that comes to the lips of the Communists as readily as any other councillor—far from it. In strict accordance with the imperative of promoting the Party, he is closely involved with the local populace, more so than other councillors. More than 75 per cent of Communist councillors claim to be in daily contact with their constituents, compared with just under 50 per cent of the Socialists and Conservatives and 41 per cent of the Independents. And when they are not talking, they are writing: more Communists more regularly are in correspondence with constituents about local affairs than other councillors (Kuroda, 1984, pp. 48–52).

To facilitate performance of the myriad services required of him, the Communist councillor, like any other, keeps in regular contact with local officials, above all the section heads (*kachō*), division heads (*buchō*), and the chief clerk, and is much more willing than his opposite numbers from other political parties to cultivate *any* member of the local administration. In part, this represents an attempt to compensate for his very limited access to the prefectural governor—typically the poorest of any local party—in part, an attempt to mobilize contacts in sympathetic public employees' unions such as the All-Japan Prefectural and Municipal Workers' Union (*Jichirō*), which is affiliated to the JSP but home to many Communist sympathizers. Much the same explanation accounts for the Communist councillors' assiduous cultivation of prefectural officials.

Interestingly, the Communist is as likely as the Conservative to short-circuit the municipal and prefectural levels of government and address himself directly to the central government. The Conservative does this in confidence of personal connections available at the national level which can be deployed so as to pressure central administration. The Communist is rather more dependent on an integrated party apparatus with high-speed lifts to the top and a detailed knowledge of the formal and informal workings of the government machine. Having learnt what benefits accrue to intermediaries who know the 'texts'—that bewildering weight and variety of instructions, decrees and circulars that structure and inform contemporary administrative practice—the Party insists that Communist councillors instruct themselves in the technical niceties of local-government operations. Critical remarks addressed to that 'minority of Communist councillors . . . who know insufficient about the dispositions of the [local] Assemblies and local government laws, bye-laws and regulations', suggest that there is still some way to go in this matter (Nihon Kyōsantō Chūoinnkai, 1982(B)pp. 115–16).

The effectiveness of the strategy hinges on the existence of an integrated party organization which, extending to the centre, embraces the local councillors through the mechanism of the intra-council party group. In fact, the Central Committee requirement that local councillors constitute party groups is obeyed to the letter. It is common practice, particularly in urban areas, for local assemblymen of all party colours to form intra-council groups (*kaiha*) within which to formulate a position at least on the more important questions. However, the Communist councillors invariably form party groups, there to discuss every and any question due to be debated by the full council (Ito, 1981, p. 113). Where the Communists are an element in a progressive coalition, two groups will be constituted: one composed exclusively of Communists, the second of Communists and their progressive allies. The first group defines positions to be adopted in the second, which defines in turn the position to be defended by the coalition in the council. In this the Communist group is unusual, all other parties being prepared to form council groups with sympathetic independents and even councillors from other parties. Only the JCP insists, at all times, on splendid isolation (Ito, 1981, p. 109).

The Communist 'cell' within the council keeps in close contact with upper levels of the party organization: a minority of JCP councillors (9.1 per cent) report that representations are made to the party hierarchy on all matters before the council, whilst for the majority of Communist councillors (81.8 per cent) it 'depends on the problem'. This can reasonably be taken to mean 'whenever the Party line is not clear or has not been decided', since 96.2 per cent of JCP councillors claim that a clash between their and the Party's opinion is rare or unheard of. If it comes to a choice between the two, the councillor favours the party line (Ito, 1981, p. 111; Kuroda, 1984, pp. 104–6). Like the archetypical Conservative-Independent notable, he is quite commonly the beneficiary of a certain 'political inheritance', a legacy of connections: 20 per cent of JCP councillors have relatives who occupied political positions before the Second World War (as opposed to 24 per cent of all councillors), and 16 per cent of Communist councillors have relatives 'in politics' in the post-war period (the figure for all councillors is 34 per cent). A councillor's father's occupation as a manager in a small- or medium-sized enterprise (32 per cent and 26 per cent for Communists and all councillors respectively) or involvement in agriculture, forestry or fishery (23 per cent and 40 per cent) guarantees a central, conspicuous position in the life of the local community and opportunities for the establishment of further contacts (Kuroda, 1984, pp. 4–36). One survey suggests that nearly 80 per cent of Independents had lived in the area they represent for more than twenty years, a claim made by only 21 per cent of Communist councillors—a similar percentage of whom had lived in the area they represent for *less* than twenty years (Kuroda, 1984, pp. 23–4).

Communist councillors are recruited from a range of occupations: small- and medium-sized enterprises (15 per cent of Communists and 30 per cent of councillors), agriculture, forestry and fishery (12 per cent and 18 per cent), blue-collar (15 per cent and 3 per cent), white-collar (12 per cent and 16 per cent), civil service (15 per cent and 19 per cent), and the professions (27 per cent and 10 per cent). The Party's dependence on the professions is greater than that of any other party, and in the Party's case 'professions' means in practice teachers: the occupational breakdown reveals the Party's dependence on Nikkyōsō, the teachers' union, widely known for its Communist sympathies. 'White-collar workers' will often mean employees from the union headquarters of a private firm, whilst 'civil servants' are often men and women engaged in public corporations such as the railways, post office and electric companies. The higher-than-average educational attainment of the JCP councillor (47 per cent versus 45 per cent of whom have attended university or junior college, Kuroda, 1984, p. 14) is probably explicable in terms of the importance of Nikkyōsō as a source of recruitment.

The Communist councillor is also younger than average: more than half of them (54 per cent versus 35 per cent) are elected to the local assembly before their 40th birthday. In stark contrast, 70 per cent of Conservative councillors and 87 per cent of Independent councillors blossom politically after their 40th birthday (Kuroda, 1984, p. 36), having served lengthy apprenticeships in the myriad organizations that knit together the life of the local community (residents' associations, housewives' associations, sports clubs, and parent-teachers' associations (Kuroda, 1984, p. 26; Jichishogyōseika, 1981, p. 15)).

Councillors who belong to the JCP are the least likely of all to have emerged through this channel and to enjoy continuing access to what is a key resource. Indeed, the Party sees the local organizations as largely an impenetrable barrier, the thicket defences of local conservatism manned by presidents who support the LDP and, abhorring the Communists, do not offer themselves as candidates for that party (Ueda, 1982, pp. 130-2). In so far as Communists do participate in local groups, it is in the newer, arguably more marginal groups, membership of which is not binding on local households and in which there are fewer opportunities for the cultivation of 'notability', the provisions of services and favours and hence the accumulation of obligated supporters—in short, the less important welfare groups concerned with traffic safety and crime prevention (neighbourhood 'watch' groups, if you like).

More than half of the Communist councillors have served in such groups. Consequently, the Party must recruit candidates for office elsewhere. Typically it does this from its own ranks: thus 52 per cent of Communist councillors have held a position in 'a' political party and 45 per cent have occupied posts in a trade union. Interestingly, the JCP is less dependent on recruitment from its own ranks than the Socialists, 71 per cent of whose councillors were once party officials and 60 per cent of whom were trade-union activists. The difference is that the Communists can draw upon a variety of ancillary organizations associated with the Party at local and national levels (Yoda, 1980, p. 92). Candidates recruited from these bodies enjoy the additional advantage of amenability to party guidance and control (Shisō Undō Kenkyūjō, 1981).

Once in office they tend to be professionals who specialize in local politics: nearly 40 per cent of Communist councillors spend 'the greater part of their time on council-related activities'. The contrast with the typical notable whose political life grows out of and is perhaps subordinate to social and occupational involvement is marked: 63.2 per cent of Independents spend no more than a 'trifling' amount of time on council affairs and only 2.1 per cent in one survey claimed to spend most of their time on council business (Muramatsu & Itō, 1980, p. 99).

The Spatial Distribution of Communist Local Government

The relatively poor representation of the primary characteristics of notability by JCP councillors is related to, and in part explicable in terms of, the spatial distribution of Communist strength. Notability is a function of a traditional social cohesion and is then most effective at the most local and rural levels of elections, so much so that nation-wide the Independents control 90.1 per cent of seats in village and small-town assemblies and are the predominant element in small towns and villages, even in the major urban areas such as Tōkyō (where Independent representation is 75 per cent of the total), Osaka (66.3 per cent), and Kyōto (80.5 per cent).

The movement from the village to the prefecture and from the countryside to the towns poses problems of scale that cannot be solved by notability, the effectiveness of which is, in any case, undermined by the socially disruptive consequences of urbanization. At this point reliance is placed less on informal networks of personal influence, although these too are mobilized, and more on a party label, which is all but indispensable in prefectural and city elections, party finances, party publications and a party electoral machine (Flanagan, 1980, pp. 131–84).

The strength of the Communists in local government varies in inverse relation to the importance of notability: accordingly, one survey of selected towns and villages reveals that in rural and isolated areas Communists comprise 8.1 per cent of councillors, while in the urban centres the proportion of Communist councillors goes up to 15.5 per cent. Currently, the JCP holds 776 (3.5 per cent) of the 22,310 village and town assembly seats contested in the elections of 1983. The Party was more successful in the election of 386 city assemblies, winning 926 (7.7 per cent) of the 12,075 seats contested, and most successful in the big cities where Communists won seventy-four (11.1 per cent) of the 665 seats disputed.

There are, of course exceptions, such as the traditional sympathy for Communist Party candidates demonstrated by the inhabitants of parts of rural Nagano and Tōhoku (Totten, 1973).

The Electoral Strategy of the Japanese Communist Party

The Incorporation of the Marginal

In towns and villages the electoral strategy of the Liberal Democrat Party, in so far as it can be said to have one, is simple—no more a matter than the coopting of notables already elected to the local councils, or at best the offer of invitations to run on the LDP ticket to notables who may wish to add this particular guarantee of access to the centre to their proven ability to get things done and thereby reassure their established voters.

This is not the case for the Communists. The sympathies of the local group leaders are overwhelmingly not with them nor concomitantly is the local organized vote. Alternative means are required. In particular, the development of specialized front organizations not only creates a reservoir of potential leadership recruits, but it also enables the JCP to provide a flow of goods and services to voters who are not already organized in interest groups who can provide the goods and services themselves or, at least, access to them. If successful, a candidate recruited from such an organization comes together with a ready-made constituency.

These socially and economically marginal elements include ethnic groups (Koreans), oppressed minorities (Burakumin), day-labourers and other unprotected, non-unionized workers in small- and medium-sized enterprises, shopkeepers, recent urban migrants, and many women. Contact is established in the tenants' association in a block of council flats or in an umbrella organization for supporters of an independent and attractive politician; in a peace march or a demonstration of concerned citizens against pollution, a cultural day for Koreans or a pop concert for the starving in Ethiopia. Once established, contact is assiduously cultivated by whatever means seem appropriate and likely to prove effective. The Association of Democratic Merchants and Industrialists has secured the allegiance of many small businessmen faced with tax problems, trying to get government loans, burdened by debts, and worried about inadequate medical insurance. The Japan Women's Association has specialized in advising women who have fallen into the clutches of loansharks. *Miniren* (All-Japan Federation of Democratic Medical Organizations) has afforded shift-workers and others who work unsociable hours a full medical service, even on holidays and late at night. The Japan Democratic Youth League has involved many lonely and isolated young urban migrants in film-shows, dances, talks and a general group life (Krauss, 1979).

The Party constantly exhorts local activists to make friends, to make friends voters, to make occasional voters regular supporters, to get those supporters to read party publications and so to make readers members of the JCP (Kuwabara, 1984, p. 275). The remarkable growth of party membership since the 8th Party Congress is eloquent testimony to the success of these efforts. A membership of about 80,000 in 1961 passed the 100,000 mark in 1964 and more than tripled by 1966, since which time, although the rate of progress has slowed, the Party could reasonably claim a membership close to 500,000 in 1985.

Organizational Aspects

The Party aims to incorporate otherwise excluded, fragmented and isolated 'unincorporated' elements who are not opposed to, but not included in and by, the groups of mainstream, incorporated social life. The target voter is often not opposed to the 'system' in principle so much as unhappy that the system has failed to include him. The task of the Party is then, it might be argued, not to challenge the system fundamentally, still less to overthrow it, but rather to stamp with approval and legitimize the disaffection of the unincorporated and to afford them alternative means of incorporation and channels for advancement. In short, the JCP is to be the inverted mirror-image of mainstream society.

This has required the Party to adapt to values and organizational styles that characterize local, particularly rural, society, and the JCP has in recent years and with some success created personal support organizations or *kōenkai* expressly for the purpose of mobilizing voters (Curtis, 1971). In many respects the *kōenkai* is the perfect organizational counterpart to local particularism. One commentator says of the *kōenkai*, 'people are drawn into such a group on the basis of areal, family, business, occupational, educational and other particularistic ties with the candidate or with someone close to him' (MacDougall, 1980, p. 67). Support is given, in the first instance, to an individual and not to a party or a programme. In return the supporter enjoys the rosy glow of community involvement and identity with the candidate and his career, and receives from the candidate small tokens such as greeting-cards, cigarette-lighters, tea-towels, etc., which symbolize his concern for and personal relation to the member of the *kōenkai*.

Contacts established with the families, friends and acquaintances of supporters lead to the distribution of relevant pamphlets and journals targeted at students, housewives, farmers and workers. At the minimum this promotes a climate that favours the electoral prospect of the councillor; at best it leads back to further *kōenkai*-sponsored events which include 'getting to know the Party' sessions in which much use is made of video-films, news-reels, posters and suchlike, presenting a youthful, wholesome and concerned image—qualities encapsulated in the person of the master of ceremonies, or local branch representative on the *kōenkai*.

The Conservatives, Socialists and Democratic Socialists have placed great reliance on the *kōenkai* as a means of winning and mobilizing votes for quite some time. In the case of the Communists, organizational and ideological values contributed to an underestimation of, and a reluctance to deal with, *kōenkai*. This changed in the early 1970s when the headlong pursuit of electoral success led to the Party's encouragement of local councillors to set up *kōenkai*. The tactic was successful, perhaps too successful: in the context of rapid party growth, the creation of support associations centred on individual politicians effectively institutionalized centrifugal tendencies that threatened the principle of democratic centralism and, in the general election of 1980, impaired the ability of the JCP to manage its vote—a vital capacity in an electoral system founded on the multi-member constituency and single, non-transferable vote. As a direct consequence, personal *kōenkai* were out-lawed and party *kōenkai* were introduced—a move that both generated widespread resentment and threatens to undermine the main strength and effectiveness of the *kōenkai* formula (JPC Central Committee, 1984, p. 603). Complaints and exhortations that continue to emanate from the Central Committee make it clear that the reformation of the *kōenkai* is far from complete; at the 16th Congress it was announced that 377 towns and villages and forty-five cities and wards were without any type of *kōenkai*, 299 *kōenkai* are only nominally party rather than personal associations and a further forty-seven are not even nominally party associations.

A major bone of contention is the register of *kōenkai* members: an important adjunct to the register of Communist newspaper *Akahata* readers, the register of basic votes and the register of members of democratic front organizations. Nominally, and in respect of the principle of independence, the local *kōenkai* keeps its own register; *kōenkai* based on an administrative area maintain registers of local *kōenkai* officials and, only 'when appropriate', full lists of the membership of each local *kōenkai* within the administrative area. *Kōenkai* organized at the constituency level keep records of officials in both the local and administrative area *kōenkai* in the prefecture, and full records of all members of *kōenkai* that operate within the constituency. The object, of course, is to integrate the *kōenkai* into a support system organized at the *To Do Fu* and *Ken* levels, within which each *kōenkai* and its members can be precisely located, and over which the Party has final control (Fukai, 1977, pp. 161–77).

In addition, the local branch (or where appropriate the district or prefectural committee) has at least one representative on the *kōenkai* committee, and aims to ensure that the General Secretary will be a sympathizer who figures on at least one of the three registers. The effect of these measures is greatly to reduce the independence of the *kōenkai*, and to ensure that the task of politicizing the local community will be pursued with as much vigour as is the task of securing the election and re-election of Communist councillors (Nihonkyōsantō Chuōiinkai, 1982(B), p. 56).

The Electoral Strategy of the JCP

The Democratic Coalition

The *kōenkai* and the democratic front organizations permit the Communists to mobilize and target sufficient votes to exploit the multi-member constituencies and return councillors to the village, town, city and prefectural assemblies. Ground rules are well developed: where the Party is weak it avoids intra-party competition by running only a single candidate in the district; when running more than one candidate, the Party's electoral managers split the district or city among the candidates and have each of them confine their posters, bills and stickers, loud-hailers and sound-trucks to their own patch; even if there is very little prospect of victory, a candidate is run as a means of making contact with any disillusioned Socialist or Conservative voters, to tap the '*je suis contre*' vote and boost party organization.

Problems of scale, combined with a convention of independence at the chief-executive level means, however, that the Party cannot, on this basis, elect mayors and governors unless it makes electoral pacts with other parties. The coalition strategy was highly effective in the mid-1970s when 103 'progressive' mayors were elected, fifty-nine with JCP backing. Striking successes were made: Tōkyō, Ōsaka and Kyōto had 'progressive' governors, and Yokohama, Nagoya, Kōbe, Ōsaka City and Kyōto City had Communist-backed mayors in 1975 when it is said that 41 per cent of all Japanese lived in prefectures or cities with progressive chief executives (MacDougall, 1976, p. 42).

The preferred formulas were a left-wing coalition of Communists and Socialists (thirty-two coalitions) and a united front of three or all four opposition parties (thirteen and eleven coalitions respectively). In so far as local circumstances permitted, coalitions were to conform to a four-point pattern: they were to be presented as a local progressive united front; the front would serve as an umbrella organization under which would assemble large numbers of groups and individuals; the candidate was to be an honest, progressive independent; and the major parties to the coalition would agree an organization framework for the campaign and a package of policies for the post-election period (Krauss, 1980; MacDougall, 1977).

Clearly, participation in such a coalition afforded the Communists a certain local legitimacy, the possibility of publicity for its policies and the sanction of a formal agreement with the Socialist Party, progress towards the long-term goal of building a united front of all democratic forces, and, above all, access to progressive non-Communist voters—the thoroughgoing exploitation of which is greatly facilitated by the Party's substantial local presence. In Hyogo prefecture, for example, there are 960 branches (cells) in Communist-affiliated unions and parallel organizations; the Democratic Students' Association has 6,800 members, the New Japan Women's Association has 4,700, the Democratic Chambers of Commerce 26,000, and the Democratic Medical Care Association 17,000; there are eleven district committees with their own offices and from two to twenty-six full-time staff, capped by the prefectural office in Kobe with a complement of no less than forty full-time employees (Foster, 1982, pp. 843–57).

In contrast, the Socialist Party has a much smaller, less effective, rather rickety outfit of, ostensibly, thirty-eight district committees, of which only fourteen have offices and seven paid officers which in turn surmount 100 branches located principally in member unions of the sympathetic trade-union federation *Sōhyō* (Foster, 1982, p. 848). The effectiveness of the JSP's local organization is on occasion further impaired by Communist penetration of labour unions nominally affiliated to the Socialists.

In such conditions electoral pacts with the Communists are as fraught with ambiguity as luncheon invitations from hungry wolves. Kyōto is a case in point: for ten years JSP–JCP collaboration pushed up the progressive vote in the prefectural assembly elections from 38.1 per cent of the total in 1959 to 46.7 per cent in 1971, when the vote began to fall away to 37.2 per cent in 1979 and down to 33.8 per cent in 1983. A disaggregated vote reveals a strikingly different picture: in that same period the Communists' *share* of the progressive vote increased, by just a nibble at first, from 17 per cent in 1959 to 27.4 per cent in 1963 and 32.1 per cent in 1967, but later by huge, mordant chunks—49.2 per cent in 1971, 59.1 per cent in 1975, 69.9 per cent in 1979, and 73.7 per cent in 1983 (Krauss, 1980, p. 411). (Table 9.2 gives these results in detail.)

LDP leaders viewed the rapid growth of the JCP with alarm and identified the Communists as the major challenge to their continued tenure of office. Consequently, legislation was passed in 1975 to curb the electoral activities of the JCP. By virtue of a revision of the Public Officers' Election Law, special camapign activities at election time were restricted, and the publication of extra issues of party papers, which reported and commented on the election, was banned. No commercial papers, magazines or trade-union or other organizations' papers could henceforth be distributed free of charge. The Party's 'legs' were tied by the extension of legal controls over trade unions, youth organizations, women's groups and traders's associations—the effect of which was to render illegal propaganda activities by these bodies at election time (JCP Central Committee, 1984, p. 462).

Table 9.2 JSP and JCP electoral results for the Kyoto prefectural
assembly, 1959–83

Prefectural assembly elections	JSP vote (%)	JCP vote (%)	Combined vote (%)	JCP vote as % of combined progressive vote
1959	31.6	6.5	38.1	17.0
1963	27.0	10.2	37.2	27.4
1967	28.1	13.3	41.4	32.1
1971	23.7	23.0	46.7	49.2
1975	17.6	25.5	43.1	59.1
1979	11.2	26.0	37.2	69.9
1983	8.9	24.9	33.8	73.7

The Current Status of Coalition Politics

The revised electoral law posed serious problems for the JCP. Moreover, prospects for collaboration with the JSP were not good after 1977. There had been tension for some time within the JSP between the right wing of the party—centred on the Eda and Sasaki factions and the New Trend Association—which favoured an anti-Communist, centrist coalition with the Democratic Socialist Party (DSP) and the vigorous Clean Government Party, and the left-wing Sakisaka faction of the Socialist Association, standard-bearers of a 'joint struggle of all opposition parties'. Setbacks in national elections triggered a bitter debate about coalition policy at local and national levels and culminated in the resignation of the JSP leadership. The new Chairman, Asukata, considered the JCP to be something of an electoral liability.

The coalition fell apart first in Kyōto, the local bastion of left-wing politics, where in March 1978 a three-way contest was held to replace the incumbent governor Ninagawa. In the event, a candidate backed by the LDP and the NLC benefited from a split progressive vote and secured election with 44 per cent of the votes polled. The Centrist candidate, backed by the JSP–DSP–CGP, took 17 per cent of the vote, and the Communist candidate, supported by an umbrella organization, 'The Liaison Conference of Various Circles for the Promotion of Democratic Prefectural Administration' which housed 4,700 different groups, captured 38 per cent of the vote (Copper, 1979, pp. 353–65).

A second leadership change within the JSP, which witnessed the emergence of Chairman Ishibashi, did not improve matters: of the thirteen gubernatorial elections of 1983 only in Fukuoka was there substantial cooperation between the JSP and the JCP and consequent electoral success. In Tokyo eventually a joint candidate was agreed, but too late to afford a real chance of victory. Indeed, a new pattern emerged: the JSP either did not back *any* candidate (Ibaraki, Akita, Ōita, Iwate and Saga) or joined centre-right coalitions with the LDP, DSP and CGP from which only the Communists were excluded (Ōsaka, Shimane, Fukui and Tottori). The JCP response was to present its isolation as evidence that the Communists were the only genuine opposition party; a Communist candidate challenged the mainstream candidate in ten elections for governor, even when, as in Iwate and Saga, there was no prospect of defeating an entrenched incumbent (Yomiuri, Shimbunsha, 1984). (Table 9.3 illustrates these electoral results.)

Much the same problem was in evidence in the elections of 145 city mayors in 1983: the Socialists ran their own candidate in sixteen cities and formed nine centrist and seventeen centre-right coalitions from which the Communists were excluded. The democratic front of Communists and Socialists operated in only nine elections—six of them in Tōkyō—and only once was successful. The JCP entered a further five centre-left coalitions as a junior partner, four of which were successful. In thirty cities the Communists ran their own candidates, fourteen of whom polled less than 10 per cent of the vote and all were defeated. Plainly, the immediate concern of the Party was not to win seats—in one city in Hokkaidō the JCP polled fifty votes, 0.8 per cent of the total—but to declare its presence and develop its local organization. Nothing has happened since 1983 that seems likely to make the JSP any more willing to enter coalitions at the local level with the Communists.

The Consequences for Public Policy of JCP Involvement in Local Government

One refrain in the local rhetoric of apoliticism is that a Communist presence is of little consequence in local government since there is not a conservative and a progressive way to clean the streets, a claim that cannot simply be dismissed by reference to the politics of no-politics. Indeed, one sober analyst argues that 'partisanship is more often a red herring than a useful guide to the regional policy-process', and concludes his study of regional politics in the Tōkyō Bay area over a twenty-year period with the observation, 'Conflicts within the region were not conflicts between progressive and conservative

Table 9.3 Electoral results in thirteen gubernatorial elections, 1983

Kanawaga	LDP–JSP–CGP–NLC–JCP		Others
	86.7%		13.3%
Osaka	LDP–JSP–CGP–DSP–NLC		JCP
	63.0%		36.3%
Shimane	LDP–JSP–CGP–DSP–NLC		JCP
	88.6%		11.4%
Fukui	LDP–JSP–CGP–DSP		JCP
	78.8%		21.2%
Tottori	LDP–JSP–CGP–DSP		JCP
	86.2%		13.8%
Hokkaidō	LDP–CGP–DSP–NLC	JSP	JCP
	46.8%	49%	4.2%
Tōkyō	LDP–CGP–DSP–NLC		JSP–JCP
	60.2%		37.9%
Ibaraki	LDP–CGP–DSP–NLC		JCP
	84.8%		15.2%
Akita	LDP–CGP–DSP		JCP
	83.6%		16.4%
Oita	LDP–CGP–DSP		JCP
	85.1%		14.4%
Fukuoka	LDP–DSP		JSP–JCP
	49%		51.0%
Iwate	LDP		JCP
	82.7%		17.3%
Saga	LDP		JCP
	83.1%		16.9%

coalitions but among localities at different stages of industrial development (Samuels, 1983, p. 234). Samuels's view is supported by an analysis of change in revenue and spending priorities for eighty-eight medium-sized cities in the 'progressive decade' (1962–74), which suggests no strong association between progressive partisanship and 'progressive' policies at this level at least (Aqua, 1979).

On the other hand, there is no doubt at all in the mind of the JCP that there is a difference and that a vote for the Party means free medical care for the aged (by municipal fiat), development of a system of providing credit to small- and medium-sized enterprises without guarantor or collateral, regulations on pollution, and increased local taxes on big businesses. Not all JCP policies will have a marked budgetary incidence. The call for 'open government', for more regular contact between citizen and councillor, and for greater popular participation in local government which has led to the creation in many municipalities of 'liaison offices' or local surgeries, is a case in point. Moreover, the Party has been associated with policy initiatives, for example, to improve social welfare and to control pollution, which do translate into aggregate financial terms but which were rapidly and generally taken up by Conservative-led local authorities with the consequence that their distinctiveness was lost. The fact that such policies were first enacted in model progressive administrations in Tōkyō, Kyōto and Ōsaka, and there proved feasible and popular, contributed greatly to the speed with which they were generally taken up (MacDougall, 1977 pp. 408–9; Ide, 1972, pp. 214–35).

The major problem in assessing the impact of Communist participation in local government on public policy is that the JCP has not yet been in a position fully to exploit the relatively small margin for manoeuvre available to local government in Japan. Local government in Japan is 'presidential', and there are no Communist 'presidents' in the prefectures and only five mayors and village heads are members of the JCP; nor, for that matter, is there a JCP majority in any assembly. As had been noted, the Party only has access to power as a partner, typically the junior partner in a coalition, clearly an insufficient basis from which to dictate policy.

'Red Kyōto', Japan's Bologna, comes nearest to but still falls far short of, an instance of Communist rule. Here the JCP holds fourteen of the sixty-three seats on the prefectural assembly, and nineteen of the seventy-two city assembly seats. However, neither the governor nor the mayor is a Communist, and the LDP is the majority party in both assemblies (with twenty-six seats in the prefectural assembly and twenty-four seats in the city assembly). Krauss says of public policy in Kyōto, at the height of Communist influence when the Progressive–Independent governor Ninagawa was enjoying his final term of office and depended primarily upon the JCP for partisan support:

the Party does not seem . . . to have been crucial to the initiation of these policies [the education, health, anti-industrialization, pro-traditional, and small and medium enterprises policies which were the hallmark of Ninagawa's progressive administration] nor does its enhanced power in prefectural politics over the last decade seem to have brought about a fundamental reallocation of prefectural government resources . . . much of the basic outline of Ninagawa's administration could already be discerned in the early 1960s, prior to the period of greatest Communist influence in the prefecture' [Krauss, 1979, p. 345].

The conclusion can be stated briefly: the Communist Party of Japan has been committed to the parliamentary road for nearly a quarter of a century. It has been eager to secure popular support and so to win elections at both local and national levels of political life. It is, however, of the opinion that given what it takes to be the very limited ability of the government of the day to control 'state power', electoral success is not sufficient to guarantee the transformation of social and political conditions which the Party intends. This being the case, the JCP is eager to ensure that, when and if it controls local and national assemblies, it will be supported by a wide range of extra-parliamentary organizations sympathetic to its cause. The task of influencing all such organizations is at least as important as, and proceeds at the same time as, efforts to control the elected assemblies. Because of this, seats in the council are seen as means as much as ends. Accordingly, the Party is eager not only to secure the election and re-election of its councillors, but to ensure also that positions in local councils are exploited so as to guarantee a maximum, favourable exposure of the Party not simply with a view to increased possibilities of electoral success, but equally with a view to the long-term socialization or, if you will, politicization of the local community. The strategy is to be pursued under the detailed supervision of the party headquarters—developments, such as the growth of personal support organizations, which tend to undermine central control are resisted. At the same time, however, adjustments have to be made to local realities if elections are to be won and influence is to be created. And so there *are* Communist *kōenkai* and JCP councillors *do* in some respects resemble the archetypical local notable even if parallel or compensatory electoral strategies have to be adopted.

Commitment to that strategy coincided with a spontaneous development of public dissatisfaction with the negative consequences of the industrialization policies pursued by a Conservative central government with scant regard to urban problems and environmental questions and insensitive to the resentments of voters who had, in one way or another, missed out on the economic miracle. This was the Party's chance, and the willingness of the Socialist Party to cooperate in a series of electoral alliances enabled it to take that chance. Party membership grew rapidly, and a significant penetration of local government was achieved.

By the late 1970s, these conditions had changed: the Progressives no longer had a monopoly on pollution; the Conservatives were re-establishing themselves in the cities; most of the socially and economically marginal voters had been mopped up by the JCP or its threateningly vigorous rival, the Clean Government Party, which was geared to the same constituency and had the advantage of a 'safe' image to reassure the floating voter; the Socialists were disinclined to risk further collaboration with a too successful Communist Party and were looking to coalitions at the centre. The growth of party membership slowed and, significantly, that of the Communist Youth went into reverse. One by one the spectacular gubernatorial successes of the early 1970s were undone and reduced by 1983 to the solitary seat in Fukuoka. The JCP's total representation in the local assemblies did hold up and even made small gains up until 1983 when serious losses were recorded.

As the Party leaders take stock in the mid-1980s, the picture is bleak: more than ever the Party is isolated at the local and national levels as the realignment at the centre of the Socialists continues with the blessing of the electorate; and as the growth of the Clean Government continues they must wonder whether the potential of the Communist local government strategy is nearing exhaustion.

Bibliography

Aqua, R., 1979. 'Politics and Performance in Japanese Municipalities', unpublished Ph.D. thesis, Cornell University.

Beckman, G. M. and Okubo, G., 1969. *The Japanese Communist Party 1922-1945*. Stanford, Calif., Stanford University Press.

Central Committee of the Communist Party of Japan, 1964. *The 9th Congress of the Communist Party of Japan: November 24-30, 1964*, Bulletin Special Issue, Information for Abroad, Tōkyō.

Central Committee of the Communist Party of Japan, 1984. *Sixty-Year History of the Japanese Communist Party*, Tōkyō, Japan Press Service.

Chihōjichi Kenkyū Shinyō Centa, 1982. *Toshika to Giin-chiiki: Rida no Yakuwari Kōdō*.

Copper, J. F., 1979. 'The Japanese Communist Party's Recent Election Defeats: A Signal of Decline?', *Asian Survey*, vol. XIX, no. 4, April, pp. 353-65.

Curtis, G., 1971. *Election Campaigning Japanese Style*. New York and London, Columbia University Press.

Flanagan, S. C., 1980. 'National and Local Voting Trends: Cross Level Linkages and Correlates of Change', in K. Steiner, E. S. Krauss and S. C. Flanagan (eds), *Political Opposition and Local Politics in Japan*. Princeton, Princeton University Press, pp. 131-84.

Foster, J. J., 1982. 'Ghost-Hunting: Local Party Organisation in Japan', *Asian Survey*, vol. XXII, no. 9, September, pp. 843-57.

Fukai, S. N., 1977. 'The Deradicalization of the Japanese Left?', Vols. I and II, unpublished Ph.D. thesis, University of Tennessee.

Fukui, H., 1978. 'The Japanese Communist Party: The Miyamoto Line and Its Problems', in M. A. Kaplan (ed.), *The Many Faces of Communism*. New York, Free Press, pp. 279–332.

Hakamada, S., 1978. *Kinō no Dōshi Miyamoto Kenji e*. Tokyo, Shinchosha.

Hayase, T., 1980. 'Chihō Giin to Gyōsei', *Hōgaku Ronsō*, vol. 109, no. 3, pp. 80–98.

Iizuka, S., 1974. *Miyamoto Kenji no Nihonkyōsantō*. Tokyo, Ikkosha.

Ide, Y., 1972. *Chihō jichi no seijigaku*. Tōkyō, Tōkyō Daigaku Shuppankai.

Ito, M., 1981. 'Chihō Giin no Daihyō Yakuwari', *Hōgaku Ronsō*, vol. 108, no. 6, pp. 101–96.

Japanese Communist Party Central Committee Publications Bureau, 1982. *16th Congress of the Japanese Communist Party: Atami, July 27–31, 1982*. Tokyo, Japan Press Service.

Jichisho gyōseika, 1981. *Jichi-kai chōnaikai to no jiyūmin jichi soshiki no jittai chōsa kekka no gaiyō*, Tōkyō.

Kansai Daigaku Seiji Keizai Kenkyūjo, 1982. *Toshi Giin no Taido to Kōdō*, no. 47.

——, 1984. *Chihō Giin no Taido to Kōdō*, no. 51.

Kim, H. N., 1976. 'Deradicalisation of the Japanese Communist Party under Kenji Miyamoto', *World Politics*, vol. 28, no. 2, January, pp. 273–99.

Kojima, Masaru, (ed.), 1980. *The Record of JCP-CPC Talks: How Mao Zedong Scrapped the Joint Communiqué*. Tokyo, Central Committee of the Japanese Communist Party Publications Bureau.

Krauss, E. S., 1979. 'The Urban Strategy and Policy of the Japanese Communist Party: Kyoto', *Studies in Comparative Communism*, vol. XII, no..4, Winter, pp. 322–50.

——, 1980. 'Opposition in Power: The Development and Maintenance of Leftist Government in Kyoto Prefecture', in Steiner, Krauss and Flanagan (eds), op. cit., pp. 383–426.

Kuroda, N., 1984. *Gendai Nihon no chihō Seijika*. Kyoto: Hōritsu Bunkasha.

Kuwabara, N., 1984. *Kyōsantō chikuiiinchō no arikata o kangaeru*. Tōkyō, Shin Nihon Shuppansha.

Langer, P. F., 1972. *Communism in Japan: A Case of Political Naturalization*. Stanford, Hoover Institution.

MacDougall, T. E., 1976. 'Japanese Urban Local Politics: Towards a Viable Progressive Political Opposition', in L. Austin (ed.), *Japan: The Paradox of Progress*. New Haven, Yale University Press, p. 42.

——, 1977. 'Political Opposition and Local Government in Japan: The Significance of Emerging Progressive Local Leadership', unpublished Ph.D. thesis, Yale University.

——, 1980. 'Political Opposition and Big City Elections in Japan 1947–75', in Steiner, Krauss and Flanagan (eds), op. cit., pp. 55–94.

Ministry of Home Affairs, 1984. 'Local Administration and Finance', in Kiyoaki Tsuji (ed.), *Public Administration in Japan*. Tokyo, University of Tokyo Press, pp. 87–107.

Muramatsu, M., and Ito, M., 1980. 'Shichōsonkaigiin no seijika to chiiki shakai no shakaikeizaiteki tokushitsu, *Hōgaku Ronsō*, vol. 107, no. 3, pp. 83–101.

Nihonkyōsantō Chūōiinkai, *Jichitaimondai to Nihonkyōsantō* 1982 (A). Tokyo, Nihonkyōsanto Chūōiinkai Shuppankyoku.

——, 1982. *Chihō giin no katsudō no tebiki*. Tōkyō.

Nihonkyōsantō Chūōiinkai Shuppankyoku, 1975. *Nihonkyōsantō to Nicchu mondai*. Tokyo, Shin Nippon Shuppansha.

Packard, G. R., 1966. *Protest in Tokyo: The Security Treaty Crisis of 1960*. Princeton, Princeton University Press.

Pohl, M., 1976. *Die Kommunistische Partei Japans: Ein Weg ohne Peking und Moskau*. Hamburg.

Samuels, R. J., 1983. *The Politics of Regional Policy in Japan: Localities Incorporated*. Princeton, Princeton University Press.

Scalapino, R. A., 1967. *The Japanese Communist Movement 1920-66*. Berkeley and Los Angeles, University of California Press.

Scalapino, R. A., and Masumi, J., 1971. *Parties and Politics in Contemporary Japan*. Berkeley, Los Angeles, London, University of California Press, pp. 125-53.

Shisō Undō Kenkyūjō, comp., 1981. 1981-nemban Nihon Kyōsan Tokei Dantai Yōran. Tōkyō, Zembōsha.

Steiner, K., 1965. *Local Government in Japan*. Stanford, Calif., Stanford University Press.

Steiner, K., Kraus, E. S., and Flanagan, S. C., (eds), 1980. *Political Opposition and Local Politics in Japan*. Princeton, Princeton University Press.

Steven, R., 1983. *Classes in Contemporary Japan*. Cambridge, Cambridge University Press.

Swearingen, R., and Langer, P., 1952. *Red Flag in Japan: International Communism in Action, 1919-1951*. Cambridge Mass., Harvard University Press.

Totten, G. O., 1973. 'The People's Parliamentary Path of the Japanese Communist Party: Part I, Agrarian Policies', *Pacific Affairs*, vol. 46, no. 2, summer 1973, pp. 193-217, and 'Part II, Local Level Tactics', no. 3, fall, pp. 384-406.

Ueda, T., 1982. 'Japanese Local Organisations: Leadership and Political Function', *Kansai University Review of Law and Politics*, no. 3, March.

Williams, Sr., J., 1979. *Japan's Political Revolution under Macarthur: A Participant's Account*. Athens, Georgia, The University of Georgia Press.

Yoda, H., 1980. 'Chihō giin to senkyokatei', *Hōgaku Ronsō*, vol. 107, no. 5, pp. 76-95.

Yomiuri Shimbun (ed.), 1984. *Sandaisenkyo no sōbunsetsu '83*. Tōkyō, Yomiuri Shimbunsha.

Zenkoku Senkyokanriiinkai, 1952. *Chihōsenkyokekkachō*. Tōkyō.

Zenkoku Shigikai Gichōkai, 1982. *Shigijai Katsudō ni kansuru jittai chōsa hōkoku*. Tōkyō.

Conclusion

Bogdan Szajkowski

This, the final part of an appraisal of Marxist local governments in Western Europe and Japan, attempts to offer tentative conclusions and a summary of the general themes based on the data and its interpretation from the chapters included in this volume.

It needs to be stressed that the importance of local authorities has increased quite considerably over the past four decades. Local government has become an essential instrument of national government and now has considerable responsibility for the provision of such essential services as education, health, road networks, the police, the fire services and social welfare. The pressing need for these services within communities emphasizes the growing importance of local institutions. In addition to supplying facilities and services, local government also performs a representative role of course, that of involving the citizens in determining specific local public needs and deciding how they are to be met.

The process of local government may be succinctly described as the determination and implementation of decisions regarding local public programmes (Humes & Martin, 1969, p. 34). The making and the carrying-out of these decisions are to a large extent indistinguishable, for wherever there is action involving decisions there is also at least some degree of policy-making in which central authorities have direct or indirect involvement.

The preceding chapters describe and analyse the principal aspects of the various Communist parties' involvement in local government. By concentrating on the changing historical environment of this involvement, these chapters give an illuminating insight to interesting and often ignored functional relationships between centrally organized and hierarchically controlled Communist parties and the wider pluralistic environment in which they function on a level concerned with somewhat narrow and parochial issues: a far cry from their original preoccupation—world revolution.

The years since the end of the Second World War have seen a major reversal of the Communists' attitudes to representative institutions in the liberal democracies. Consequently, Communist parties operating in Western Europe and Japan have steadily built secure foundations in local government. Local political power has had a moderating influence on the Communists and inevitably has led to a future acceptance of the established political system. The Communist parties discussed in this volume, with the exception of the PCP, have used local government in moderate ways. It is interesting to note that the strength of their following, measured by their election results, is somewhat larger than the support they receive on a national level. Furthermore, this observation applies equally to those polities that have a long tradition of Communist party direct involvement in the political process, for example, France, Italy, Finland and Japan, and those of Greece, Spain and Portugal where the Communists operated clandestinely for many years.

Two main, but not mutually exclusive, explanations for this relative strength in local government suggested by the contributions in this volume appear to be particularly interesting. First, it would seem that the electorates of the countries analysed in these studies may be willing to give the Communists more support on the local level because of the narrow framework of sub-national politics which offers only a limited and, in national terms, relatively insignificant prospect of policy-making and policy implementation. In other words, it is not expected that the Communists would be able to carry out their full revolutionary programme on a microcosm level. Second, the small scale of sub-national politics may be significant, since alliances of various types (political and personal) are much more easily constructed on a local level than on a national scale. Consequently, voting for local alliances may appear to be much more acceptable to a local electorate. In addition, it is worth stressing how much more personal and direct in scope and contacts is the nature of voting for a local government, where votes often support a known member of a local community rather than a political party as represented by a distant political figure.

For the Communist parties, involvement in the sub-national political process serves several main purposes, some of which are not different from those of other parties. These include, among others: expansion of their power base and increased political involvement; utilization of politicization that occurs in and around these institutions for the party's benefit; creation and maintenance of channels of recruitment to both local and national elite positions; training of party activists; possibilities of political experimentation that would be ideologically and politically cost-effective; prospects of educating the citizenry in the party's policies and programmes. In addition, local politics offers the Communists an experience in participatory dynamics—a scaled-down government involvement that builds up the party's experience and expertise for the future. However, what makes the Communists' involvement different from that of other parties is that local government serves for Communist parties on the whole as a channel of implementation of centrally perceived and determined policies. In other words, the opening for political participation is made only within the formula of a party programme which comprises not only national but also clearly delineated international issues. These issues are determined by the central leadership and executed in accordance with the principle of *democratic centralism*, a hierarchical chain of directives that is unique to Communist parties.

Democratic centralism also allows the central leadership of the party to reformulate local issues substantially and to manipulate the mechanics of sub-national government including the selection of local activists. Essential Lenninist practice prevents the acceptance of spontaneous action not derived from the Communist party itself (Middlemas, 1980, p. 335). This may at least partially explain why Communist-controlled local government, with one exception, has not put forward new ideas for sub-national policy. It must be acknowledged that local government institutions are the manifestations of a country's social and political heritage. Thus, for example, in Spain and Portugal, where there is a weak tradition of participatory democracy, the Communists also distrust popular mobilization; hence their very traditional approach to local government. The same, however, cannot be said for France, Denmark, Sweden, Norway and Finland, which have strong traditions of citizens' involvement in running their national and local affairs. Yet neither in these countries have the Communist parties produced any novel approaches at the local level. The Communist parties in these countries appear to opt for 'safe' administration and prefer to emphasize that their foremost local accomplishments are sound administrative competence and efficiency.

The exception is, of course, Italy, where the PCI has been successful in formulating and applying novel and innovative local cultural policy that distinguishes it not only from other Italian parties but also from Communist parties elsewhere. It should be remembered that local government has been the PCI's main concern ever since the Party's expulsion from the central government in 1947. Consequently, over the years local government has become the ground where it can demonstrate its pragmatism, innovations and experiments.

The impact of sub-national units controlled by the Communists on the party's national policy and the country's central government is another important theme emerging from the chapters included in this volume—to what extent the monolithic nature of the Communist parties allows for the assertion of local identity. The interplay between central and local party apparatus in terms of policy-making is, with the exception of Italy, very much in favour of the former. As pointed out in the introductory chapter, local politics is an extension of the national and international policies of the

Communist parties, which is bound to limit local initiatives and to increase tensions between central and local government. These chapters have shown that in most cases the balance of power is heavily in favour of central institutions and elites. A particularly sharp example of this is Portugal where, as José Amodia points out, local policy is no more than an echo of what the PCP is doing elsewhere. The Party often neglects local themes in favour of national issues of the day. Thus, for example, the last local elections in Spain and Greece were also run on national and international issues such as the membership of NATO and the European Community. Leninist centralism mixes poorly with liberal democratic representative institutions in general and with sub-national authorities in particular. In Italy, however, the local government strategy of the PCI has changed from one of using local party organizations to carry out national policies, to giving sub-national politics the opportunity to make a contribution to the shaping of national policy.

Communist-controlled local government helps to extend as well as to maintain party rule. It serves as a training ground for future national leaders and as a redoubt of communist strength even in the face of national electoral setbacks. It is nevertheless worth pointing out that a retrospective look at the local involvement of the Communist parties analysed in this volume gives some evidence of their strategic planning in response to local circumstances. With the exception of the PCP and KKE, the other parties discussed in this book concern themselves increasingly with calculations related to their national and local political context rather than what is loosely termed 'ideology'. However, at the same time, as the main thrust of the chapters shows, each of the parties considered faces serious policy, participatory and institutional dilemmas if they are to maintain, let alone expand, their local community involvement. Most of the problems arise no longer from the historical perspectives that beset Communist parties' development during the inter-war period, but from the limitations imposed by their Leninist structure. The path of nursing local inititives and insisting on obedience to central decisions at the same time is a treacherous one and, in the long run, must either bring about change in the highly centralized organizational structure and thus lead to the liberalization of the Communist parties or risk further loss of support on a sub-national level.

Bibliography

Hume, S., and Martin, E., 1969. *The Structure of Local Government*. The Hague, International Union of Local Authorities.

Middlemas, K., 1980. *Power and the Party: Changing Faces of Communism in Western Europe*. London, André Deutsch.

Nelson, D. N. (ed.), 1980. *Local Politics in Communist Countries*. Lexington, Univeristy of Kentucky Press.

Tannahill, N., 1978. *The Communist Parties of Western Europe*. London, Greenwood Press.

Index

(*Note*: page numbers in *italics* indicate an article by the author indicated.)